19 May '94

For Richard

[signature]

SAVED FROM OBLIVION:

INTERDEPENDENCE THEORY IN THE FIRST HALF OF THE 20TH CENTURY

SAVED FROM OBLIVION:

INTERDEPENDENCE THEORY IN THE FIRST HALF OF THE 20TH CENTURY

A study on the causality between war and complex interdependence

JAAP DE WILDE

Dartmouth

Aldershot · Brookfield USA · Hong Kong · Singapore · Sydney

© Jaap de Wilde, 1991

All rights reserved. No part of this publication may be reproduced,
stored in a retrieval system, or transmitted in any form or by any
means, electronic, mechanical, photocopying, recording, or otherwise
without the prior permission of Dartmouth Publishing Company
Limited.

Published by

Dartmouth Publishing Company Limited
Gower House, Croft Road
Aldershot, Hampshire GU11 3HR
England

Dartmouth Publishing Company
Old Post Road
Brookfield, Vermont 05036
USA

ISBN 1 85521 141 6

Printed in Great Britain by
Billing & Sons Ltd, Worcester

Contents

The West-West context. The East-West context. The North-South context. Global challenges. Politicians and interdependence.

A typology of structural interdependence. Qualifications of structural interdependence: a) confrontational interdependence; b) constructional interdependence. Doubts about empirical research.

Three paradigms in IR-theory. The origins of Realism and Structuralism. The post-war origins of Pluralism. The hidden tradition of Pluralism.

Morgenthau and functionalism: the State is dead — long live the State! Mitrany versus Morgenthau? The flirtations of functionalism and Realism.

Sovereignty as a solution. The "state fixation" of political writers. From "order state" to "service state". Sovereignty bypassed — the threat-system surpassed. Grass-root functionalism. The problem of war is defined the wrong way.

The background and the challenge. The chaff: a liberal-christian, eurocentric paradigm. Change has become a constant in the twentieth century. The neglect of interdependence and its results. Learning interdependence. Awareness is crucial but not enough. Policies of interdependence. From cosmopolitism to individualism and from parochial autarchy to world economy: two sides of the same coin. Constructional interdependence changes the nature of power. What about the future?

Political thought is itself a form of political action. Political science is the science not only of what is, but of what ought to be.

E.H. Carr (1939)

Introduction

The main task of Peace Research is to study the causes of war and the conditions of peace. With this objective in mind, in 1962, professor Bert Röling (1906-1985) founded the Polemological Institute within the Faculty of Law at the University of Groningen, the Netherlands. This study aims to contribute to that objective.

Interdependence theory is studied because interdependence in world politics is sometimes seen as a cause of war and sometimes as a condition of peace. Supporters of both views have a serious point. Interdependence is a relation between two or more actors, and, like all relationships, it is therefore a source of conflict. The actors involved affect one another's behaviour, which can be both pleasant and irritating; the irritation may cause conflicts, and their management can involve threats and acts of deliberate and organized destruction (political violence). On the other hand, interdependence by definition implies a measure of reciprocity, which limits the options for conflict management.

In view of this apparent contradiction, it is important to notice from the outset that, when interdependence is connected with the absence of political violence, this should not be equated with the

1

absence of conflict. Interdependence is a source of conflict. But conflicts under interdependence are characterized by all kind of constraints, and these constraints may stimulate more sophisticated forms of conflict management than the primitive killing or mutilating of people or the threat to destroy (parts of) their civilization. To quote Charles E. Merriam, peace is not the end of struggle but the finer organization of it (see page 169).

The awareness of constraints made Robert O. Keohane and Joseph S. Nye hypothesize, in 1977, that governments will not use military force toward one another, if they and the peoples they represent are involved in a complex network of interdependent relations. The more complex the network of relationships in which countries are involved, the stronger the constraints on all-out war. One constraint may be that the employment of force with respect to a fierce conflict on one issue is likely to rupture mutually profitable relations concerning other issues. This explains for instance why many writers about interdependence have stressed economic relations among countries as an incentive to peace. Moreover, other actors might get involved, because of unavoidable chain-reactions. This will complicate the assessment of the risks of aggressive military policies.

Another constraint may be that, given such a complexity of interests, it will be very hard to make a clear-cut hierarchy of national interests and thus to define policy objectives for which these ruptures are an acceptable price. Also, some very important policy goals in modern national societies, such as public economic and ecological welfare, by their nature cannot be served by the use of military force.

Furthermore, the existence of multiple channels provides a variety of instruments for power politics. This variety leads to an increased competition with military options in times of crisis. In case of complex interdependence, escalation ladders may be longer and there may be more emergency escapes for the conflicting parties to back out without losing face. In short, constraints like these might increase the safety margin within international relations, despite the increase of conflicts that accompanies growing interdependence.

The "how", "why" and "when" of these constraints are the concern of this study. But it is not an empirical analysis. I am not measuring indicators and characteristics of complex interdependence, such as information flows between actors, networks of issue-specific activities, import-export percentages of Gross National Products (GNP), the measure of global social mobility of (specific groups of) people, densities in cross-border traffic, the number of economists and ecologists working in foreign policy departments, the number of political scientists in advisory boards of multinational corporations, the number of joint ventures, the number and character of governmental participation in international organizations, the size of transnational activities and the number of non-governmental organizations with international activities, the sensitivity or vulnerability to sanctions, the measure of symmetry among actors, etcetera. Such empirical research should indeed take place in order to tell us more about interdependent relationships. But, though empirical research is important, when it comes to test hypotheses about the causality between war, interdependence theory has not yet reached the stage in which empirical findings can achieve the status of empirical evidence.

The measurement of social variables may be difficult, their interpretation is still harder, because it requires theory. Theories provide frameworks for the interpretation of facts. As long as the framework is insufficiently defined, there is no use in endlessly accumulating new and more detailed data, because this will not help to take away the fundamental defects. When it comes to hypotheses about the relationship between interdependence and the role of the military component in diplomacy, there are still many of these defects. For that reason I have chosen to restrict myself to the conceptual and theoretical level.

The defect that is addressed in this study concerns the neglect of early theories about interdependence. The critics of the interdependence thesis in particular have pointed out that the presumed link between peace and interdependence is not new. They pointed at Norman Angell, for instance, who propagated the promise of interdependence as far back as 1909. But Angell has been generally known as a classic liberal, placing his confidence in the merits of free trade. Furthermore, two world wars have taken place despite

3

all this interdependence. Some people even argued that they took place because of all this interdependence. The title of Angell's book, *The Great Illusion*, therefore, seemed to sum up the quintessence of his own ideas. Why pay renewed attention to them?

One of the reasons is that pre-war literature about interdependence has never been critically examined with the explicit objective to distil those parts which are still useful for current theorizing. Political science as a distinct discipline started in 1919 and every student in political science learns what was wrong with its first phase, which lasted to about 1939-1945: it is utopian, idealistic, eurocentric, moralistic, legalistic, naïve in its descriptions, dangerous in its predictions, in short, mainly of historical value. All this is true, and evidence is easy to find, also in the work of the authors discussed in this volume. But, simultaneously this criticism is simplistic, because it reveals only part of the story. It is a myth to think that half a century of serious research by concerned, well-trained intellectuals has yielded merely rubbish. The baby has been thrown away with the bath water. Before passing judgment, the pre-war contribution to the development of a consistent theory of interdependence has to be analysed. In this volume I hope to do so.

To that end, I have tried to break with a tradition that, in my opinion, has unwillingly contributed to the neglect of the literature written in the period 1900-1950. In this study, I stress in what ways the work of Angell, Muir, Delaisi, Merriam and Mitrany can contribute to the improvement of contemporary theories on International Relations. The aim is to save the good parts of their work from oblivion. The rest can be forgotten. The general tradition in reviewing contributions to science, however, seems to work the other way round: the good parts are forgotten because critics take their credit primarily from their ability to lay bare the shortcomings of the works they review. The bad parts are stressed, the rest is taken for granted. This is a very inefficient method of accumulating knowledge. Probably the development of political science is hampered by this practice. Don't read Angell, for he is an Idealist! Forget about Mitrany, for functionalism doesn't work! Keep away from interdependence literature, for it repeats the simplistic war-does-not-pay thinking of the nineteenth century! I have tried to break with that tradition, and have concentrated mainly on the

4

aspects which in my opinion do contribute to interdependence theory.

This volume is structured as follows. The first two chapters place interdependence theory in its disciplinary and historical context. They reflect the contemporary state of affairs. Moreover, in the first chapter the concept of interdependence is defined and elaborated into a typology which aims to provide a framework for all the different specific applications of the term. Both chapters have an introductory character and provide the background against which the intellectual history of the pioneers of interdependence is placed.

Chapters 3 to 7 deal with the contributions of these pioneers: Norman Angell, Ramsay Muir, Francis Delaisi, Charles Merriam and David Mitrany respectively. Though the chapters are not meant to be biographies, I have decided to include a certain amount of biographical information because the historical context and the personal circumstances in which the five authors developed their ideas on interdependence and related subjects add much to the understanding of these ideas. In chapter 8, the insights of the authors are combined and the debate about the feasibility of pursuing a policy of growing interdependence is re-opened.

To give the reader a hand, the synopsis provides summaries of each chapter.

Many people have contributed to the preparation of this dissertation. Very important were the two conferences about "Interdependence and Conflict in World Politics" that were organized by the Polemological Institute in November 1986 in Groningen and, in cooperation with the Inter-University Centre, in June 1987 in Dubrovnik, Yugoslavia. Not only did these two conferences culminate in a volume about interdependence theory, edited by professor James N. Rosenau (Institute for Transnational Studies, University of Southern California) and professor Hylke Tromp (Polemological Institute, University of Groningen), but they also resulted in valuable discussions and numerous international contacts. Moreover, the constructive criticism and useful suggestions of Rosenau and Tromp, who were kind enough to supervise this manuscript, contributed greatly towards structuring my thoughts about the complexities of interdependence theory. Where I failed to do so, they should not be held responsible.

International contacts are essential to any student studying International Relations (IR), and in this respect the Dubrovnik Summerschools on "Political Violence" fulfilled an important function, as did professor Chris Mitchell's invitation to work for a month at the City University of London (October 1987). In this respect the international Pugwash conferences on "Science and World Affairs" and the conferences of the International Peace Research Association (IPRA) should be mentioned, too. In different ways, these conferences visualized the importance and difficulty of questions such as how to define and how to translate the social responsibility of sciences, and how to organize a fruitful debate among scientists from many, fundamentally different social backgrounds and national traditions.

The difficulties of answering questions like these are not only typical for the international context in which IPRA and Pugwash operate. Even in a small country, like the Netherlands, contacts among institutes, and, at times, also within them, are characterized by dialogue and cooperation as much as by indifference to each other's research projects. Still, the discussions with my colleagues at the Polemological Institute, in the interdisciplinary research group on "Security & Development" and at several seminars and conferences at other Dutch universities, have been very stimulating and important to my work.

The administrative support from the Polemological Institute has been substantial: Elly Pilon, Astrid van Dort and Erik Schuil assisted my work when needed and took care that the conditions for doing research were optimal, while Digna van Boven continued to collect relevant literature even after her working conditions as a librarian had become far from optimal. Peter Kruijt and Ramses Wessel contributed considerably to the continuity of the research project on interdependence at the Institute (which includes a yearly interdisciplinary course for graduates). Instead of fulfilling their military service, they collected literature, reviewed articles, prepared research proposals, published case-studies, helped to organize courses and conferences and constantly kept the discussion about interdependence alive. The index of this volume was made by Ramses Wessel, too. Hans Peterse had the difficult task to correct my English; except for chapter 3, which was largely corrected by Karen Shostak. Hans van der Dennen made the manuscript camera-ready and constructed the tables, figures and graphs. I thank them, and all other present and former members of the Polemological Institute, for their positive contributions and the pleasant cooperation.

Outside the Institute, I was kept in tune by all my musical friends of whom especially Anke van Huis should be mentioned for reasons best known to her.

Jaap de Wilde
Groningen, August 1990.

1   The concept of interdependence in political science

This study is about interdependence in world politics. It has been inspired by the hypothesis that there is a causal relationship between levels of interdependence and the use of political violence. This hypothesis can be formulated in different ways, ranging from rather loose rhetoric, like "peace is a joint venture", to more rigid formulations: "the attractiveness of applying violence for political purposes decreases, as the complexity of patterns of interdependence increases, despite an increase of conflicts accompanying growing complexity" or "increasing structural and cognitive interdependence enlarges, by means of a process of social learning, the safety margin within a given society". It is not so much the exact phrasing which matters in this study, but the development of the general idea that a policy of growing interdependence can offer a solution for situations characterized by mutual war-preparation and eventually lead to the disappearance of interstate warfare.

This chapter is divided into three parts. First the varous political incentives to study interdependence theory are mentioned. Then the concept of interdependence will be explained semantically, resulting in a typology of interdependence. Thirdly, the position of interdependence theory within the broader context of political science is pointed out.

The West-West context

That interstate warfare and even the threat of it can disappear, is supported by the fact that, during the second half of this century, war has been unthinkable among many countries, notably those with high welfare levels. This observation was, for instance, made by Bruce Russett and Harvey Starr, who, in *World Politics: the Menu for Choice* (1981) claimed that a good example of stable peace in the realm of international politics can be found in the relations among the countries of the Organization for Economic Cooperation and Development (OECD).[1] The OECD, founded in 1960 to replace the Organization for European Economic Cooperation — in its turn founded in 1948 with a view to the distribution of the Marshall-aid — is composed of Australia, Austria, Canada, the 12 EC-countries, Finland, Iceland, Japan, New Zealand, Norway, Sweden, Switzerland, Turkey, and the United States of America. Yugoslavia is an associated member and normally the European Commission is also involved in the OECD-activities.

With the exception of short acts of violence between Greece and Turkey about Cyprus in 1974, no military confrontation at an interstate level has taken place among these countries since 1945. Between France and Germany, sworn enemies for over a century, war has become unthinkable (provided that until 1990 this only applied to the western part of Germany). With a proviso concerning Greece and Turkey, it can be stated with reason that the twenty-four OECD-countries have not been occupied in mutual war-preparations and that the governments of these countries have ruled out the threat or use of military force against one another in their diplomatic relations. That is no slight achievement and if we know how this situation has come about we will know something about the "causes of peace".[2]

One of these causes may be that, overall, West-West relations can be typified by "complex interdependence".[3] Though the governments formally represent independent, sovereign nation-states, they actually seem to function as regional councils in one international society. They are members of many intergovernmental organizations and their subjects participate in a large number of transnational relations and organizations. In this respect the "Pax Americana" differed substantially from the "Pax Sovietica", which challenges the second main thesis about the causes of stable peace, namely that the hegemonic position of the superpowers is responsible.

The unconceivability of war among the OECD-countries supports the thesis that there is a causal relationship between levels of interdependence and chances of war. The OECD, as an organization, also seems to be aware of that link, judging by some of its reports: in 1978 the OECD published a report entitled *From Marshallplan to Global Interdependence*, in 1982 followed by *Economic and Ecological Interdependence: A Report on Selected Environmental and Resource Issues*, and in 1987 the report of the symposium for the twenty-fifth anniversary of the OECD was published with the title *Interdependence and Co-operation in Tomorrow's World*.

The East-West context

The other part of the thesis, namely that a policy of stimulating interdependence could offer a solution for situations characterized by mutual war-preparation, is supported by the developments in the East-West context since 1985. From 1945 up to 1985 the conceivability of war, unstable peace, between East and West was a basic fact of life. In that period East-West interdependence was not complex at all, enmity and mistrust were dominant, and mutual deterrence was the principal form of interdependence. According to many scholars and politicians this military stalemate, however costly and wasteful, was the best attainable, given the anarchical character of the international state-system. Others denied this axiom about international anarchy and claimed that improvement would be possible by stimulating relations that would introduce new actors, institutions and interests in the East-West arena, that might offer new behavioural options, finally resulting in a new behavioural culture. In short, a policy of interdependence seemed to be required. Such a policy means that a social actor (normally a government) will actively and purposely stimulate the growth of transnational and international relations among the inhabitants of two or more countries. A policy of interdependence implies that political, bureaucratic and juridical barriers between countries are reduced, that cross-border contacts are stimulated, that joint ventures are subsidized and that new intergovernmental juridical regulations are developed to manage the extension of contacts.

Such an option was, for instance, the main theme in the pamphlet "Managing East-West Conflict. A Framework for Sustained Engagement", published in 1984. Its signatories include Robert McNamara (former Secretary of Defense, USA), Helmut Schmidt (former Chancellor, Federal Republic of Germany), Edward Heath (former Prime Minister, Great Britain), George Kennan (former US Ambassador to the Soviet-Union), Saburo Okita (former Foreign Minister, Japan), Cyrus Vance (former Secretary of State, USA), John McCloy (former Chairman, Chase Manhattan Bank), Pehr Gyllenhammer (Chairman, Volvo Sweden), Pierre Trudeau (former Prime Minister, Canada), Bruno Kreisky (former Chancellor, Austria), and some twenty other (former) politicians, scientists, and businessmen of standing from Western Europe, Japan, and Northern America. In the preface to their joint statement Joseph Slater (President of the Aspen Institute) characterized the direction in which this group was looking for an alternative to the deadlocked East-West confrontation:

> "As John J. McCloy, one of our wisest and most experienced members, has said, the West needs 'a philosophy of interdependence' which will 'challenge the Soviet Union to positive action'."[4]

Yet, it was the Soviet-Union which first adopted such a philosophy of interdependence; challenging the West to positive action. (A philosophy of interdependence points at the moral justification of a policy of interdependence at a higher level of abstraction: the general expectation that growing interdependence improves the relations between the countries concerned.)

11

This shift has fundamentally changed the value of many publications on East-West interdependence. Ever since 1945, the general assumption underlying all research that aimed to contribute to the improvement of East-West relations had been that the causes of the Cold War would not be eliminated. Shortly after the revolutions in Eastern Europe in November 1989, Dieter Senghaas pointed out that politicians and political scientists at best aimed to achieve a "Zivilisierung des Konfliktes"; the East-West divide should be made tolerable. No one seriously considered the option that the Cold War could be ended permanently; let alone that this could be achieved by unilateral action from within the Eastern bloc.[5]

This unexpected option, however, has been carried through and this revolutionizes political science as it has revolutionized the political structures in Eastern Europe. It influences the research agenda of interdependence theory as well. It is, for instance, no longer relevant to study the political contribution of the "innerdeutsche Beziehungen" to the "Zivilisierung des Konfliktes", or to study the effectiveness of the structural economic boycot of East-West trade by means of the Cocom-lists. The question *whether* East-West trade should be increased has been replaced by the question *how* East-West trade should be increased. This suggests a shift in the relevance of the literature: the expertise of traditional research on ways to improve East-West relations should be applied to other political theaters (for instance to study the possibilities of conflict-civilization between India and Pakistan, the Jews and the Palestinians, Mexico and Texas, North and South Korea), while the insights from the studies on West-West and North-South interdependence should be applied to the new European context.

The North-South context

It is not just Western trilateralism and the East-West context which constitutes a challenge to the study of interdependence. Though a policy of interdependence seems to be a promising answer to the socio-political problems in Europe, this is not to say that such a policy is an answer to every problem that is in danger of escalating into political violence. In fact, certain types and levels of interdependence can be looked upon as sources of political violence themselves. One might for instance hypothesize that the North-South relations are at right angles to the presumed causality between the abolition of war and interdependence: the existing web of relations is complex enough, but it is primarily associated with the spiders living in it, catching flies. Do the countries of the South also need "a policy of interdependence", to challenge the North to positive action?

Such has been tried; but sofar it has failed. In the early 1970s the countries of the South discovered their so-called commodity power: because of an economic boost, the consumption of raw materials in the industrialized countries increased. Much capital was invested in raw materials too, as a result of the inflation and the instability on the exchange markets that followed the break-down of the Bretton Woods monetary system (1972-1973). Furthermore, the oil-policy of the Organization of Oil Exporting Countries (OPEC), leading to the oil-crisis of 1973, seemed to prove that the South could use its commodity power successfully. This all stimulated the "Group of 77" to devise a coordinated programme for a New International Economic Order (NIEO).[6] The programme was defended at the gatherings of the United Nations, the Conference on International Economic Cooperation (CIEC) and UNCTAD IV and V. Representatives of the Southern countries are said to have proclaimed interdependence at these conferences as a tactic against the North to point out that its responsibility towards the South was inescapable. But, as a NIEO was not achieved, it has also been claimed that these representatives were in fact using the word interdependence only as a tactic to preserve the favoured position of ruling elites within their home countries.[7] Anyhow, the attempt to formulate a policy of interdependence failed at the very moment that the political circumstances seemed to be optimal. Scepsis in the developing countries about the need to improve interdependence theories, therefore, is understandable.

Simultaneously, however, one should consider the alternatives; does a policy of independence, autarchy and state sovereignty provide a more promising future for the developing world? The challenge to political science here is obvious.

13

Global challenges

The East-West, West-West and North-South incentives to the study of interdependence suggest a geo-political or area-specific approach of IR, but that impression is misleading. The incentives can also be structured according to an issue-specific approach. First of all there are many studies on economic issues, such as interdependence in monetary affairs and banking or interdependence in trade relations. Specifically relevant to political science is the literature on the national security implications of increasing economic interdependence.[8]

Secondly, interdependence is one of the main themes in the study of international organizations and regime formation.[9] An example frequently used in interdependence literature in relation to the problems of regime formation, concerns the problems about how to formulate the law of the sea. Or, in the words of Ernst Haas, how to manage "ocean space"? At least the following interests are involved here:

> "fishing, mining, merchant shipping, pollution control, underwater communications, oceanographic research, innocent passage through territorial waters, recreation, maintenance of law and order, the peaceful settlement of disputes, conservation of *all* living resources of the sea, maritime safety and ownership of vessels, slavery, piracy, the drug traffic, the development and diffusion of new ocean-related technologies, the use of underwater nuclear explosions, arms control."[10]

These are completely different interests, involving rather different interest groups, but serving one of them may be opposing the interests of others. In other words, within "ocean space" the many specific issues are strongly interdependent without any coherence in their different interests. Should the involved actors defend their own interests in a "free market" or has the process to be governed by some kind of "ocean space government"? In either case knowledge is required about the character of the existing interrelations and the expected impact of changing one of the variables.

Thirdly, interdependence is at times mentioned as the cause of specific, relatively new forms of political violence. It has for instance been hypothesized that terrorism is a typical side-effect of growing global interdependence: through the world media, symbolic small-scale actions can have a worldwide impact. This makes dramatic acts of violence more attractive to extremist groups; terrorist actions can hardly be kept secret from the public. Simultaneously, however, terrorism shows that state boundaries provide little security in the present-day world and that international cooperation is imperative if it is to be suppressed.[11] Thus, one might question whether an increase of terrorism is the price to be paid for growing interdependence or whether terrorism profits from the traditional impotence of governments to cooperate effectively, while securing their sovereignty in domestic affairs.

This uncertainty about what causes the problem — interdependence or governmental unwillingness to cooperate — is not restricted to observations about terrorism, but a central feature in the analyses of many issues: the threat of scarce natural resources, the unjust distribution of welfare combined with ruthless repression (torture, disappearances, political murder, structural exploitation and "Verelendung" of parts of humanity), the potential destruction of the eco-systems on which the human species and other highly developed forms of life depend, the uncontrollable effects of modern warfare and the likewise uncontrollable production of and trade in weapons (with the accompanying waste of labour, capital and energy), are issues that dominate the political agendas all around the world. *Disarmament, Development* and environmental *Preservation* (DDP) are the catchwords for these global challenges, of which the urgency is clear, but to which the traditions of government are hardly adjusted.[12]

They seem to be caused by forms of global interdependence, but their solution seems to require even more global interdependence. To find an answer to that paradox is another stimulus to study interdependence theory.

Politicians and interdependence

The last incentive to be mentioned here is provided by the fact that politicians actually refer to interdependence on many occasions, in regard to many different issues. Politicians can appeal to interdependence in order to take the wind out of the sails of those opposing their policy proposals: global interests should take precedence over local, ethnocentric interests; or, one step further: the only way to serve the local, ethnocentric interest in the longer run would require that immediate priority is given to the global interest. For reasons like that, the European Community has the right to meddle in the activities of "our" Dutch fishermen, and for that reason the International Atomic Energy Agency (IAEA) intervenes in the "national" industrial security procedures of its member states. The effects of an overfished North Sea or of accidents with nuclear power stations, like the Chernobyl accident in 1986, are inevitably international in scale and "thus" too important to leave prevention solely in the hands of local decision-makers.

Similarly, an appeal to global interdependence can counter (neo)mercantilistic and protectionistic tendencies in times of economic recession. While the essence of mercantilism is that national economic and political interests should have priority over considerations about economic efficiency on a global scale, the essence of interdependence is that global efficiency has in fact become the national interest.

But, appealing to the same logic, the International Monetary Fund (IMF) and the World Bank have intervened in the domestic economic policies of "sovereign" developing countries, forcing some of them to economize beyond the point of social elasticity, stimulating either civil war or fierce repression. Internationalization of interests gave the theocratic regime in Iran occasion to meddle with the freedom of press and speech in Great Britain, as has been exemplified by the Salmon Rushdie affair (1989-1990). Internationalization of interests has turned the United States into a busy-body in Latin America; if not to fight communism, then to fight drugcartels.[13]

In short, national interests have a global impact; global interests make themselves felt nationally. Students of International Relations have the task to point out whether an appeal to interdependence is justifiable or an improper mystification of traditional, nationalistic and ethnocentric power politics; a mystification of the principle "You depend, I rule".[14] To this end one should know what relevance an interdependence theory has to understanding world politics in general. Answering that question means posing many others and with that, one enters the jungle of empirical and theoretical problems to which this study is devoted. What is interdependence? With what types of thinking is the concept associated and to what issues and actors is it applied?

A typology of structural interdependence

The concept of interdependence does not mean the same to everyone in political science.[15] Its purport in relation to development issues and the North-South divide is not necessarily the same as its meaning with respect to the East-West context or to the trilateralism of West-West relations. This is confusing. Some critics therefore argue that the concept of interdependence is quite meaningless. It is seldom carefully defined, and talking about interdependence often contributes to the confusion in political debates, rather than ending it.[16]

It is certainly true that in the literature one comes across several essentially different applications of the word interdependence, leading to rather diverse answers as to its empirical reality and its political implications. Despite the differences, however, they can still be framed together in a meaningful way.[17]

When used in political science, "interdependence" in general refers to *independent social actors*, who wish to preserve their identity, but who are also *structurally affected by one another's behaviour* (whether they like it or not). In German: "Die Akteure sind selbständig aber nicht unabhängig".[18]

The reasons for this mutual affect may be two-fold: the actors are involved in each other's affairs, or they are part of the same system. Of course, these two sources of interdependence do not necessarily exclude one another — if actors are part of the same system they are indirectly involved in one another's affairs, and reversely, many systems are based on the involvement of two or more actors with each other. But the distinction is of great importance in a practical sense. A lot of confusion in the literature results from the fact that statements on the systemic level are wrongly compared with statements on a behavioural level.

Suppose, for example, that someone characterizes the relationship between the Ancient Greek city-states Athens and Sparta as a perfect example of high-level interdependence, because both were part of the same system: the Greeks shared many rules that regulated diplomacy and the conduct of warfare, they had the same religion and culture, they shared a common inheritance and agreed on who were the "barbarians"; in short, they were all part of Hellas and every city-state was tied to the fate of the system as such. This claim (that Sparta and Athens were highly interdependent) will not be understood, however, by someone who uses the word interdependence only in reference to tangible relations and the vulnerability of the situation for changes in these relations. Looking at such direct involvement and its existential value, the interdependence between Athens and Sparta was not that impressive. Originally, the polis was autarchic and until the fifth century B.C. trade volumes were low. Moreover, from the fifth century onwards, Athens and Sparta were leaders of rival military blocs, who avoided making themselves vulnerable by having relations in other fields. Thus interdependence was low and insignificant.

Both arguments make sense, both logically and empirically. But they cannot be compared, unless the two different levels of abstraction are taken into account. Apparently, one must distinguish the interdependence at the system's level from the interdependence in day to day interaction. These differences can be worked out in a simple typology of three types of structural involvement.

The first type refers to the intertwinement of activities of actors or even the (partial) integration of actors. If in this sense one is speaking of, for example, the economic interdependence between two countries, one refers to all economic cross-border relations in which actors residing in these countries are involved. Even if within these relations a formal division of property is present or can easily be restored, one is allowed to speak of interdependence because an actual division of property would have direct consequences for the actors and countries involved. The reciprocal effects of a unilateral retreat from the relationship are quite concrete and directly traceable. They can be put on a sensitivity/vulnerability scale. They are explained in terms of the consequences of specific behaviour, rather than in terms of system-dynamics. (Reciprocal effects can, of course, be both positive and negative.) This type will be called integrative interdependence.

The second type of structural involvement is related to the first, but here the emphasis is not on the intertwinement of activities, but on a human-made superstructure: some form of formal, institutionalized governance with juridical responsibilities that replace or go beyond those of the participating actors. "Governments" are the most familiar examples of this. They are linking all kinds of social actors into one "national" household, thereby stimulating the further development of functional specialization within the State. But most of the literature in this context focusses on "international organizations" as superstructures that coordinate specific issue-areas, such as the specialized agencies of the United Nations Organization. In this context interdependence is not of an integrative type, but of a functionalist type.

In relation to the Athens/Sparta example, these two types of interdependence refer to the tangible relations between the people living in these cities. Do they trade with one another; do they fight; do they communicate; are there other actors involved?

The third type of structural involvement refers to the Hellas-type of interdependence; the existence of a system, or even an "organic whole", a body: the individual actors depend upon one another because they inevitably and involuntarily belong to the same system. The fate of every element in the system is linked to the fate of the system as a whole and through that to all other elements. The interdependence here is of an "automatic" nature; that is, no direct interaction between different actors is required to make them interdependent. The concept refers to chain-reactions, feed-back processes, action-reaction patterns. The effects on social life are explained in terms of system-dynamics rather than in terms of individual behaviour. The world, for example, is such an organic whole in an ecological sense, a military and an economic sense.

In sum, this gives the following typology:

19

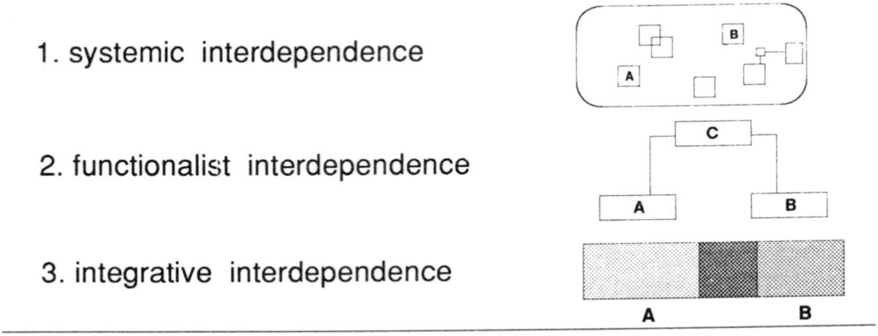

1. systemic interdependence

2. functionalist interdependence

3. integrative interdependence

figure 1   *Three types of structural interdependence*

Thus, when interdependence means that independent social actors are structurally affected by one another's behaviour, this may be systemic, functionalist, or integrative in nature.

In case of systemic involvement, the interdependence among the actors is restricted to the fate of the system, and thus restricted to the behaviour and the behavioural options which willy-nilly affect or can affect the system. (Example: the individual acts of car-driving and cutting tropical trees are put on the agenda of world politics because the accumulation of these acts affects the functioning of the eco-system on a global scale and, through that, the functioning of the actors depending on that eco-system.)

In case of functionalist and integrative involvement, the interdependence among the actors is related to their direct interactions, and thus restricted to the behaviour which determines the continuation or the disruption of the relationship. (Example 1.: De Gaulle decreased the measure of integrative interdependence among the West-European armies when he withdrew the French army from allied NATO-command. Example 2.: The governments of the European countries increased their functionalist interdependence when they decided to extend and institutionalize the CSCE-process.)

There are no clear-cut dividing lines between the two behavioural types. Empirically, functionalist and integrative interdependence may be difficult to distinguish. Many organizations, NATO is a good example, contain aspects of both: NATO is an example of functionalist interdependence when it comes to its political structure (the memberstates are politically sovereign and, officially, NATO only orchestrates consensus), while it is an example of integrative interdependence in military terms (NATO-forces are under allied command and operate as a unit). An empirical distinction between systemic interdependence and the two behavioural types seems easier to make, provided that the actors and levels of analysis are correctly defined. When, for instance, research is done on the interaction between the members of a political party, the party itself is in fact the macro-structure that determines the systemic interdependence, while the behaviour among subgroups and individuals within this structure can be characterized by functionalist or integrative patterns of interdependence. In research about the political behaviour in a specific society, however, the same party can be defined as one of the actors within the larger framework of this society. In other words, discussions about what should or should not be called systemic interdependence and what is or is not behavioural interdependence will be confusing when the level of analysis remains obscure and when the actors are not clearly defined.

In general it can be said that systemic interdependence is a pre-limiting condition of politics; the Hellas of Athens and Sparta. It is a macro-determinant of social life. Functionalist and integrative interdependence exist within this framework, as other behavioural options exist within this framework, such as isolationism, aloofness or imperialism and colonialism. When people say that the world has become interdependent, they are pointing at this systemic interdependence. The world has become one society by growing interdependent (meaning that independent social actors can affect one another's behaviour or behavioural options worldwide) and as a result this world society has become the macro-perspective within which social behaviour should be analysed. (How and why this process of growing interdependence took place is the subject of chapter 2.) In early times the family or the tribe provided a macro-perspective for the analysis of social behaviour; the region and the continent have also played that role. Now it is the globe.

Illustrative is that, in February, 1989, the Kayapó Indians from the basin of the Amazon river demonstrated at a meeting of the

World Bank to protest against the international financing of the plans of "their" Brazilian government to build barrages in the Amazon river with the aim to improve the Brazilian economic infra-structure in order, among other things, to pay its huge debts to bankers in America, whose bankruptcy could in turn cause a global economic crisis. It shows that not even people who wish to live in isolation can find structural conditions on earth which guarantee that they can safely do so. As the freedom of action in micro-economics is ultimately determined by macro-economics, so the freedom of action in ethnocentric or in state-centric politics is ultimately determined by the macro-dynamics of a world society.

Qualifications of structural interdependence

Obviously, qualifications have to be made, because the impact and importance of the global dimension differ from one area to another. World records in sports and Olympic Games are certainly a token of the world society which has evolved, but they are not essential to social life. Also, the impact of a breakdown of the world economy is qualitatively different from the impact of a third world war or the impact of terrorism, while the impact of ongoing disasters, like poverty, hunger, torture or environmental degradation is different again. Moreover, not every part on earth is similarly affected by the same event.

Another reason for making qualifications is that social actors can be interdependent at different levels and in different ways at one and the same time. Two business firms might be deadlocked in fierce competition, yet both favour a healthy market. Their interdependence at the system's level is characterized by "shared interests", while the interdependence in their direct relationship is antagonistic and of a zero-sum type. The shared interest in the market constrains their competing strategies, and their competition constrains efficient cooperation — double investments are likely. For similar reasons the often grim conflicts between employers and employed seldom end in blowing up the factory; both depend on it.

Interdependent relations thus have to be qualified. For this purpose a second typology can be made, which cuts across the first one. Interdependent relations appear in two extreme forms.

a) confrontational interdependence. The first qualification is based on the traditional dychotomy between power and dependence. Dependence, in its meaning of "subordination", "being subjected to", is the antipole of power; dependence as impotence, as being powerless to act on one's own account. Inter-dependence in this meaning refers to a "mutual subjection". There is a stalemate: thanks to the other(s) neither side can reach its goal. In this restricted meaning interdependence can be seen as a key-concept in balance of power theories. This is the first extreme way in which the concept can be qualified: *interdependence as the consequence of the mutually perceived necessity of obstruction or competition* — the image of "two scorpions in a bottle", as used by Oppenheimer in 1953 to describe the dangerous impotence of the superpowers.

> "[T]he prevailing view is that we are probably faced with a long period of cold war in which conflict, tension and armaments are to be with us. The trouble then is just this; we may anticipate a state of affairs in which two Great Powers will be in a position to put an end to the civilization and life of the other, though not without risking its own. *We may be likened to two scorpions in a bottle, each capable of killing the other, but only at the risk of his own life.*"[19]

Sometimes this is labelled negative interdependence. But one should realize that this stems from a normative attitude towards this type of interdependence, and is not a mathematical expression of empirical findings. (Third parties may favour a stalemate between two other parties and thus call it positive.) A better denomination has been suggested by Dieter Senghaas: "Konfrontative Interdependenz" or confrontational interdependence.[20] Apart from the military and ideological relations between East and West, he mentioned the Sino-Soviet relations, the relations between Iran and Irak and between Egypt and Lybia as examples of this type of interdependence in recent history (during the 1980s).

In the realm of military strategy, the logic of confrontational interdependence was in fact already developed by Carl von Clausewitz. In *Vom Kriege* (first published in 1832-1834) he isolated the logic of warfare artifically from its social context and tried to lay bare its intrinsic dynamics. Because a war is unthinkable without an enemy, the success of planning depends on the reactions of the antagonist, just as his success depends on our reactions; warfare is caught in the logic of chess without being subject to the rules of chess. According to Clausewitz, in the abstract this caused (a) a mutual tendency to use violence to its extreme; (b) a mutual tendency to strive for complete subjection; (c) a mutual tendency to use all available forces and powers, including optimal investments in material and immaterial means of resistance.[21] (An interesting aspect of Clausewitz' reasoning is that he concluded that these dynamics towards absolute warfare were only realistic when war could be isolated from the rest of the social intercourse. In reality there would always be all kinds of modifications (constraints!) to temper these intrinsic tendencies. Here, the rules of chess enter the game. It is the task of politics, Clausewitz argued, to determine the balance between what is probable in practice and what is possible in theory.)

b) constructional interdependence. Obviously, the concept of interdependence does not owe its popularity to this negative sense. Its good reputation is due to the opposite extreme: *interdependence as the consequence of the mutually perceived necessity of cooperation —* the image of a symbiosis, a relationship of mutual advantage. This form of interdependence follows from another meaning of the word dependence, namely, "need" or "want". If different units need one another for their well-being (or merely think they do), one could speak of positive interdependence.[22] The economic and political relations among the OECD-countries are an obvious example.

Sometimes this is referred to as symmetrical interdependence, but this is an unsatisfactory term, because it suggests an equal distribution of costs and benefits, which is empirically doubtful and theoretically not a precondition of a symbiosis. The label "cooperational" interdependence, as opposed to confrontational interdependence, does not work either, because this gives the false impression that relations of this type are free of conflict and full of harmony. I therefore propose to call it "Konstruktive Interdependenz", constructional interdependence.

This quality is dominated by a dogma that is at right angles with the ideal of independence: two can do more than one. In this sense dependence, and especially interdependence, is not the antipole of power, but indeed a source of power: one for all, all for one. Cooperation creates a *surplus value* none of the actors involved can create on his own. In other words, the actors are interdependent as far as the surplus is concerned (but still independent with regard to the rest of their activities).

Basically, the cooperation creating the surplus value can take two forms. First, the actors can unite their resources; a labour union. This can be seen in political coalitions, business mergers, military alliances and, indeed, labour unions. Secondly, the actors can arrive at a division of labour. Here the surplus value results from specialization and the exchange of the products so obtained (trade). A lot of the literature on interdependence is based on the idea of an (international) division of labour.

In both instances (union and division of labour) the cooperation will not be free of conflict: the distribution of costs and benefits (also in an immaterial sense), the working conditions (micro: the interpersonal relations; macro: the political climate), and the tension, inherent for each partner in the cooperation, between the individual identity and the collective identity are constant sources of potential conflict.

Distributional problems are often formulated in terms of asymmetrical versus symmetrical interdependence. Specific relationships can show a strong asymmetry, and thus a net dependence, which is, of course, a source of conflict.[23] The North-South context is an obvious case in point, and the unequal distribution of welfare within virtually every country is another. But also in case of presumed symmetry, conflicts will exist, for instance about the distribution of the costs and benefits involved. Moreover, there will always be the danger that, in the course of time, the symmetry will evolve into asymmetry.

25

Such a symmetry-scale — a qualification in terms of the distribution of costs and benefits — points in fact to a third dimension of interdependence. If the first dimension is the structure of interdependence, and the second, the qualifications expressed by the typology of confrontational and constructional interdependence, then the third dimension is concerned with the relative positions of the actors in the structure in terms of comparative costs and benefits — the measure of symmetry.

Apart from "mutual subjection" (negative extreme) and "mutual need" (positive extreme) interdependence can also mean "being mutually influenced", which has a more neutral connotation. This is based on a third meaning of the word dependence, "being influenced by", which is present in sentences like: "a good harvest depends on the weather" or: "employment in the FRG depends on the exchange-rate of the US-dollar" (the dollar-rate influences the export-possibilities of German firms and, through that, the employment).

Mutual influence again refers to the structure of the relations. An indicator frequently referred to in this context is the measure of sensitivity or vulnerability of the actors involved to changes in their relations or to changes in the system. This indicator, however, has the disadvantage that, in general, it is unilaterally defined:[24] what is analysed is the sensitivity or vulnerability of one actor in respect to manipulations of its relations by other actors. It tells us something about dependence; the reciprocity is not considered, while reciprocity is the crucial aspect of interdependence when it comes to constraints on unilateral behaviour. Only when the sum of the different measures of sensitivity of all actors is taken, the measure of mutual influence can be known. In this way only, a sensitivity/vulnerability scale can be an indicator of mutual influence.

Both typologies can be combined:

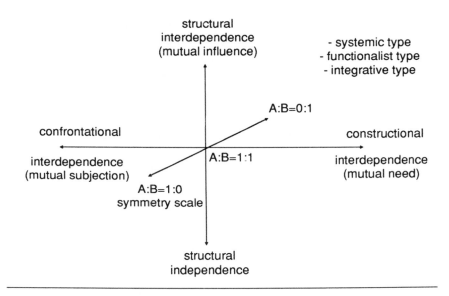

figure 2   *Qualifications of structural interdependence*

To sum this up:

- Structural interdependence can be operationalized into a three-dimensional concept, which expresses how given actors are mutually affected by one another's behaviour.
- The first dimension concerns the degree of mutual involvement (the measure of existential value of the interdependence).
- The second dimension concerns the character of the mutual involvement (confrontational and constructional aspects).
- The third dimension concerns the (a)symmetry of the mutual involvement (the distribution of costs and benefits).

Doubts about empirical research

A fundamental question concerns the application of this model (or any other model of interdependence for that matter). Can it for instance be operationalized empirically? To this end one has to

27

develop specific indicators of the three dimensions of interdependence: what is meant by "mutual influence" and what is not meant by it; when is one allowed to speak of "mutual need"; what points at "mutual subjection"; how does one measure symmetry? Basic to these questions is the more general problem whether the above model should be applied universally or in a discriminatory way. Are all social relations to be measured in terms of mutual dependence or only some of them? What is e.g. the use of typifying certain relations as extreme forms of "asymmetrical interdependence" if they are in fact exploitative, repressive, dictatorial or in other ways dehumanizing? Should not relations be qualified with the word that expresses their essence best? If exploitation is their essence, let's call it that! In that case there is a limit to the use of the concept; interdependence is used discriminatorily; a relationship is interdependent or not. Interdependence theory, then, becomes a theory about specific relations (as opposed to a general theory about politics).

On the other hand there is still good reason to initially analyse all social relations in terms of mutual dependence, before passing judgment. This implies a universal or a holistic perspective. Interdependence theory here generally means *analysis in terms of the relative dependency positions of actors with respect to specific values* (as opposed to traditional analysis in terms of the relative power positions of states with respect to national interests or, in case of marxist oriented theory, of social classes with respect to class interests). By taking an initial distance such an analysis can reveal the structure on which the injustice rests. Weak spots might be detected, and as a result the net-dependent actors might discover a certain margin for manipulation, as the net-dominant actors might discover specific sensitivities or even vulnerabilities.

In this way, interdependence theory becomes a general theory about politics (as opposed to a theory about specific relations) and knowledge about the variations in the degrees of interdependence in all its dimensions becomes central to its application.

But the dilemma is that this "neutral", strictly scientific stand might prove to be politically inopportune: reference to interdependence might be seen or actually be misused as an attempt to obscure structural exploitation: parasitical relations under the cover of a symbiosis. This criticism was uttered, for example, by the Chinese delegate to the United Nations Special Assembly Session, Deputy Premier Deng Xiaoping in 1974:

> "Moscow's imperialist fallacies are even more undisguised than the so-called 'interdependence' advertised by the other superpower, which actually means retaining the exploitative relationship."[25]

The other dilemma, however, is that, in the absence of a clear dividing line between parasitical and symbiotic relations, the discriminatory use of interdependence is doubtful as well. Except for extreme, obvious cases, the debates on the question whether a situation is interdependent or not will therefore probably reflect normative interpretations, rather than scientific findings.

One possible way out of these dilemmas is improvement of the model by seeking empirically verifiable indicators of interdependence. This will make the model more convincing. However, in this study I have chosen not to make an attempt in that direction. The main reason is that evidence is theory-dependent. Empirical research is always based on sets of implicit and explicit axioms, and when these axioms are debated empirical "evidence" loses much of its convincing power.

Moreover, in order to develop a thorough empirical model of interdependence, more is required than just the above typology. Interdependence has been defined as a relationship between social actors, but this does not define the actors themselves. That definition depends on other theoretical considerations: is it justifiable to restrict research to the relations among governments only, or do we have to include social movements, international organizations and multinational corporations as independent social actors? Even if that question is answered, the kind of data about their relations that are required to measure interdependence must be defined. This, again, involves implicit a-priori axioms about what is thought to be relevant: to what extent are psychological, cultural, economic or historical data relevant? Which disciplines should be involved and how can their know-how be matched in one single operationalization?

Then there is the question about what exactly is to be measured. In many cases it may be doubted whether it really is *inter*-dependence that is measured, rather than dependence. The elasticity of the import-curve and the demand for foreign goods and services, for instance, are first of all state-centric indicators of economic dependence: the elasticity determines the costs of losing a trade relation. Similar kinds of state-centric indicators have been developed for export-dependence or the gross formation of fixed capital abroad. Long-term foreign investments and investments in the trade sector may indicate a measure of vulnerability to disruptions in foreign countries, but, again, it says something about dependence only. The reciprocity is not measured.

A problem with a second type of indicators is that their political relevance is not clear. What can, for instance, be concluded from statistics about personal mobility (emigration, tourism, student exchanges, foreign workers, business elites) or from statistics about communication (like cross-border mail traffic or T.V. satellite connections)? Also the political weight of economic costs is hard to determine, even if the costs are accurately known, because the perceptions of the actors involved remain obscure. Whether and to what extent an actor is willing to make sacrifices on one issue in order to be successful on another issue cannot be concluded by measuring economic data only. In short, evidence is theory dependent.

To understand the theoretical controversies about interdependence, one has to be aware of a more fundamental problem, that is at the root of political science as such. Interdependence theory fits in a specific tradition of Euro-American political thought, and as such it competes with other paradigms about world politics. To understand the thinking on interdependence it is first of all necessary to know its position within political science.

Three paradigms in IR-theory

During the 1980s a consensus was reached with regard to a basic classification of theories of world politics. The main catchwords may differ, but essentially Western political science knows three perspectives: Realism, Pluralism and Structuralism.[26] This tripartition partly stems from the disputes, the fundamental differences of opinion, which are so typical of the short history of the theory of international relations; a forced polarization in which each perspective takes its own identity from the denial of the others. The term Realism is an obvious inheritance of this, as it insinuates that competing views are irrealistic and free-floating.

Partly, the tripartition also stems from a more neutral demand: the demand for political sciences to be taught as objectively as possible. Especially in Great Britain efforts have been made to describe the state of the art in political science.[27] In 1985 Michael Banks presented a general survey which is summarized in table 1.

These three perspectives form a triangle in which the existing literature can be located. Because of their partly polemical origins, the characterizations of the paradigms look a bit like caricatures and actual divisions along these lines tend to stigmatize the literature. Yet Banks ventures to make such a division, and in doing so he reveals a second distinction in the IR-literature, namely between classical texts (everything written before 1918), traditional texts (the period between 1918 and the 1950s and 1960s), and contemporary literature (roughly from the late sixties, early seventies onwards).

This distinction is based primarily on the history of Realist writings, and, with a somewhat different time-scale, Banks also applies it to Structuralist literature. In his treatment of the Pluralist paradigm, however, he restricts himself to contemporary contributions.

table 1 *Characterization of the three paradigms in the Western study of international relations.*

	Realism	Pluralism	Structuralism
character-ization of world system:	politics of power & security	politics of interdependence & transnationalism	politics of dominance & dependence
	state anarchy; billiard ball model; state-centric.	world society; cobweb model; multi-centric.	centre-periphery; octopus model; multi-centric.
main actors:	nation-states; governments; IGOs.	governments; IGOs; (I)NGOs; social movements; departments; individuals.	social classes; economic and political elites; MNCs.
main subject:	struggle for power; alliances; national interest; military strategy.	global challenges; interdependence; transnational interests; issue-specific approach.	economic power; exploitation; class/elite interests; historical materialism; "dependencia".

(IGO = Intergovernmental Organization; (I)NGO = (International) Non-governmental Organization; MNC = Multinational Corporation.)

Note that interdependence theory is defined here as a subfield of Pluralism — the school of thought. This does not mean that interdependence is equated with pluralism — the concept. A difference between interdependence and pluralism is that pluralism expresses the multiple-actor character of societies, while interdependence points at the relations among the actors.

The origins of Realism and Structuralism

Historically, Realism can be traced back to the work of Thucydides (460-396 B.C.), Machiavelli (1469-1527), Hobbes (1588-1679) and Von Clausewitz (1790-1831). The works of Aron, Carr, Niebuhr, Herz, Lippmann, Morgenthau, Bull and Wight form the traditional texts of this paradigm. "This group provides the background reading for any study of contemporary theory in IR", Banks writes.

> "The majority of introductory texts continue to draw heavily upon it; the subfield of strategic studies has grown directly from it, and its theories form the unstated paradigm for many accounts of the foreign policies of individual states."[28]

Here Banks expresses a point of view which is present in most textbooks.

There is, however, still another intellectual inheritance which has made an influential contribution to this paradigm, but which is seldom if ever mentioned. This inheritance is formed by nationalistic theories. Persons like Gottfried Herder (1744-1803) and Giuseppe Mazzini (1805-1872) taught the doctrine that nationality is the only just foundation of statehood, and that the limits of states ought always to be determined, not by the accidents of conquest or dynastic inheritance, but by the natural affinities of peoples. Once a nation-state is formed, either by unification or by separation, a "natural" organic whole has come into existence, which seems to function as a closed actor.[29] The state centricity and the sacrosanctity of national sovereignty rights within the Realist paradigm stem from this doctrine of nationality.

If we look at all its roots, it will be recognized that contemporary Realism is primarily a theoretical abstraction from the struggle for power among the military rulers and the ethnocentric peoples on the European continent.

Banks locates the roots of Structuralism in (a) the early Christian and humanistic attention for social justice and personal development, (b) the philosophy and moralism of Immanuel Kant (1724-1804), and (c) the dialectics of Hegel (1770-1831). Here, the

33

traditional literature includes the work of Karl Marx (1818-1883), Friedrich Engels (1820-1895) and, somewhat later, the work of Lenin (1870-1924). Apparently, Banks intends to make Structuralism a reservoir for political theories that are concerned with vertical power relations: the "automatic" exploitation of one group of people by some other group, given a specific social structure. (In that sense, Realism is a reservoir for theories of horizontal power relations: the struggle among equals for better positions in a specific social structure.) But if this is indeed his intention, then the traditional phase should include more branches of political theory than just Marxist theory. One could for instance include documents like the encyclical *Rerum Novarum* (1891) of Pope Leo XIII, in which Catholic social theory is formulated.

But there is a good reason why Banks should be pardoned for concentrating on the Marxist-Leninist branch only. As the tenor of this branch is against the grain of the political establishment, the scientific value of historical materialism has long been neglected by the mainstream of political science, especially at the universities in the United States.

> "Once the study of IR became institutionalized in universities, most of its professoriate regarded structuralist ideas as false, or unduly normative, or politically subversive."[30]

It is indeed quite unlikely that scholars with other opinions would have been able to collect any funds for research during the Palmer Raids of the twenties or the McCarthyism of the fifties. "Natural" selection, therefore, kept this perspective on world politics outside the mainstream of the US-dominated political sciences. Especially the work of Immanuel Wallerstein (since the early 1970s) may change this situation.[31] (It is telling, though, that Wallerstein is working and living in France as much as in the USA.)

In Europe, and also in Latin America, structuralism has had better chances to develop, as is witnessed by neo-Marxist literature, the "Dependencia" school, and the work of Johan Galtung. Still, American studies remained dominant in the field, and British researchers (see note 27) must be credited for giving Structuralism its present place in the paradigm debate.

The post-war origins of Pluralism

Though Banks is aware of a clear intellectual tradition of Realism and Structuralism, which dates back to the ancient classics and early Christianity, he considers Pluralism a new phase in the development of political theory. According to Banks — and this opinion is shared by many others[32] — the emergence of the Pluralist paradigm is *exclusively* a reaction to the dominant position of Political Realism after the second World War.

The so-called anomalies of the Realist paradigm (these are political events that can only be explained in an ad hoc manner, independent of the central assumptions about the working of the international system) became increasingly evident. Insofar as Banks is aware of a Pluralist tradition, it concerns such exposures. He mentions, for instance, the work of David Mitrany (1888-1977), who, already in 1933, pointed at the possibility of a peaceful and voluntary integration of nation-states (functionalism). But, according to Banks, the development of Pluralism into a distinct paradigm took place in the 1970s. He even calls his compatriot and teacher John Burton "by far the most important contributor to the new paradigm".[33] That judgment will not be readily subscribed to by his American colleagues.

Fact is, however, that in the second half of this century it became increasingly difficult to carry out research using state-centric models. This was primarily a result of the steady growth of IGOs (from about 100 in 1945 to about 250 in 1970) and the explosive growth of internationally operating NGOs (from about 800 in 1945 to some 2000 in 1970). Table 2 illustrates this development. One important feature of the IGOs cannot be expressed in this table: they have been institutionalized and have their own bureaucracies. The political weight and the extent of independent decision-making of, for instance, the present-day NATO stands in no comparison with the political weight of the ad hoc military alliances of before 1945. In a historical perspective it is quite obvious that the growth of IGOs and INGOs is more than just a level-of-analysis problem or a neglectable development in the realm of "low politics".

35

table 2   *Growth in IGOs and INGOs in the world from 1909-1988* [34]

year:	1909	1951	1960	1968	1972	1976	1981	1985	1988
IGOs:	37	123	154	229	280	252	337	378	309
INGOs:	176	832	1255	1899	2173	2502	4265	4676	4518

(In comparison: in 1988, the number of nation-states, defined as self-governing units, was 167, of which 159 were member of the United Nations.)

At a purely theoretical level, Realism increasingly caused difficulties, too. A number of social crises in the early 1970s called into question the primacy of military security issues over economic welfare issues. Especially, the military failure of the USA in Vietnam, the breakdown of the Bretton Woods monetary system, and the OPEC oil-embargo should be mentioned here. The failure of the USA to win the war in Vietnam (1964-1975) showed the illusory nature of the axiom that resort to war is the ultimate solution to political problems. In this case it was not. Even more importantly, the strong domestic opposition against the war showed the illusory nature of the axiom that the nation-state is a coherent actor, represented by a government serving the national interest. This active role of public opinion in foreign affairs (through the media) also showed the irrelevance of a strict distinction between the realms of domestic and foreign politics. The protests were broadcasted worldwide by television and thus had a direct political influence outside the traditional channels of diplomacy.

The breakdown of Bretton Woods was also connected with the Vietnam war. In 1944 the British Ministry of Finance lost its struggle with the USA Department of Finance about what should have become the key currency in the new, post-war exchange system. Britain defended John Maynard Keynes' proposal to create the "bancor" (a stateless currency, the value of which would be deduced from a basket of national currencies) but in 1944 the US-dollar was as-good-as-gold and the superpower status of the USA was indisputable, so it was the dollar which got a key role in the monetary world. In the 1960s this hegemonic position was lost. Part of this is explained by the recovery of Western Europe, Japan and the world economy in general. The other reason, however, is the neglect by the American Administrations of the effects of its ambitious domestic and foreign policies on the balance of payments. The huge costs of the Vietnam-war were an important factor in putting the convertibility of the dollar into gold under pressure. In August 1971 President Nixon had to abandon this convertibility and, after a new devaluation in 1973, the Bretton Woods system was dead.

In the same year OPEC cut off the oil supplies because of the Western support of Israel in the fourth Israeli-Arab War. From a traditional perspective, this was the world turned upside down: an economic cartel (not a nation-state or a military alliance) proved able to give the world an uppercut with an economic fist driven by commodity power. One reaction was to invest still more money and energy in military defence: larger oil reserves, rapid deployment forces, etcetera. But the notion of military power as the ultimate means to protect "the" National Interest also came to hang in the balance. Pluralism evolved out of this criticism.

The hidden tradition of Pluralism

The above explanation of the origins of Pluralism is correct but incomplete. Actually, Pluralism has a rich tradition, but this is generally neglected or remains hidden.[35] There are several reasons for this. Part of the explanation is that the generation of political scientists that dominated the 1970s had its background in an unhistorical, if not, anti-historical sociological training. Knowledge of the world before 1945 was not deemed to be essential for the analysis of the social developments of the present. It is typical that in 1977 in a quantitative analysis of the quality of textbooks on political science, historical explanations were measured among the minuses instead of the pluses.[36]

Another part of the explanation is to be found in the Euro-American culture (in science, as elsewhere) that attributes a high value to originality, innovation and the opening up of new horizons. Whether one is re-inventing the wheel, is a question which is not asked very often.

But the most interesting part of the explanation is to be found in the apparent success of Political Realism in both the United States and Europe. As noted before, the tripartition between Realism, Pluralism and Structuralism is partly based on disputes which are fundamental to the discipline of political science. To a certain extent the three paradigms and their characterizations (see table 1) have always been competitive. During the first phase of the competition between them Structuralism was immediately side-tracked: because of the success of the Russian Revolution (1917) marxist-oriented views were suspicious even before political science was established and institutionalized at the universities (a process which intensified after 1919). Structuralism remained offside until the post-war period of decolonization and the rise of the North-South and human rights issues. Pluralism, on the other hand, was dominant at the universities during the interbellum, but it finally lost the first round, precisely for that reason.

To understand this, one has to be aware of a third classification of theories of world politics. That is the distinction between Idealism and Realism.

During its institutionalization phase in the twenties political science was dominated by liberal, legalistic and moralistic views. This was largely due to the influence of the ideals of the League of Nations and President Wilson's peace policy. In one of the most widely used textbooks on IR-theory Holsti wrote that:

> "[M]ost work in the field during this decade had a normative orientation: Writers were less concerned with the variables or conditions affecting government behavior in external relations than with judging the policies of states according to their own values."[37]

We are told that these writers (Holsti does not mention them by name) believed that a rational and moral political order based on universally valid principles was attainable. To reach this ideal they put their trust in education, reform of antiquated social institutions, and the sporadic use of violence (at the level of mere police actions).

This optimism and idealism was brought down, first of all, by the course of history: the rise of totalitarianism in Europe, the great economic Depression, the failure of the League, and, finally, the second World War. Secondly, the Idealist School was attacked by theorists like E.H. Carr and Hans J. Morgenthau, who (not without justification) were looking in their work for the "basic forces" that determined the reality of IR and who were not primarily interested in the "moral principles" which ought to be determinant.[38] The continuation of the Cold War, immediately after the second World War, completed the demise of Idealism and, in fact, of all research and theorizing during the interbellum. According to Rosenau:

> "The advent of World War II led to a great stress on 'realism' in the study and teaching of IR, on recognizing that international actors are often aggressive and self-serving in their behaviour, and the cold-war period of the 1950's and 1960's perpetuated and legitimized the presumption that the central tendencies in world politics move toward conflict."[39]

The 1950s and 1960s, therefore, were characterized by the dominance of the Realist paradigm at the universities, as well as in the praxis of foreign policy. According to quantitative data, even in 1973-1974 Morgenthau's *Politics Among Nations* was still the textbook most frequently referred to in introductory IR courses at American universities.[40]

But with the condemnation of Idealism, the more serious developments of the Pluralist paradigm were thrown aside, too. Actually, the genesis of political science was reduced to a simple cliché. And that is an impoverishment of the discipline.

In *Perspectives on World Politics* (1981) Smith, Little and Shackleton give a striking illustration of this:

> "After what E.H. Carr has described as the *initial 'utopian' phase* of the study of world politics, there developed during the late 1930s and 1940s a definable focus on the politics of power and security."[41]

They introduce Pluralism ("the politics of interdependence and transnationalism", as they call it) as a reaction to Realism at the end of the sixties. Next, they point at the analogous development of Structuralism; "the politics of dominance and dependence". About the "utopian phase", half a century of research and theorizing, not a word. It is as if in the beginning the soil of political science was waste and empty, until Realists planted a scientific tree.

When in the 1970s the criticism of Realism entered a new phase, little reference was made to the pre-war tradition of Pluralism. Such reference would have meant an identification with a track of which the new Pluralists, like the traditional Realists, automatically assumed, as it seems, that it had come to a dead end in the discrepancy between desirability and reality. This generation of scientists and politicians had witnessed the war in its childhood or had even fought in it, and as students they had read and heard mostly Realists, among whom were many migrants who had fled the European continent. Therefore, the criticism brought forward in the 1970s was really new to them and they wanted it to stay that way.

Yet, it is evident that the Pluralist tradition dates from before the war. The critics of the new Pluralist literature were the first to mention this. Especially interdependence theory fell victim to their attempts to force the paradigm debate of the 1970s into the old dichotomy of Idealism and Realism. By exploiting the fact that the "utopian phase" was under a taboo they discredited the political purport of interdependence theory. It has inspired the present author to take a closer look at the early writings on interdependence, and the critics earn the credit for having provided the challenge to do so.

2   The era of global interdependence: when did it start?

Two histories of global interdependence

The great migrations of the period between 375 (the year in which the Huns destroyed the empire of the Ostrogoths at the Black Sea) and 568 (when the Longobards settled in Italy) are early evidence of the fact that the fate of societies in one region of the globe (Europe in this case) is linked to developments in societies located at the other end of the globe. The Chinese had destroyed the second empire of the Huns in Turkestan, which drove part of them to the West; also, many Asian tribes were forced to migrate due to climatic changes, population growth and lack of land. Lust for adventure, war and looting played a role, too, but these factors are of secondary importance as they had also been present in earlier periods, when they had not led to a chain-reaction of migrations. The result of the chain-reaction was that the Germanic peoples, on the run for the pressure from Asia, moved into the West Roman Empire, sometimes as allies, sometimes as plunderers, but in both cases accelerating the breakdown of the Empire. But the people at that time did not and could not know what caused these developments. To them, the invasions of the Huns were similar to an earthquake.

Nowadays, there is a fundamentally different situation. At a Pugwash Conference in Dagomys (USSR) in 1988 the American biologist and population-expert Paul Ehrlich hinted at the possibility of new migrations in the near future. The causes would be partly the same as the ones just mentioned: overpopulation in combination with climatic changes. His warnings were supported by reports of the Worldwatch Institute and the United Nations Environmental Programme (UNEP). The greenhouse effect is expected to lead to a rise in the sea level of up to one meter by the year 2050. Under such circumstances large deltas, as in Bangladesh and Egypt, will be flooded. This means a loss of about 15% of the habitable land in these countries which will cause about 13-14% of their population to be displaced.[1] Even if part of the population were to drown in apathy or because it is unable to escape, India, Birma and the higher parts of Bangladesh can expect at the least some ten million "environmental refugees" to enter their territories. (In Bangladesh there lived about 114,7 million people in 1990.) How are they to shelter and feed them; what will be their political rights; how will the local communities react? How many hundreds of thousands will be hosted by other countries? Even at present many people in "civilized" countries, like the Netherlands or Germany, think they already have a serious refugee, immigrant and migrant-workers problem.

The difference with the year 375 is that in the twentieth century people have the ability to be aware of such interdependence, and therefore can at least try to prevent disastrous events by dealing with the causes — in this example the greenhouse effect, the primitive system of maritime defence in Bangladesh and the problem of population control in Asia (the World Bank has put the cost of a substantial protection plan for Bangladesh at US-$ six billion). It is the difference between "lack of knowledge" and "negligence".

As has been argued in the previous chapter, interdependence is one of the key-concepts in the study of world politics, used to describe the unification of humanity into one single political system — the emerging world society. An extension of the typology of structural interdependence that was developed in chapter 1 concerns the role of perception. The emergence of the world society implies two processes: first, the history of the "physical" unification of different societies (for better or for worse) into one whole. This is the structural dimension of interdependence, as described in chapter 1. Second, the history of the "psychological" awareness of this unification; the *cognitive dimension*.[2] In other words, when we trace the origins of the present era of global interdependence, we have to describe both the history of the emerging global dimension in local politics, and the history of the awareness of that dimension.

The combination of the two is essential. From a present-day perspective the world can (and should) be analysed in terms of a unitary "system" from its very beginning, but this refers essentially to the structural dimension and our present perception of the past. We have grown accustomed to the idea that the world in, for instance, a geological, a biological, a climatological or a geographical sense is and has always been functioning as a whole, meaning that events occurring in one part of the globe affect events taking place in (remote) other parts of the globe. This kind of structural interdependence can and at times did affect human societies. But for as long as it did not exist as a factor in political decision-making, there is little use to talk about global interdependence. Mere facts do not shape political conduct. In order to enter the realm of politics, that is in order to become a subject of social manipulation, the global dimension of life has to be recognized (which, of course, does not imply that it is thereby accepted or correctly understood). The cognitive dimension of interdependence implies that externalities are internalized, and politicized.

The discovery of interdependence in the 1970s

At first sight the awareness of global interdependence might seem a product of the 1970s. In a dispute on Realist theories of International Relations (the paradigm-debate) especially North-American scholars stressed the global dimension of world politics and its priority over "local" dimensions, like America's national interest. The paradigm of Political Realism, which had dominated the study of International Relations in the western hemisphere from about the forties to the seventies, was held responsible for the neglect of interdependence. Events like the Vietnam-war, the breakdown of the Bretton Woods monetary system, and the OPEC oil-crisis showed only too clearly that the USA was loosing its leading position in the world. The USA increasingly became an ordinary member of the world system instead of its leader, but it had been blind to this process and it was the Realist paradigm which was blamed for this.

In an article reviewing the literature on interdependence of the 1970s Joseph Sassoon captured this changing perspective in the study of IR, when he concluded:

> "There is widespread awareness of the fact that interdependence, in the forms it has assumed over the past decade, is a historically new phenomenon, which cannot be interpreted according to the schemas (or myths), which might have been applicable to the far more static international situation of the fifties and the sixties."[3]

Not only in the science, but also in the practice of politics the awareness of global interdependence came to the fore. In 1975 Henry Kissinger stated:

> "The traditional agenda of international affairs — the balance among major powers, the security of nations — no longer defines our perils or our possibilities. ... Now we are entering a new era. Old international patterns are crumbling; old slogans are uninstructive; old solutions are unavailing. The world has become interdependent in economics, in communications, in human aspirations."[4]

Perhaps what Keohane and Nye suggest is true, namely that Kissinger merely used phrases like these for rhetorical reasons, trying to gain domestic support for his foreign policy initiatives; perhaps there was more to it: "We have a real belief in interdependence — it is not just a slogan", Kissinger stated in 1974.[5] But illustrative for the 1970s is that reference to global interdependence could serve rhetorical purposes (see chapter 1, pp. 16-17). Moreover, Kissinger proved not to be an exception. President Nixon in 1972, President Ford in 1974, Alexander Haig in 1981 and 1982, George Shultz throughout his service as Secretary of State, and even President Reagan were all, at one time or another, referring to global interdependence.[6]

In the 1970s the awareness of global interdependence was further stimulated by another incentive. In the Reports to the Club of Rome, as well as in the bulk of the so called "global village" literature, the awareness of the global dimension of local politics lies at the heart of the subject matter. Here again people saw themselves as standing at a dramatic moment in human history: *Mankind at the Turning-Point* as Mesarovic and Pestel's book was called.

"The world community appears as a 'system'", they wrote, "by which we mean a complex of interdependent parts, rather than a mere grouping of predominantly independent entities, as it was in the past. Consequently, a disruption of normal conditions in any part of the globe soon begins to make its effects felt all over the world, as many recent events show only too clearly."[7]

Recurring discoveries

At a closer look, however, the seventies were far less dramatic a period in the emerging era of global interdependence than the literature suggests. Article 76 of the Charter of the United Nations, for instance, already mentions the need "to encourage recognition of the interdependence of the peoples of the world". The Charter was drafted in 1945. In the early sixties President John F. Kennedy defended his "Grand Design" in similar terms as Kissinger defended his policies in the seventies. In 1962 he even proclaimed to be ready for a "Declaration of Interdependence".[8] (According to Röling, in 1975, at the celebration of the then 200 years old "Declaration of Independence", such a declaration was indeed formulated.[9])

For the political scientist the discoveries of the seventies were not as novel as the literature suggests, either. For example, in 1956 Ernst

Haas and Allen Whiting's *Dynamics of International Relations* opened with a chapter entitled: "The Facts of Interdependence and Their Denial". There are even earlier statements:

> "We have entered a new era, the era of interdependence; and this interdependent world is threatened with chaos because it has not learnt how to adjust its institutions and its traditions of government to the new conditions."[10]

This was written in 1933 by a British historian, Ramsay Muir, in an effort to explain why the Balkan-war of 1914 had become a world war. In the same year David Mitrany, in his study on the progress of international government, concluded that:

> "the doctrine of absolute sovereignty cannot for a moment be upheld in the face of the actual interdependence of States ... Our problem is to create acceptance for a new set of principles through which emphasis shall be placed upon the duties of States as much as upon their rights, upon their interdependence rather than upon their independence ..."[11]

It was under the influence of the first World War that Muir and Mitrany discovered interdependence. In France, Francis Delaisi had come to the same conclusion in 1925. But even before the shock of the first World War, the fact that the political reality had changed fundamentally had already been acknowledged by some authors:

> "our vocabulary is a survival of conditions no longer existing, and our mental conceptions follow at the tail of our vocabulary. International politics are still dominated by terms applicable to conditions which the processes of modern life have altogether abolished. ... The cause of this profound change, largely the work of the last thirty years, is due mainly to the complex financial interdependence of the capitals of the world ... This interdependence is the result of ... the incredible progress of rapidity in communications ..."[12]

46

This statement was made in 1909 by Norman Angell, at that time a journalist in Paris. In his pamphlet *Europe's Optical Illusion* he used arguments like these to warn the public and the politicians that the policies they pursued would make war inevitable, while the fruits of victory would not be what the antiquated axioms about politics promised them to be. The same line of reasoning was present in the work of Jean de Bloch who in 1897 quite accurately predicted the destructiveness of modern warfare.

"What is the use of talking about the past when you are dealing with an altogether new set of considerations? Consider for a moment what nations were a hundred years ago and what they are to-day. In those days before railways, telegraphs, steam ships, etc., were invented each nation was more or less a homogeneous, self-contained, self-sufficing unit. ... All this changed. ... Every year the interdependence of nations upon each other for the necessaries of life is greater than it ever was before. ... Hence the first thing that war would do would be to deprive the Powers that made it of all opportunity of benefiting by the products of the nations against whom they were fighting. ... The soldier is going down and the economist is going up."[13]

The discovery of interdependence in the 1980s

"It took time for our society and the Soviet leadership to develop an interest in the new mode of thinking. We pondered a good deal. We criticised ourselves and others and asked ourselves difficult and challenging questions before we saw things as they are and became convinced that new approaches and methods are required for resolving international problems in today's complex and contradictory world, a world at a crossroads." (Mikhail Gorbachev, 1987)[14]

Since 1985 interdependence has become a key-concept in the political statements and scientific writings in the Soviet-Union as part of the "New Thinking". Vadim Sagladin, for instance, stated in May 1990 that "we in the Soviet Union recognize interdependence as one of the most important results of the historical process". He concluded that interdependence can be the starting-point of a security and peace policy.[15] It seems to be especially Minister of Foreign Affairs Shevardnadze who is placing his confidence in the philosophy of interdependence; a philosophy in which shared interests outweigh competitive ones.[16] This perspective seems to be dominant throughout his Department. Soviet Deputy Minister of Foreign Affairs Vladimir Petrovsky, for instance, stated in July 1988:

"We have a different way of seeing the world since 1985. We see that interdependence matters; we no longer have a simple picture. We are working very hard to overcome the enemy image which was created on both sides. War makes no sense. Each system (capitalistic and communist) is evolving in terms of its domestic affairs. That's the only way to prove which system is better in the long run. In a world of global dangers you can't export revolution or counter-revolution."[17]

Illustrative for the changed worldview is that in May 1988 the journal *International Affairs* (Moscow) organized a conference for "the younger generation" of Soviet international affairs scholars on "The Soviet Union in an Interdependent World". In the same spirit as Norman Angell one of the participants, Konstantin Pleshakov, claimed that:

"The world today is prepared objectively for the concept of interdependence ... But it is not ready psychologically. Herein lies a great danger."[18]

And his colleague Aleksandr Medvedev added:

"It is common knowledge that the modern world economy is characterised by greater economic, financial, political, ecological, scientific and technological and informational interdependence of states. The deepening involvement of each country in the international division of labour is, in fact, an imperative, irrespective of the country's size and its economic and military potential."[19]

This "imperative" was the main theme also in a Report of the Soviet Academy of Sciences about International Economic Security, published in 1987.[20] It opens with a paragraph under the heading "Dangers of Interdependence". The authors discuss the advantages of a stronger commitment to the international division of labour over against the disadvantages of the resulting vulnerabilities to outside events. The Report also concludes that, in view of the already existing levels of interdependence, the "bloc-type systems of economic security" are completely ineffective and out of date. Apparently, economic security requires additional ties, which go beyond the blocs.

The similarities with the American literature of the seventies are striking. The Special Report of the Department of State "Toward a Strategy of Interdependence", published in 1975[21], seems almost to have been obligatory reading in Moscow. The authors of this report distinguish "natural" interdependence from "optional" interdependence. And that is exactly the distinction which is made by their Soviet colleagues. The first refers to the historically grown international intertwinements and linkages in economics and politics. The second refers to a deliberate strategy aiming to reduce the tensions in the world that are the result of the "natural" interdependence.[22]

Though interdependence only became a central concept in the policies of the 1980s, it appears that within the Soviet-Union already discussed in the 1970s. Marshall D. Shulman mentions an article in *Izvestia* (February 1973) by Vladimir Osipov, entitled "The Logic of Coexistence", in which it is stated that:

"the global nature of the interdependence of states makes anachronistic foreign policy concepts of former centuries based on the opposition of some countries to others and the knocking together of military alliances."[23]

This points at a tradition of using the term interdependence in the

Soviet-Union as well. It would be interesting to know to what extent this type of reasoning has influenced the generation that took office in the mid-1980s.

The conquest of distance

From the beginning of this century up to the present one comes across statements about the emergence of global interdependence. During his visit of Copenhagen in June 1989, even the Pope spoke about the "growing awareness of planetary interdependence" as an important stage in the birth of "a new and better era".[24] These statements share four arguments:

1. (descriptive:) the world has fundamentally changed over the past decades;
2. (explanatory:) the reason for this is that the communities in the world have become increasingly interdependent;
3. (prescriptive:) as a result "old", traditional thoughts should be put aside;
4. (predictive:) if not, disasters will occur, some of them on an unprecedented scale.

The history of the discovery of these arguments reflects the developments of the cognitive dimension of interdependence.

The history of the structural dimension has followed a different path. This path is easy to trace, insofar as it concerns the technological developments that have helped to open up the world. Though technology is not an independent variable (it is itself a product of civilization and social needs) its development provides the most impressive and tangible evidence of the unification of the world into one single socio-political whole.

But, for another part, the history of structural interdependence is a bit more complicated. Interdependence has been defined in terms of behaviour (integrative and functionalist interdependence) and in terms of system dynamics (systemic interdependence). It should be noted that in the case of *social* sciences this systemic interdependence is restricted to (indirect) behavioural effects. This means that the fundamental systemic interdependence of all species in regard to, for instance, the cosmic fate of planet earth, or to, for instance, the climatic changes on that planet, are recognized as such, but not dealt with *until* (a) people start to recognize this global dimension of their lives, or (b) people attain the potential capacity to influence the actual working of the global dimension of their lives. In this regard technological developments provide a yardstick for the history of the structural dimension of the global interdependence of communities.

It can be argued that the history of the structural dimension of global interdependence in this sense starts in the sixteenth century: "ever since the European peoples began to expand their trade, their ideas and their methods of organization over the rest of the world".[25] In the empire of Philip II of Spain the sun did not set — Europeans had discovered the rest of the world, and the rest of the world got in touch with the Europeans, whether they wanted or not. The Spanish empire disappeared, but the conquest of distance continued, stimulated by the process of state formation, by missionary spirit, commercial spirit and adventurism, by wars of religion, by nationalism and imperialism, in short by a complexity of social factors and accelerated by technological innovations.

The revolution of communication of the nineteenth century in particular had far-reaching consequences. Before the steamer, overseas contact depended on the winds. During the long journeys one was completely cut off from the world. The oceans formed the natural frontiers between societies. But by the nineteenth century they had been transformed into, to use the words of Margaret and Harold Sprout, the "highways" of the world:

"For thousands of years the oceans and larger seas ... presented a formidable barrier to human movement and served more to separate than to integrate the widely scattered aggregates of humanity. All this changed rather abruptly following the historic voyages of the later fifteenth century. [T]he oceans and larger seas provided highways [and] until well into the twentieth century, the surface of these waters carried virtually all intercontinental commerce

51

and much of the local traffic between coastal points on the same continent."[26]

Overland transportation and communication revolutionized likewise. For centuries, land travel had hardly witnessed any progress. "It may be doubted whether a traveller or a message could pass from Rome to Paris more rapidly at the end of the eighteenth century than in the prime of the Roman Empire", Muir says.[27] The American economist Eugene Staley calculated that, in the year 1790, a traveller from Boston needed five days to get to Philadelphia or Atlantic City. In 1938, when Staley did his research, he or she would be able to reach London, Paris or Rio de Janeiro in the same time.[28] In 1990 Staley's traveller can easily round the world in that time, while an American or Soviet ICBM can reach Moscow or Washington respectively within twenty minutes.[29] In 1933, Muir concluded that:

> "In peace as well as war the annihilation of distance has transformed the relations of men. ... It is not possible to exaggerate the effects upon world politics and upon economic life of this extra-ordinary revolution. In many respects, and for many purposes, the world has shrunk to the size of a market-town. Nothing has contributed more to make the whole earth interdependent than the conquest of distance which has been achieved during the last century."[30]

Social learning

The first event in history in which all peoples on earth were directly or indirectly involved and *realized* that they were, was the first World War. "The Great War was itself the final proof that the whole world had been brought within a single political system", Muir remarks. The reaction was likewise unique: for the first time in history an institution was created with the explicit goal to prevent similar disasters in the future by serving humanity as a whole. This was the League of Nations. In that sense the year 1919 can be taken as the starting point of the era of global interdependence.

The experiment failed — partly because the idea of world government was too much a reflection of national state structures (in which the efficiency of government strongly depends on national loyalties and a monopoly on the legitimate use of violence — factors not present on a global level); partly, because the participants (governments) owed their existence primarily to another mandate, namely the direct promotion of ethnocentric interests despite their international implications; partly, because there was no tradition in or experience with conflict-management from a global perspective. (Compare the struggle for survival of young democracies, like for instance the Weimar Republic in Germany in the 1920s.) Finally, the failure was also partly due to the fact that the United States of America in particular sought aloofness from conflict through neutrality and withdrawal. Britain sought to do the same through a policy of appeasement.

The failure of the League became evident when the lesson that had provoked her formation was repeated: a second world war occurred. Again an experiment in world government followed, the United Nations Organization. At many points this experiment has been trapped in the same pitfalls as the League. There are, however, also substantial differences. The specialized agencies in particular fulfil important roles in the management of global challenges. The International Monetary Fund (IMF), the World Health Organization (WHO), the General Agreement on Tariffs and Trade (GATT), the International Atomic Energy Agency (IAEA) and the United Nations Educational, Scientific and Cultural Organization (UNESCO), to mention a few, have become independent actors in the political arena ("selbständig aber nicht unabhängig"). The policies pursued under their flags can be criticized, but the fundamental point is that their existence is not primarily linked to the promotion of territorially-bound interests. The agencies were created to map out specific issue-areas and to deal with them from a global perspective. They are examples of increased functionalist interdependence as they have the explicit task to deal with the dynamics of global systemic interdependence. This mandate is promising. But the long tradition of state-centric practices and dogmas might easily frustrate it.

Obviously, there is a discrepancy between the structural and the cognitive dimensions of interdependence; between the conditions of global interdependence and the struggle for local independence. This discrepancy points to a process of social learning, which is partly triggered by disasters — by the perils of interdependence.[31] Disasters (caused by the neglect of interdependence) may make people adjust their minds and behaviour to the conditions they reveal. How to manage global interdependence becomes an issue on the political agenda. World wars provoke the question how to manage escalation processes; Chernobyls provoke the need of more efficient global control agencies.

But one of the complicating factors is, of course, that the awareness of the conditions of interdependence does not automatically imply that these conditions are taken for granted. Haas and Whiting pointed out that "aloofness", isolationism, is one of the possible reactions to global interdependence.[32] Attempts to back out and to create an insular position within world politics are a logical reaction to the awareness of the conditions of interdependence, especially when this awareness is enforced by disasters.

This aspect is often neglected. Muir and Angell, for instance, both thought that, as soon as people discovered their interdependence at the systemic level, they would understand that the only way to cope with its dynamics is by creating interdependence of the functionalist and the integrative types. In the words of Muir:

> "An interdependent world ... which consists of independent nations claiming unlimited sovereignty and striving after self-sufficiency ... must be a very insecure and precarious world, unless and untill the component nations have learnt to recognise and accept their interdependence, to base their whole policy upon it, and to establish in co-operation the institutions necessary to make interdependence tolerable."[33]

Haas and Whiting agree that this is the ultimate sensible answer, but they also point out that the ultimate answer is not necessarily the first one.

Therefore, the era of global interdependence is characterized by the continual uneasy relationship between the conditions of inter-dependence (the structural dimension) and their acceptance (the cognitive dimension). This uneasiness has led the so-called "inter-dependencists" to concentrate on two kinds of predictions for the near future: a fatalistic scenario and an idealistic scenario. The fatalistic scenario spins out the disasters humanity will face if policies remain based on the conditions of a past world. The idealis-tic scenario predicts the end of such threats to civilization, if people come to recognize and accept the global dimension of politics as a limitation to ethnocentric behaviour and as an invitation to sharing the responsibility for the fate of humanity as such. Especially in the early writings on interdependence this dichotomy is present: inter-dependence means trouble, but only as long as it is neglected.

The continuity of change

"To stress that world affairs are marked by growing inter-dependence is not to imply that theretofore individuals and groups were self-sufficient and independent. People have always been interdependent. The tendency to rely on others for basic services that sustain individual and community life is as old as human history itself. What is new about inter-dependence is the global scale on which it is presently un-folding. For centuries the work and lives of people have been organized around and through the nation-state. In recent decades, however, rapid scientific and technological advan-ces have precipitated profound changes that are transform-ing relations both within and among nation-states."[34]

This statement points out the various challenges the argument of this chapter leads to. First of all there is the question if there remain any arguments to stick to 1945 or even 1973-1975 as the starting-point of the era of global interdependence. Obviously, the conquest of distance did not stop in 1919 and it is not stopping now. Satellites, space-shuttles, nuclear energy, the fibreglass cable, the micro-electronic revolution, computer networks, etcetera, all have their impact on the social structure of the world. But are these innovations changing the system fundamentally time and again, or are they just a development within it or perhaps even the result of the system's dynamics?

The reverse challenge is, of course, provided by the question why we should not go back further than 1919. Why not take the International, founded in 1889, as a beginning? Mihály Simai, for instance, quotes the Communist Manifesto (1848) as one of the first sources noticing global interdependence:

> "In the 'Communist Manifesto' ... Marx and Engels wrote that by exploiting the world market the bourgeoisie had internationalized the production and consumption of all countries. They pointed out ... that national seclusion and self-sufficiency were being replaced by a 'universal interdependence of nations'."[35]

Others have mentioned the work of Adam Smith, John Stuart Mill and Richard Cobden in the British liberal tradition, Grotius in the juridical tradition, Rousseau in the French, and Kant in the German philosophical tradition, as possible origins of contemporary thinking on interdependence. Though additional research is required, the impression remains that the global dimension of politics was not really an integral part of these men's work. While they all certainly contributed to the development of the cognitive dimension, their work is predominantly limited to the European theatre. Rousseau, for instance, described the complex entanglement of the European states in the eighteenth century. He is surely revealing some of the characteristics of interdependence, but not of *global* interdependence.[36] Originally, the theory of Communism, too, was only applied to the European world. Despite its international aspirations, the idea of a World Revolution was only appropriate to countries having an industrial proletariat; not even Russia was included.

More difficult to answer is David Mitrany's challenge to taking 1914-1919 as the turning point.

> "[A]bout the beginning of the twentieth century ... world

56

interdependence was at last recognized to be as real as European interdependence."[37]

Looking at the tradition of international organization which culminated in the League, he mentioned that, in 1906, the Inter-Parliamentary Union replaced the ideal of forming a European federation by the ideal of a global League of Nations. But the main landmark, in his view, are the Peace Conferences in The Hague in 1899 and 1907. At these conferences the notion of a "Directorate of the Great Powers" was replaced by the notion of a "Common Council of all the Independent States of the World".

> "[These conferences] marked, in fact, the beginning of a new international era. ... the coming together of all sovereign members of the society of nations, as well as the declared purpose of their gathering, implied at last a recognition of the unity of the civilized world."[38]

However, in one breath Mitrany observed and disproved the typical nineteenth century character of these conferences. They were concerned "with the rules of war rather than with ways of peace" because "warfare was still accepted as the chief instrument of international change". He therefore concluded that, in the end, the historical meaning of the The Hague Conferences was restricted to what they implied rather than to what they achieved. In comparison with that, the shock of the first World War and the Covenant of the League of Nations made a much greater impact. In the words of James Joll:

> "whichever way you looked at international relations before 1914, the First World War and its consequences forced a radical change of view and made it increasingly hard to apply the old categories, both practically and theoretically, however much people went on trying to adapt their old ideas to new experiences. ... it was no longer possible to think in terms of a *European* balance of power. ... The war had made impossible a return to an international system based on the balance of power in Europe alone."[39]

However, far more important is the question to what extent the conclusions of contemporary research and theorising are affected when a historical perspective is accepted. Does the conclusion, that "old", traditional theories should be put aside because the world has changed fundamentally, still make sense if these changes are not the product of "recent decades"? Indeed, critics use historical arguments to conclude that it does not. Kenneth Waltz quotes Asa Briggs who in 1968 characterized the turn of the century as "the belle époque of interdependence".[40] Waltz uses this characterization to support his thesis that interdependence leads to war rather than to peace:

> "Today the myth of interdependence both obscures the realities of international politics and asserts a false belief about the conditions that promote peace, as World War I conclusively showed. ... Logically it is wrong, and politically it is obscurantist to consider the world a unit and call it 'interdependent'."[41]

Yet, reading Angell, Delaisi, Merriam, Mitrany and Muir, one gets the impression that it is exactly World War I that proved that the false beliefs about the realities of international politics were a part of the axioms of state-centric power politics. Angell predicted two world wars for that reason. Taking responsibility for world politics was seen as a luxury, not as a necessity. But because of the increasing interdependence, it had long become a necessity, as World War I and World War II conclusively showed. The strict interpretation of sovereignty rights, combined with the strict separation of domestic and international politics, was criticized by all five authors discussed in this volume. They observed how this hampered international organization. Another recurring theme in their work is the problem that the geographical borders of the welfare-state do not coincide with the borders of the order-state. This problem has been paramount throughout the twentieth century, in particular because people tried to manage it with a state-centric solution in mind. Policies of protectionism and imperialism were among the results: conquer every territory you need for production and sales, and protect yourself against the rest of the world. According to Muir,

Merriam, Delaisi, Angell and Mitrany, state-centrism blinded governments and their subjects to the pragmatic logic that, when you cannot destroy your neighbours, you somehow have to accept their presence. Searching the "somehow" is the struggle of the twentieth century.

It is my thesis, therefore, that placing contemporary interdependence into its historical context will reinforce the criticism on state-centric theories about power politics, rather than undermine it.

This does not imply that all arguments will stand the test of an historical perspective. Especially some of the arguments about transnationalism have to be re-examined.

First, transnational actors are no novelty in politics, and neither is their political importance. The church is an obvious example, but the trading companies of the seventeenth and eighteenth century could also be mentioned. In 1640, for example, Portugal split off from Spain and hence wanted to end the war with the Dutch in Brazil. Both the Dutch East- and the West-Indian Trading Companies petitioned strongly against this, as it would mean an end to the lucrative raids on Portugese ships and the plunder of trading-posts. A similar event took place in England in 1745, when British merchants rejected peace with France and Spain for commercial reasons. And what to think of the Fuggers in Augsburg, who, in the first half of the 16th century, controlled the European led-, silver- and copper-production and financed the wars of Charles V? These were non-state actors of prime importance in matters of war and peace.

Secondly, it is necessary to qualify the thesis that growing interdependence stimulates a fragmentation of government. This fragmentation is shown by the independent international relations of virtually every governmental department; the so-called transgovernmental relations. In the Special Issue of the journal International Organization on transnational relations and world politics, edited by Keohane and Nye, this argument was used to undermine the paradigm that nation-states are closed actors, and that a clear distinction can be made between domestic and foreign policy. Empirically this has been confirmed by e.g. East and Salomonsen.[42]

But the conquest of distance and the resulting interdependence also has a reverse effect: the control of governments over their representatives abroad is much larger than it was, say, a century ago. The role of ambassadors and embassies has changed fundamentally. The ambassador has become an agent of economic promotion and tourism, rather than a policy-maker and an interpreter of local developments. The press covers the news and if something really important happens, the Minister of Foreign Affairs or the President will fly in him or herself.[43]

It is important to note that these revisions of contemporary interdependence theory at the same time reinforce the criticism on the state-as-actor thesis. If ambassadors and colonial rulers could and did act independently from the state they represented, if merchants did not agree with governments about the "national interest", if Jacob Fugger the Rich was in fact more important than the Emperor, why then do we have theories which tell us that the world society is "a system of 'billiard-ball' states in intermittent collision"?[44] Why, if the Doctrine of Sovereignty is a myth, do people base their political behaviour on it?

The ahistoric character of contemporary writings on interdependence makes these writings unnecessarily susceptible to criticism. It is a challenge to examine the extent to which the current theories on interdependence can profit from the early contributions to this paradigm. My thesis is that this test will enrich contemporary interdependence theory with a strong and impressive intellectual tradition.

3 Norman Angell (1872-1967): ancestor of interdependence theory[1]

Not successful, merely right

In 1912, on the initiative of Lord Esher and with support of former Conservative Prime Minister Arthur Balfour, the industrialist Sir Richard Garton put up the money to establish the Garton Foundation.[2] The stated object was "To promote and develop the science of International Polity and economics as indicated in the published writings of Mr. Norman Angell."[3] This enabled Angell to spread his ideas about the senselessness of war. "Norman Angellism" became a movement, with which over a hundred organizations identified themselves, especially in Britain. War and Peace societies, International Polity Clubs and even Norman Angell Leagues came into being. Many bankers and businessmen sympathized with Angell's ideas, as they were part of the network of interdependence he attached so much value to. In 1913 the journal *War and Peace* was established as "A Norman Angell Monthly" and *The Great Illusion*, Angell's best known book, appeared in no less then seventeen languages (including Chinese, Russian, Tamil, Urdu and Marathi) and more than a million copies were sold.[4] Then the First World War broke out and in September 1914 Angell wrote his balance sheet: "No, we have not been 'successful'. We have merely been right."[5]

Right about what? *The Great Illusion* was first published in 1909 as a pamphlet entitled *Europe's Optical Illusion*.[6] It stated that people were living under the illusion that military power could make a country wealthy; that the trade, territory and colonies of a defeated enemy could be profitably added to the wealth of the victor and that international financial interdependence could be disrupted without damaging trade. Angell did not oppose military defence as such, neither was he a pacifist, but he criticized the "war spirit" in public opinion, the chauvinism and the underlying fatalistic view, held by many, toward the inevitability of war. Simultaneously, however, he had his own doubts about whether peace could be preserved: the false axioms were self-fullfilling. He thus warned that Britain's policy, if unaltered, would make war unavoidable.

In 1910 the book *The Great Illusion* appeared as an expanded version of the pamphlet. Among other things, Angell added a chapter on the economic nonsense of war-reparation payments. Not surprisingly, therefore, he was among the first in 1918-1919 to criticize the conditions of the Treaty of Versailles. He warned of its adverse consequences and called for the preservation of the alliance in peace time. Twenty years later, in 1938, Angell again turned against the logic behind British policy and predicted that, for essentially the same reasons as in 1914, this would lead England into war again. His ideas did not go unnoticed, as is witnessed by the Nobel Prize for Peace which he was awarded in 1933. The Nobel Committee even called him "the great educator of public opinion [who had done so much to] remove the wrong conception that war benefits anyone."[7] Yet, in 1939 the balance-sheet could have read the same "not successful ... merely right".

This is not, however, the way Angell is remembered at present. He is generally considered to belong to the Idealist School of international relations. He is said to be a utopian because he considered it possible to "abolish" war, because he was an advocate of the League of Nations, because he trusted in the power of education to reform and believed in the ability of economic interdependence to promote peace. The very wars that Angell predicted were interpreted as proof that his ideals were utopian.

Part of this image also stems from misinterpretations of his work. The most serious and obstinate of these is that he stated in *The Great Illusion* that war had become unthinkable because of international economic interdependence. As J.D.B. Miller noted in the most recent Angell biography:

> "If one mentions Angell in intellectual company one is likely to have him identified as the man who proved that war was impossible, only to be refuted by World War I."[8]

In this chapter the idealistic, utopian image of Angell's work is demystified and qualified. This is not actually a goal in itself; my interest springs from the important role played by the concept of interdependence in Angell's work. In exposing the illusory nature of the policy being followed, as well as in laying the foundation for an alternative course, Angell based his argument on the consequences of international socio-economic interdependence. Angell's utopian image therefore also extends to contemporary interdependence theories. This is not favourable for the evaluation of these theories. The authors of the concept of interdependence do not enjoy being identified with Angell, while the critics are more affectionate: after two world wars it should be obvious that just this sort of trust in interdependence is the real great illusion. Both are erronous. Any theory of world politics in which interdependence is a central concept, would benefit by an analysis of Angell's ideas on interdependence.[9]

The temporizer idealist

Several factors make it difficult to assign Angell to a particular school of thought. If one calls him a classical liberal in the free trade tradition, one is faced with the fact that he was a Labour member of the British Parliament (1929-1931). If one calls him an advocate of the League of Nations because he was active in the League of Nations Union and sympathized with Wilson's ideas, there is the fact that he deemed plans for a world government to be unrealisable. Angell was a practical man who was interested in applicable, realistic politics, and who had little patience with academic hair-splitting. Yet, he was a theoretician who strongly advocated the study of international policy and international economics. It is characteristic of him that even saying that he was British does not do him justice. Ralph Norman Angell Lane, as he was baptized, was educated mainly in France and Geneva, emigrated to the United States when he was seventeen, worked as a journalist in Paris from 1897-1913 and spent most of the second World War in the United States. Not surprisingly, the title of his first book was *Patriotism under Three Flags* (1903). (The book was signed under the name Ralph Lane. The name Norman Angell was first used for the pamphlet to keep this distinct from his work as managing director of the Paris edition of the *Mail* and especially to avoid a conflict with his employer, the future Lord Northcliffe.)[10]

Angell's membership in the Labour Party is assumed to have been largely opportunistic; a left turn with doubts, as he called it. His enthusiasm for the League of Nations was certainly more sincere, but again opportunism may have played an important role in it. The League offered a possibility for change and this opportunity had to be taken. This, however, did not lead him to an uncritical surrender to ideals that were unrealisable in the short term. For example, many supporters of the League of Nations strove for extensive disarmament, something which Angell rejected. In *The Great Illusion — 1933* (an updated version of the pre-war book) he noted:

> "the practical political conclusion ... is not to insist that the world make suddenly one huge jump from armed anarchy to a world without force or arms at all."[11]

In 1935 Angell even joined "The Focus", a lobby supporting Winston Churchill, whose ideas Angell in principle opposed. For years, Churchill had argued in favour of increasing armament expenditures, but, according to Angell, without making clear the purpose and the causes. By 1935 (a year after receiving the Nobel Price for Peace) he knew cause and purpose himself. Angell recognized that all European countries persisted in the fallacies he had criticized since 1908 (the cause), and he recognized the necessity to block the specific translation of these illusions given by the totalitarian regimes, especially Hitler's dreams of *Lebensraum* (the purpose). In *The Great Illusion — Now* (1938), little sympathy for the League of Nations is to be detected, although he still considered international cooperation to be necessary and the only definite way to deal with the causes.

Angell's political activities, and their sometimes pragmatic nature, are therefore one of the factors that make it difficult to label and pigeon-hole him. Another is the changing historical context in which he wrote. The first of his more than forty books was published in 1903, and the last in 1958. Angell's alarm about the emotionality of the "public mind" and his emphasis on the positive effects of international interdependence remained constant, but his argumentation on these subjects underwent an — only logical — development while his views on related matters changed under the influence of events. Thus, *The Great Illusion* (1910) was directed against the "jingoes of the right", while *The Steep Places* (1947) (according to Miller Angell's post-war political testament) took a stand against militant leftists for whom the Soviet-Union was a model.[12] In *The Great Illusion — Now* (1938), however, Angell agitates against the Bolshevik scare because he, with an eye to Hitler's ambitions, saw the Soviet-Union as Britain's natural ally and because he felt that Moscow had abandoned the idea of world revolution.[13]

Judging from Miller, however, the consistency of Angell's opinions is remarkable. This is especially true of his long-term vision. In the short-term, he continually set himself against specific expressions of deeper-rooted illusions. The more vehement the expressions, the further were the countermeasures he advocated from the ideals that he nevertheless deemed realisable. Angell clearly tried to blend the practically realisable with the theoretically possible. This testifies at least to an attempt at realism, but not all of the frictions between expediency and principle were convincingly resolved.

Angell's idealist image

In 1980 Paul Taylor described Norman Angell as one of the leading figures of the Idealist School. According to him, belief in the possibility of a world government is characteristic of this school. International organization, cooperation among sovereign states, would form the basis of such a government.[14] Indeed, Angell's work bears some of the marks of the Idealist School listed by Morgenthau, but not all.[15]

Angell had complete faith in the possibility of international organization and cooperation among sovereign states. But, he felt that it did not pay to sketch blue prints for a world government, because they would not be realisable within the foreseeable future. In 1938 he wrote that:

> "No attempt is made to draw up schemes of world government. There have been many such in the past, as there will be many in the future. ... the better they are as a piece of logical governmental mechanism, the more remote they are likely to be from the familiar, the everyday ..."[16]

Be the fine plans what they may, Angell suggested, what matters is an analysis of the forces that stand in the way of their realization.

> "To discover why ... nations persisted in methods of security which condemned them to insecurity so great that the end must be destruction, was the purpose of *The Great Illusion*."[17]

That sounds realistic.

His analysis led him to criticize two widely accepted axioms in particular. The first is that military conquest would result in economic prosperity; the *"conquest pays"* axiom. The second concerns the method of national self-preservation; a method in which every country attempts to ensure its own defence by denying it to another. This principle can be traced back to the logic that superior force is the best defence; the *"national superiority"* axiom.[18] This axiom is based on the logic behind the survival of the fittest, and it is firmly grafted onto Social Darwinism, which was widely accepted at the turn of the century. Angell called it the logic of cannibalism. "It is quite clear that I must eat you, or you must eat me. Let us come to a friendly agreement about it." Obviously, international order based on such logic is unthinkable: "Security for one has to be purchased at the insecurity of the other."[19] This can only have one result: war.

Naturally, both axioms have much in common, but it is useful to differentiate between them because it then becomes clear that the arguments Angell advances to rebut each axiom are essentially different. These differences then help determine to what extent Angell belongs to the Idealist School.

Angell attributes his idealist image primarily to his criticism of the first axiom. Morgenthau, for example, places him in the "war does not pay" tradition.[20] George Modelski mentions Angell in the same breath as Cobden, Adam Smith and Kant, who, he says, all saw free trade as the certain road to peace. Modelski traces this line through to the current literature on interdependence.[21] Joshua Goldstein quotes Angell to rebut the presumed idealism of Keohane and Nye:

> "Norman Angell, writing in 1914 ... argues that economic interdependence has made war 'irrelevant to the end it has in view', since war no longer benefits the winner. All of this sounds rather like Keohane and Nye's (1977) view of the 1970s; yet World War I broke out within a year of the above writings."[22]

There are also those who concluded from Angell's criticism of the "conquest pays" axiom that he believed that war could not be fought any longer. "Norman Angell ... tried to prove that war had become impossible", Forest Grieves wrote in 1977.[23] Reiner Steinweg wrote in the introduction to a volume (which aims to teach the lessons of history!) that Angell had argued that war based on power motives had lost all reason.[24] In 1989 Richard Rosecrance put it even more strongly:

> "Norman Angell's *Great Illusion*, neglecting past precedents, suddenly declared in 1912 that the economic interests and

interdependence of the great powers would prevent war. But this short term and limited perspective was shown to be wholly inadequate in 1914."[25]

Miller names Barbara Tuchman (1964) and Albert Wohlstetter (1974) as the propagators of this myth, which grew up shortly after the appearance of *The Great Illusion*. It was strengthened especially by the fact that E.H. Carr frequently cited Angell as an example of misguided utopianism. In *After All*, Angell complained of the stubborn survival of this myth. "Perhaps it will never die", Miller writes.[26]

Interdependence, prosperity and conquest

In rebutting the "conquest pays" axiom, Angell does not use idealistic arguments, but primarily theoretical and empirical economic ones. The structure of the modern, economically developed world differs from more primitive economic structures in that war no longer achieves the positive economic goals that it did previously. A country's political and economic frontiers are no longer necessarily the same.

> "Can we [England] get Canadian wheat or Australian wool without paying for it ...? If the German conquered those territories could *he* get those things without paying for them?"[27]

Wealth and trade cannot be conquered. In a modern economy, plundering another country is actually dumping goods in one's own market, with the destruction of the foreign consumer market and domestic unemployment as the result.[28] Cornelia Navari summarized this argument as follows:

> "the real wealth basis of modern society lay in its social institutions. Modern wealth was, thus 'intangible' ... it lay not in goods but in the system of production of goods, in its credit worthiness, in its security of contract and in its com-

munications system. It did not lie in material but in institutions, behaviour and ways of thought."[29]

This argument, of course, also applies to the axiom of national superiority. According to Angell, military superiority was no longer a prerequisite for prosperity. He cites as examples the prosperity of small European countries, which was certainly at the same level as that of Great Britain, France or Germany. In a military respect they were nothing.

> "If the common doctrine be true, the financiers would not invest a pound or a dollar in the territories of the undefended nations."[30]

The behaviour of investors and financiers indicated that, in practice, they attached little importance to the military strength of a country. On the other hand, they were themselves not aware of this, and their thinking was dominated by the antiquated axioms. They invested without qualm in countries that were in no way able to militarily defend their assets, but at the same time, they clung to the notion that without her fleet, England would be robbed of every penny she had.[31]

One of the fundamental changes, Angell believed, is that wealth in an economically civilized world is primarily based on credit and commercial contracts. This is the product of an economic interdependence which itself arises from an increased division of labour and highly developed communications. International finance is also largely interdependent. Disruptions in New York automatically lead to financial and commercial disruption in London, forcing financiers in both cities to work together: not out of altruism, but out of economic self-preservation. Furthermore, the financial world is intertwined with trade and industry. Industrial production only results in wealth if the product can be sold. Wealth for one is therefore dependent on the purchasing-power of the other, which implies that the other must also be able to sell his product, since his wealth rests on the same principle.[32] Regardless of competition and the associated conflicts, there is thus a high degree of systemic interdependence in markets. According to Angell, it is therefore in one's own self-interest to eschew traditional conquest. If one wishes to conquer a country without damaging one's own economy, then one must respect the enemy's assets. This undermines the "conquest pays" axiom, conquest is economically futile.[33]

Modifications of the economic futility of war

There are some major theoretical arguments against this thesis. The first counter-argument is that the small countries were free-riders, who took advantage of the balance of power between the Great Powers. Dougherty and Pfaltzgraff refer in this respect to J.H. Jones, who in 1915 attacked Angell's arguments on this ground.[34] Doubtful about this argument, however, is that before the first World War and during the interbellum period the small countries were not at all sure that the balance of power would protect them from occupation and, therefore, the financiers could not be sure either. There were no free-riders, there simply was a hierarchy among countries in terms of military capacities. The lack of collective military security was even one of the main issues Angell addressed during the interbellum. If there was a causality between national military superiority and the economic security of foreign investments, the financiers showed no awareness of that in their behaviour.

A second counter-argument is that Angell's thesis has restrictions which he does not mention. Implicitly, he is talking about military conquest among countries with modern economies. This can also include (former) colonies, but when colonialism is restricted to stripping foreign soils of their natural resources it does matter who "owns" the colony in military terms. Angell did not realize that plunder of raw materials does not have the effects of dumping goods, provided that such resources are not available domestically.

In other words, he does not specify in how far his thesis is valid with respect to the relations between countries with modern economies and those with undeveloped, traditional agricultural economies or among countries with both modern and traditional economic sectors. What measure of industrialization is decisive; what measure of import/export orientation is decisive; what measure of public participation in the economic activity is required, before the systemic economic interdependence reaches a level that makes conquest of rich territories futile? As Angell concentrated on the European theatre, apparently these countries had reached such a level. The measure of their economic development at the turn of the century therefore can be extrapolated into a possible yardstick, but Angell himself did not provide one.

Another questionable axiom in Angell's thinking is that he implicitly equals the national interest with the public interest, which implies a neglect of the specific group interests of ruling elites. Military power can be used to destroy a serious competitor of a producer at home (which is, in fact, the most radical option within protectionistic policies). This is not in the general interest of the public (they have to pay the price of protectionism: the military effort and the artificial prices for protected goods that are higher than they would be in case of free trade), but it may be in the short-term interest of the ruling elite who decides on the use of military force. In 1911, Francis Delaisi predicted war between Germany and Great Britain for economic reasons of that kind.[35] On the other hand, however, the essence of systemic interdependence in modern economies is the impossibility of limiting the military destruction to one specific major competitor as a kind of precise surgical operation. Destruction of major economic actors disrupts the entire network of relationships these actors are part of. Thus, apart from political risks in the sense of interference of third parties, disapproval from foreign public opinion, increased enmity among the countries involved and escalation into all-out war, it may cause direct economic costs because of monetary instability, reduced purchasing power on export-consumer markets (due to increased unemployment in the country of the attacked actor), reduced attractiveness of the home-market for foreign investors because of the adventurous policy, etcetera. These reciprocity costs have to be taken into account in order to assess the costs and benefits of a surgical military act of destruction. Fact is, though, that Angell concentrated his argument not on the destruction of economic potential but only on its conquest by occupying the country where the economic potential is located.

In how far, Angell asked himself, does annexation produce a real increase in prosperity for the population? Can trade channels be stimulated or established by superior military power? To what extent can the British Navy actually protect British trade?[36] These are concrete questions designed to determine the economic usefulness of war and the possibilities of a military defence of prosperity. There is no appeal to morality in this connection:

> "Industrialism and commercialism are as full of cruelties as war itself — cruelties, indeed, that are longer drawn out, more refined, if less apparent, and, it may be, appealing less to the ordinary imagination."[37]

A blind faith in the blessings of free trade is difficult to reconcile with this statement.

It is therefore surprising that Angell has retained his idealist image based on his criticism of the "conquest pays" axiom. More surprising yet is the fact that the aspects of Angell's work that *are* idealistic have not been used to support that image. This idealism is apparent in Angell's criticism of the "national superiority" axiom in particular.

Survival of the fittest or cannibalism?

Angell's criticism of the "national superiority" axiom is primarily directed at the short-sightedness of its logic. The statement that war is close when various countries attempt to guarantee their security by aiming for military superiority is quite level-headed. "When we say 'Si vis pacem, para bellum', we must apply it to all parties." Angell also saw no good in the resulting balance of power:

> "Neither side, in fact, desires a balance; each desires to have the balance tilted in its favour."

And because military power is so difficult to measure, an arms race is the obvious result. Regardless of intentions, this alone leads to explosive situations. As Angell said way back in 1915:

"You cannot indefinitely pile up explosive material without an accident of some sort occurring; it is bound to occur."[38]

However, Angell rejects the "national superiority" axiom not only because of its logical inconsistency, but also because he scorns the identification of the population with the nation-state, preferring to see it exchanged for an international orientation.

Although Angell felt little for a blueprint for a world government, he deemed a rational international political order, based on universal principles, to be desirable and even realisable in the long term. In this, he most clearly fits the characteristics of the Idealist School. The "national superiority" axiom was an obstacle to the formation of this order and for that reason had to be opposed, too.

Still, subtlety is required in discussing this idealism. It is based partly on normative preference but also partly on observation. Angell detected heightened international activity in communications, trade, and financial transactions. This activity resulted in a genuine increase of social, political and economic processes. In combination with the international character of modern economy, the result was a growing interdependence. From this he concluded that a nationalist political system ignored the cross-border interests of the population. Moreover, the increased international traffic would increase the chances of unintentional clashes unless it were regulated.

"[The] multiplication of human contacts ... do not of themselves make for peace; they may quite easily make for war ... unless we get new rules for the road (as we had to have with the coming of the motor car)."[39]

To this end, the nation-state had become too limited a unit of social organization. If one wanted to avoid clashes (including war), then the formation of an international order was required.

According to Navari, this points at an important transformation in liberal thought. Here, the free trade argument was fundamentally modified (free trade led to unwanted collisions); the axiom about the "invisible hand" which steers the market mechanism was denied. The liberal thought of Adam Smith (1723-1790) and Richard

Cobden (1804-1865) rested on the assumption that markets were the underlying, natural condition of social life. But, Navari points out, Angell argued that there was nothing natural about them: markets could be created or disturbed, and existing markets thus were always the result of historical, social processes.

> "This conception marks a vital shift in the tradition of liberal internationalism: the shift from its old natural law to its modern sociological form; from timeless principle to structural-functionalism."[40]

Angell was not indifferent, however, to the form the international order should take. It should be based on cooperation and equal rights, democratic principles which were already available in a number of countries and which he felt were universally applicable. He ascribed the fact that not everyone was convinced of this to the survival of illusions.

Angell realized that because of these illusions, the principles of democratic internationalism had to be defended, and that because of increased interdependence, this defence was no longer possible on a purely national level. Defence was only possible through the formation of a military alliance of Western democracies, supplemented by any country prepared to respect the same norms internationally. Already in 1918 Angell wrote that:

> "the survival of the democracies, insofar as that is a matter of the effective use of their force, depends upon their capacity to use it as a unit, during the war and after."[41]

The more dangerous the illusion in political practice (think of the German quest for *Lebensraum*, which was in complete agreement with the "conquest pays" axiom), the more important and indispensible is military power.

Because of his democratic ideals and the continued existence of the illusions, Angell himself also fell back upon the quest for military superiority, therewith allowing the "ultima ratio" of military force to enter his thinking. He did continue to emphasize, however, that the formation of a military alliance should not mean an increase in one's own security at the cost of another's:

> "Such an alliance ... is not "encirclement", because member-
> ship is open to all on equal terms; we offer to others the
> precise principle of defence we claim for ourselves."[42]

The army should not serve nationalist ambitions, but the laws that
protect the interests of all peoples.

Nowhere in the (Western!) literature is Angell assigned to the
Idealist School because of this plea for (Western!) democratic principles and the collective defence they would require. Even the way
in which he pictures this alliance-formation is not criticized. As far
as democracies are concerned, Angell argued, an alliance cannot be
based on force and domination; that would run counter to the
principles that must be defended. Therefore, voluntary cooperation
can be the only way; the voluntary, mutual acceptance of universal
rights, paper guarantees; in short, moral primacy.[43]

At this point, the true students of the Realist School should rise
up. Morality in power is idealism to the extreme. It is directly
contrary to the "realist law" that they who strive unscrupulously
for power will dominate the world. And it conflicts with the nature
of the international state system, the quest for sovereignty, political
autonomy, economic independence and other sacred cows of the
nation-state.

Last warnings in 1938 — Angell's theory in practice
(How to stop Hitler, when you share part of his illusions?)

Norman Angell's protest against these sacred cows was not
restricted to the theoretical level. He tried to device practical
answers to the challenges that dominated the political agenda in
his days. These attempts are worth recalling because they reflect
his awareness of the reciprocity in politics.

In 1938 Angell considered the emergence of the totalitarian regimes
the biggest problem in politics. To meet their threat, he proposed a
so-called "dual peace policy".

75

"Peace demands a dual policy; resistance to claims of exclusive possession, combined with an offer of real equality of access, of economic rights; partnership."[44]

The aim was to make international cooperation attractive to Germany, Italy and Japan, while simultaneously forming a defensive military alliance against countries that resisted cooperation. It is the combination of both tracks which was expected to have an impact on the dictators.

Angell assumed that the dictators were familiar with the risks and the costs of warfare. They could know, for instance, that the first World War had dislodged regimes that had sat in the saddle longer than their own. The dictators knew that in the last resort their survival depended upon popular support and that repression could not be made waterproof. Angell also realized that Germany, Italy and Japan saw themselves as Have-Not states, which made the status quo unacceptable to them. He therefore proposed the following:

1. Germany, Italy and Japan were to be invited to stand with Britain "for the establishment of a Fact-Finding Commission to answer such questions as whether the Have-Not states are at a disadvantage in their access to raw materials, and if so, what is the nature of the disadvantage".
2. The Have-Not states had to accept the free publication of the findings of such a Commission within their territory.
3. Britain ought to make it clear that it stood for the umpire principle in those cases where sincere difference of opinion existed. The Have-Not states had to be invited to accept such impartial judgment or, when they did not accept a specific judgment, "refrain from war as a means of correcting what they regard as unjust".
4. "[S]ince the whole case of the principal Have-Not states is that the status-quo becomes with the passage of time inequitable", they were to be asked to agree with the creation of institutions of peaceful change.[45]

It was not unthinkable, in Angell's view, that the Have-Not states would refuse one or more conditions of this first track. He, therefore, recommended a second one, the immediate creation of a military alliance:

5. "[England] should make it clear that we and other states accepting those principles form a defensive alliance or confederation based on the principle that an attack on one is an attack on all."[46]

But didn't Britain pursue a policy as proposed in the first track already? Angell did not think so. In principle, convening conferences was a correct method. However, since 1918 there had been many conferences without any result: they all failed because the public did not realize the price of success. Therefore, the many suggestions in 1938 for convening a new world conference in order to resolve the economic, territorial and political disputes could not lead anywhere either. Illusions were omnipresent.

First of all, all parties at the negotiation table shared the illusory thought that national self-preservation implied that their home countries must be stronger than any potential aggressor. This was most evidently illustrated at disarmament conferences.

> "No wonder the conferences fail ... It is [conceived as] a meeting in which each member feels that he is being asked to increase the danger to which his nation is to be exposed."[47]

Secondly, the mere idea that peace could be assured by territorial revisions was very dangerous. In *Mein Kampf,* Hitler literally stated that his final objective was to obtain enough land for about 250 million Germans "on this continent" (in 1938 Germany had a population of about eighty million). The required territory could be found in Russia.[48] The "Lebensraum" thesis could only be dealt with by correcting the economic fallacy which gave rise to it; by dealing with the illusion that self-sufficiency is a precondition to welfare. But how could England at the negotiation table expose an illusion in which the British believed themselves?

Thirdly, there was the idée fixe that governments could preserve peace at home while remaining indifferent to the peace in other places. The British government claimed that she had secured the peace, and the public believed it.

> "What the phrase [that peace had been secured] really means, of course, is that war has not so far come to us; that it has only come to Manchurians or Abyssinians or Chinese or Spaniards or Czechs, and oppression and torture only been applied to Jews, or Social Democrats, or Pacifists or foreign Christians; and that their peace is not our concern."[49]

Now that the German threat had become unmistakably obvious to everyone, Angell continued, the public reacted by demanding more armament. Simultaneously, however, there was a strong public demand to support General Franco in Spain — apparently, a democracy ruled by a people's front of republicans, socialists, communists and syndicalists was more dreadful than a rightwing military dictatorship.

Deterrence is political

In Angell's opinion the confidence in deterrence by tremendous armament spending was completely unwarranted for at least three reasons. First of all it was rather questionable to what extent weaponry provided any real security for the civilian population. "The trenches may be safer than our homes; our soldiers safer than our babies."[50] The development of the (conventional!) airforce had reduced the insular position of Britain, as a result of which London would be situated at the front.

Secondly, Angell realized that a far-reaching militarization of society posed a threat to the security of the people in itself: the armament would become too costly, would bear too heavily on the taxpayer, and would usurp accumulated savings. In the longer run inflation would be the inevitable result of increasing loans for unproductive purposes.[51]

Thirdly, Angell made it clear that it was not just military power which mattered but political intentions. Military superiority does not deter by itself. He illustrated this by pointing at the combined military power of England, France, Belgium, Russia, Japan, Italy, Rumania and, later, the United States during the first World War.

"Here was overwhelming power, as the final victory proved. But that overwhelming power did not deter the aggressor, nor prevent war. Nor did it ensure effective defence."

Why did this superior power fail to deter? The answer is patently obvious:

"The power did not prevent aggression because the putative aggressor did not know that he would have to meet the power."[52]

In 1938 the situation was no different. Would England join the Soviet-Union to fight against Germany or Japan, or would it remain neutral, Angell asked himself. Would England support Germany and Japan in their struggle against Soviet Communism? Would England drop France as an ally the moment its government turned socialist, as it had dropped Spain? To Angell's great annoyance these questions did not receive any attention in the public debate. The public was interested only in armament itself; the supposed shortages of aircraft, granates or one or the other type of cruiser.[53]

In effect this last point came down to a call for a firm military alliance which overruled the interstate conflicts of its members. Such a plea had indeed been part of Angell's work since 1918, when he wrote *The Political Conditions of Allied Success*. But a military alliance as such was insufficient to deter a potential agressor. Without a policy along the first track, there could be no peace. Germany should be offered the means needed to realize higher standards of living in a non-violent way.

"For in the absence of peaceful means of obtaining them she will quite certainly fight for them. As we should."[54]

79

Such an offer had never been made to Germany, not before the first World War, not at the Versailles conference, and has never since. The reason of this is obvious: England feared that that would go at the expense of its own economic position.

Democratic internationalism and collective security

The democratic internationalism pictured by Angell is based on the fundamental equal rights of all people. These rights are actually limited to one principle: first and foremost, the goal of an international order is to guarantee that physical power is not the final judge.

The problem with the existing order was that countries based their mutual defence on the "isolated power of each". The armies' job was to allow a country to be its own judge. Angell strove for an order under which countries would base their mutual defence on the "combined power of organized civilization". Like the police within a state, the army's only task would be to prevent the parties to a conflict from taking the law into their own hands by relying on their force.

> "The proper function of force [is] to cancel out force in human relations, to see that it [does] not decide disputes."[55]

In addition to wars in self-defence, Angell accepted the idea of military interventions to (re-)establish order. In this respect Navari mentions that Angell judged England's policy in India and Egypt, and even the conquest of Algeria by France, to be sound forms of "real-politik". In *The Great Illusion* he wrote:

> "Where the conditions of a territory is such that the social and economic cooperation of other countries with it is impossible, we may expect the intervention of military force, not as the result of the 'annexationist illusion', but as the outcome of real social forces pushing for the maintenance of order."[56]

Navari, however, does not mention the preconditions Angell connects to the formation of an international policing task. Angell realized that before a police force can be created, something more is needed, namely an agreement that it is necessary. After all, in a domestic situation, a police force can only function if there is a social consensus on the need for the rules it enforces. This consensus does not mean surrendering to superior force. It is an expression of self-interest, and is, according to Angell, based on the realization that people within a society are dependent on one another, that is, it is based on interdependence.

> "[A] realization of interdependence — even though it be subconscious — is the basis of the social sense, the feeling and tradition which make possible a democratic society in which freedom is voluntarily limited for the purpose of having any freedom at all."[57]

Angell refers here to two aspects of interdependence. A normative aspect and a pragmatic aspect. The former concerns the notion that if one wishes to avoid falling victim to pressure and domination, one must (a) control one's own tendency to use violence, and (b) be prepared to collectively resist pressure.

> "It is as certain as anything can be, that men cannot protect their own interests effectively unless they are prepared to defend the interests of others, that is to say, the law which protects others."[58]

This normative argument culminated in his plea for a protective union of Western democracies.

More pragmatic is the awareness that when there is a high degree of interdependence, violence hinders rather than helps in the protection of one's interests. The more dependent people are on one another and the higher the quality of the mutually required performances, the more individuals, groups and countries will realize that cooperation increases their chances for success better than the use of force and domination.

81

"To the degree to which we are really dependent on someone, our physical power over him is limited; to the degree to which the service we demand of him is difficult, needing for its performance knowledge, tools, freedom of movement, he can use those things to resist the power we try to exercise over him."[59]

This is what in contemporary literature is referred to as the measure of mutual sensitivity and vulnerability which limits the military options, simultaneously creating new, more civilized instruments for power politics.

Despite the normative aspects of this statement, Angell was not aiming at a normative choice between cooperation and force. If victory in a war could provide greater material or spiritual advantage than cooperation, then it would be unwise and unrealistic to choose for cooperation. In that case, Angell said, international anarchy would be preferable to international order.[60] It was from this notion that the need arose to deflate the illusions that led to a real preference for anarchy over order in international society; a preference for the "isolated power of each" determining the course of international affairs.

All nations were certainly prepared to condemn armament, economic nationalism and international distrust in the abstract, but in practice it became obvious that

"each one individually clings to his armament, adds to his tariff, invents new modes of economic nationalism, and insists upon an absolute national sovereignty which must make international order impossible and the prolongation of anarchy and chaos inevitable."[61]

Angell was of the opinion that political thought on this subject was still based on the conditions that existed before the Industrial Revolution. The idea that conquest, territorial expansion, force and domination were *necessary* for increased prosperity belonged to a phase of economic development which had already passed — a phase in which war could be lucrative. Angell considered the type and extent of interdependence between economically developed countries to be such that the "isolated power of each" had become counterproductive in the international sphere.

It is, of course, distinctly idealistic to strive for democratic internationalism, for it implies a consensus on the idea that every individual, group and nation has a right to its own opinion and that respect for those opinions means a voluntary limitation on everyone's freedom of action. Indeed, in the 1930s, when one Western democracy, the United States, still had a war-scenario ready for an invasion by another Western democracy, Great Britain, these ideals must have sounded totally utopian.[62]

At first sight Angell's plea for democratic internationalism seems not only idealistic but also unrealistic. In many countries even today, people are unable to achieve a consensus of any sort even at the national level. And where it has been achieved, the consensus is constantly under pressure. But, as Angell wrote when he defended his ideals in 1938, do we have to conclude that, simply because a constitution can fail "every State must inevitably drift to the conditions of South American Republics where every general election is a civil war"? Must we conclude that "civil war is the proper or inevitable method"?[63]

Though these rhetorical questions have little to do with analytical skill, they point at an aspect which in the debate about Realism and Idealism has been obscured. Angell's protest here concerns what nowadays is called worst case thinking. The question of whether or not war between nation-states is unavoidable has little to do with the opposition between Idealism and Realism as it is described in the literature. The Realists, with their trust in a military balance of power combined with skillful diplomacy, cherish the same ideal as Angell, with his faith in democratic internationalism based on interdependence: that conflicts can be settled without war.

The real opposites: idealism — fatalism

In 1938 Angell summarized the conclusions of *The Great Illusion* as follows:

"The conclusion to be drawn from the argument of this book is not that, since war is profitless, the danger of attack is past. Men are not guided by the facts, but what they believe to be the facts. Only when the futility is realized will the futility deter. One-sided disarmament is therefore of no avail and is not here advocated. But, while maintaining our arms, we must maintain our efforts to create a new order based on the recognition of those mutual obligations between nations which are necessary for fruitful cooperation. Such efforts are now unpopular so that statesmen dare not make them and take the risks involved. The necessary will can never exist so long as we believe that cooperation between nations is contrary to the laws of nature and of life and beyond man's power. *This book is designed to undermine that satanic fatalism; to prove that, though truly war will not stop itself apart from human endeavour, man can, since he makes war, also make wars to cease.*"[64]

In the period following the first publication, little seemed to remain of mankind's ability to abolish war. When the book appeared, the crisis in the Balkans was already imminent. In 1912 the first Balkan War began, the second followed in 1913, and the crisis of July 1914 ushered in the "Great War". Afterward, man's attempts to abolish war took the form of the League of Nations. But the attempt to safeguard peace and encourage international cooperation failed. In 1931 Japan invaded Manchuria; in 1936 Italy annexed Abyssinia, Germany occupied the Rhineland and the Spanish Civil War broke out. In 1937, the Sino-Japanese war became a reality. In the meantime, England tried to avoid war by negotiation. The Munich Conference of September 1938 was the notorious pinnacle of this appeasement. In that year Angell repeated his statement: "man can make wars to cease". Less than six months later, on March 15-16, 1939, German troops entered Czechoslovakia. Britain finally faced facts. Appeasement was abandoned, general national service was instituted, and war declared on Germany on September 3. Angell himself went to the United States to argue for American participation in the war. The second "Great War" was followed by some 160 smaller ones, of which approximately thirty-two were still in progress in 1989.[65] If man is able to put an end to war, he does not seem to be very willing.

The most fundamental criticism of idealism (Angell's in this case, but the same is true of the idealism in the Realist School) is that the existence of war *proves* that it is inevitable. Taken in the absolute, this means that no form of peace policy can or will be successful for very long. According to this perspective, neither disarmament, deterrence, balance of power, peaceful coexistence, SDI, mutual dependence, autarky and autonomy, development aid, religions, the principles of sovereignty, nor human rights can guarantee peace for a long time or even lead to the abolition of war (which, in the end, is a far less ambitious goal, since it is restricted to the abolition of organized military violence). Even a defence of these ideals with the argument that they have never actually been realized or con- sciously maintained does not mollify the fatalist: this failure simply proves that man is not able to abolish war.

As Angell observed, for the true fatalist war is comparable to a natural phenomenon. It happens whether people want it or not.[66] The phenomenon can be studied, it can be predicted, it can be prepared for, but it cannot be prevented any more than a seis- mologist can prevent an earthquake.

Despite his resistance to such fatalism, Angell is ambivalent on this point. "War may be inevitable. Perhaps. I do not know. Nobody knows".[67] He then uses a metaphor which frequently appears in contemporary peace research as well:

"Disease is certainly inevitable; yet in the West, plague, cholera, leprosy have been wiped out. Is that no gain?"[68]

He (likewise as in current usage) expands the metaphor for the struggle against fatalism as follows:

"The people in the East don't want cholera. But they don't see the relation between mediaeval sanitary conditions and the disease which kills them ..."[69]

So, what is needed is a change in "sanitary conditions".

But what sort of change? Angell does not believe that human

nature itself can be changed, nor does he accept the view — which, according to Morgenthau, is so typical of the Idealist School — that man is basically good. He definitely had his own normative viewpoint on what is good (equal rights and cooperation), and what is evil (force and domination); but he found the question whether man is by nature more inclined to one or the other to be of secondary importance. Angell has a more neutral starting point, namely the axiom that man will try to act in his own best interest. Where this requires violence, he will use violence; where this requires cooperation, he will use cooperation. That man is disposed to fighting is part of his nature, according to Angell, but what he fights for is determined by his needs for survival, his traditions and habits, education and way of thinking.

> "We now see that it is irrelevant and unworthy to fight about religion; we could as easily come to see that it is irrelevant and self-defeating to fight about our nationalisms."[70]

Two factors have a decisive influence on the choice between cooperation and violence. The first concerns the social circumstances in which the choice is made; the second the determination of what one's own interests are. These two factors continually occupied Angell and can be recognized in the main themes of his work:
• the "public mind" (relating to the determination of one's interest);
• interdependence (relating to social structure).

For a fair assessment of his views on these matters, one must keep in mind exactly what one is criticizing: the idea that war as such could be abolished or the argument that encouraging socio-economic interdependence results in interests which are not served by war, thus discouraging the decision to wage it. The former involves a discussion of the usefulness of a peace policy, the latter a discussion of how to carry it out. If one rejects Angell's ideas because war (between nations) is simply inevitable, one cannot simultaneously argue that war can only be prevented by military deterrence based on superior or even equal force. Yet this confusion of arguments is implicit in criticism by the Realist School.

If one is a fatalist and feels that war is inevitable, then the important question should be: which policy has the least disastrous consequences in the event of war, the quest for optimal military deterrence or the quest for an optimal blending of interests? If one does not consider war to be inevitable, then one must ask: what provides the best guarantee against it, a military stalemate (balance of power), national superiority (hegemony) or a lack of material and social interests in warfighting?

Irrationality: a hurdle Angell could not leap

Concerning public opinion, Angell actually only worried. He was convinced that deep-seated convictions could be changed. He cited, among other things, the fundamentally altered view of the justice and normality of slavery, polygamy, autocracy, the duel and corporal punishment. But the changes he felt were necessary for his time did not happen.

Angell was puzzled by one of the dilemma's of democracy. Democracy was the most preferable polity — he even championed international democracy — but that does not imply that decisions collectively taken are correct ones by definition. (Correct, meaning truly serving the interest of the people.) As long as public opinion is dominated by illusions, policies will be directed by them.

"John Smith" (there is no "Jane" in Angell's work) is a political amateur, who is only willing to take notice of policy issues in his spare time. Politicians and journalists fight to gain his attention in these scarce moments.[71] In this struggle, those confirming his illusions are most likely to win.

> "None of us likes to be told that his ideas are wrong, the things he usually does utterly foolish, and the newspaper which should habitually do this would lose circulation, and the politician who did it would lose votes. What both do normally is to win approval by confirming existing error."[72]

Moreover, the ability of politicians to pursue reforms in spite of the public will is limited by the intrinsic nature of democracy. The proper task of the politician "is not to change the common mind but to represent it". At best the politician can profit from existing pressures for change, but "it is the business of those outside politics to prepare the ground for the wiser politician".[73]

Despite his constant struggle against prevailing views, the illusions continued to dominate thought. Better education and information were the only other remedies he could think of, but what he understood this to mean remained unclear, according to Miller. Angell never solved this problem and, according to many of his critics, the reason is his extreme reliance on rationality and the independent power of reasonable argument. Irrationalism and bureaucratic short-sightedness are aspects of political decision-making which he recognized as such; they were central to his fatalistic future scenarios: the illusions will cause war. But he could not incorporate them as an intrinsic element in his idealistic scenarios: to abolish war, irrationality had to be abolished first, it seems.[74] Angell wanted the choice between cooperation and violence to be based on a sober weighing of interests, not on propaganda campaigns, sentiment and habit. Social conditions could then be given its proper weight as a factor in the decision. Increasing socio-economic interdependence was the key-condition that could open the door to the abolition of war.

Angell's concept of interdependence

Angell provided no strict definition of interdependence, and he used the word in different contexts. That is not to say, however, that he did not use the concept consistently. At the core Angell interpretated interdependence as a *structural linkage of fates*, a "Schicksalsbündnis". In economics, this referred to an *intertwining of interests* (integrative interdependence): complementary interests resulting from a division of labour (specialization), the cobweb-structure of monetary interests, and the complex relations between finance and trade. In politics the "structural linkage of fates" referred to *inevitable mutual influence* (systemic interdependence): in essential areas, one cannot ignore the interests of the others, whether they collide or run parallel. (For Angell, these essential areas were the pursuit of prosperity for the population and the maintenance of democratic norms and values.) In a different context, Angell used the word interdependence to refer to processes of change: particularly the *quantitative increase* of cross-border socio-economic and political processes and the *qualitative change* in economic relations. The quantitative increase involved both the intensification of contacts (the density and speed of communication), and the geographical spread of contacts (the "conquest of distance"). The quantitative increase was explained by improvements in communication- and transport-techniques. In this respect Angell saw the Industrial Revolution as a turning-point.

By mentioning these processes of change, Angell implicitly gave a clue as to other factors that made up his concept of interdependence. The *intensity*, the *spread* and the *quality* of relations qualified the "mutual influence" and the "intertwining of interests", and determined the nature of the "linkage of fates". In other words, for Angell, interdependence indicated a community of fates which:

- is characterized by (a) an intertwining of interests and (b) (more passively) mutual influence; and which
- is qualified by (a) the intensity of contact (density and speed of communication), (b) the geographical spread of contact and (c) the quality of mutually required performances or services.

The political implications that Angell associated with increased international interdependence arose from what he considered to be a high score on these qualifications. From the increased "intensity of contact" combined with their enlarged "geographical spread", he concluded that international organization and legislation had become necessary. He thus called for recognition of the fact that, although autonomous national policy-making continued to be possible, the political consequences could no longer be controlled autonomously, and that a successful prosecution of policies without international coordination could no longer be guaranteed. The external factors on which one depended in practice, therefore, had to be duly considered in the decision-making process. This, in fact, was a plea for increased functionalist interdependence, based on the awareness of increased systemic interdependence.

Considering the increased "intensity of contact" combined with the higher "quality of required performances", Angell concluded that force and domination were ultimately counterproductive.

> "Very simple forms of service like ... the cutting of sugar cane, can be compelled by the sheer compulsion of the slave-driver's whip. But you cannot get your appendix cut that way. ... In that circumstance you come to a voluntary agreement, bargain, contract, fees."[75]

In this sense, interdependence encourages self-control in the use of violence on the one hand, and cooperation and negotiation for the successful defence of one's interests on the other.

Together with the previous conclusion (the recognition of the role played by external factors in "autonomous" policy-making), this is expressed in Angell's statement that democratic internationalism is the only firm foundation for an international order.

These conclusions are definitely idealistic: interdependence *should* lead to international organization, to the destruction of outdated axioms and to equal justice. An interdependent structure apparently does not automatically bring this about; common sense and goodwill are required as well. In this sense Angell can be seen as an exponent of the Idealist School. On the other hand, however, the analyses on which he based his conclusions are considerably more realistic. A key element underlying his conclusions is the notion of mutual vulnerability. According to Navari and Baldwin, the concept of vulnerability even formed the heart of Angell's theory of interdependence.

> "[With interdependence] He meant a condition entailing potential harm, one moreover in which economic, as well as social and political, relationships were such that rupturing them produced costs."[76]

Vulnerability is the condition that results from the modern system of production, which is based on a division of labour. If man ignores genuinely increased socio-economic interdependence, if he refuses to adapt the assumptions underlying policy to conform to fundamental social change, then war will be inevitable.

4 Ramsay Muir (1872-1941) and the lessons of the first world war

In 1983 William Diebold, Jr. retired from the American Council on Foreign Relations. He had worked more than forty years for the Council, and thus his valedictory address gave an eye-witness account of half a century of American involvement in world politics: the isolationism of the 1930s, the advance towards economic and military hegemony, the key role in the formation of the post-war structure of Western cooperation, the decline of this cooperation in the 1970s, and, finally, the depression in the early eighties; different policies, changing governments, changing agendas, depths and heights. Diebold looked for the long-term perspective of this all, and the common denominator he came up with was "global interdependence". "The basic challenge is well-known", he said, and then he quoted Ramsay Muir:

> "We have entered a new era, the era of interdependence; and this interdependent world is threatened with chaos because it has not learnt how to adjust its institutions and its traditions of government to the new conditions."[1]

It is one of the rare quotations from Muir in contemporary literature.[2]

In fact, Diebold repeated the answer Muir himself gave to the same question. Muir's *The Interdependent World and Its Problems* (1933) is *his* eye-witness account of half a century of history; an account in particular of his struggle with the question why he, a professor in Modern History, failed to understand modern history when it was made. In that sense, the development of Muir's thinking itself explains the importance of the *cognitive* dimension of interdependence.

The Interdependent World and Its Problems deals with the perils of interdependence, the dangers and risks of being mutually dependent, and it deals with the fruits of interdependence, the surplus value of being mutually dependent. Muir's thesis is cryptic: world war is one of the risks of global interdependence, yet the end of war is its necessary consequence. What is remarkable about this thesis is that in it two arguments are combined that in contemporary literature are considered as one another's opposites. Some claim that warfare in situations of complex interdependence loses all purpose and thus will disappear. Other maintain that the most devastating wars in history occurred and will occur in situations of complex interdependence. Muir maintained the first, without denying the second: in case of increasing global interdependence war loses all purpose, but wars that do occur despite that fact will manifest themselves on a global scale. This thesis reflects the lessons Muir learned from the experience of the first World War.

In this chapter, first Muir's life is described and compared with that of Norman Angell. The purpose is to exemplify the importance of incorporating a global perspective in public education and science. Second, the short-comings of Muir's reasoning are explained by laying bare the eurocentric, liberal-christian paradigm which is typical, not only for him, but for the spirit of his age in general. Next, Muir's observations about interdependence are reviewed.

Man of the middle class

In his memoirs, which, unfortunately, remained unfinished, Muir typified his own life as "the story of a typical man of the middle class in a critical period of British history".[3] Though he wrote these words in 1940, he did not merely refer to the ongoing war of that year, but to the entire period since his birth in 1872. That period was critical in two related ways: (a) the world had changed radically, and (b) most people failed to notice that. In 1933, in retrospect of his college years, Muir put his finger on the sore spot:

> "It never dawned upon us that we were about to be faced with problems more complex and fundamental than any that Aristotle or Hobbes or Rousseau had considered: problems affecting not the organisation merely of a city, or of a Nation-State, or of a linked group of peoples such as those of Europe, but the organisation of a whole world, consisting of infinitely various peoples intimately linked together politically, culturally and economically."[4]

Why this blindness for changes that were so fundamental and so patently obvious in retrospect? Muir, once again about his college years at the end of the nineteenth century:

> "nobody offered us any penetrating thought, or even challenged us to think for ourselves, about the tremendous problems created by the transition to a world-economy which was then taking place."[5]

They studied Aristotle, Hobbes and Rousseau and that was it.

But the characterization "man of the middle class" plays a part too. Muir's political consciousness was only aroused at the late age of 41, when he, as a visiting professor, travelled through India from September 1913 to May 1914. The confrontation with the caste system, the multitude of peoples and religions, some of which were quite belligerent, and the part of the British in this whole, fascinated him, especially because of the question how such a country could ever become a democracy.

93

The first World War further mobilized his political awareness and made him conscious of this "critical period in British history". In great contrast to Norman Angell, who had announced, as early as 1909, that, if policies remained unchanged, war in Europe would be inevitable, Muir was completely surprised by the war. This was even literally true: A few days before England declared war, Muir was still in Germany. The *Frankfurter Zeitung* and the *Kölnische Zeitung* ("among the most liberal and the most reliable newspapers in Europe")[6] contended, even after the Sarajewo incident, that war was unthinkable, especially with Britain. A telegramme from his worried brother brought him back to reality. Upon arrival in England (after an hazardous journey through the Netherlands and Belgium) he was struck by the local reports, which told a completely different story.[7] The contrast with Norman Angell is telling.

Why perception matters: comparing two lives

Ramsay Muir and Norman Angell were both born in 1872. Also, both of them were British, and both were active politically, which, again in both cases, resulted in a short and frustrating membership of British parliament. In the end, both of them also were interested in interdependence. These similarities provide an interesting background for comparing their lives, and for showing that not only the conditions of interdependence matter but also the awareness of these conditions.

Up to the first World War, Muir's life was indeed exemplary for the British middle class. Muir's father, whom he lost at the age of eleven, was a minister and Scottish, like his mother. Muir grew up in the village of Birkenhead, destined to become a clergyman, too. But, thanks to great financial sacrifices by his mother, a small inheritance and a special scholarship, he was able to study at the University College in Liverpool and, for some years, at Oxford University. In 1898 he received his degree in the Classics and a year later in Contemporary History. In that year (1899) he became an assistant lecturer in Liverpool and his greatest ambition was to found an independent university in that city.

In that he succeeded. In 1905 the bureaucratic and political struggles were won. Muir was appointed professor at the new University of Liverpool. In that capacity he was invited by the American Society for University Extension, in 1906, to make a lecture-tour through the United States of America. Besides two short vacations in Norway and Switzerland respectively, this was his first trip abroad.

"All my life, hitherto, even when I was at Oxford, had been centred in Liverpool, which had latterly completely engrossed me."[8]

In the USA he focused completely on university life, and his report shows no signs of the political awareness that was incited by his voyage through India in 1913.[9] After this voyage through India (where he was also much occupied with the British university system) he was bestowed a chair in Modern History at the University of Manchester.

Up to that year, Muir had published about the history of Liverpool (in 1906 and 1907), about "Peers and Bureaucrats" (1910), and he had made atlasses of history in cooperation with his brother-in-law George Philip. All these years he lived with his mother as much as possible ("she liked to have her chickens under her wing"[10]). That was the world of Ramsay Muir between 1872 and the first World War.

Norman Angell was also born in a small village (Holbeach in Lincolnshire), but he was educated at the Lycée de St. Omer in France, a commercial school in London and, for just a year, the University of Geneva. In Geneva he got his first experience with journalism. At an early age he expressed the wish to change the world, but as he soon found this to be too ambitious, he decided to emigrate to the USA to become a farmer, a cowboy. He was seventeen at the time!

Five years later, in 1897, he resigned to the fact that he was a better writer than a ploughman (as a farmer he constantly went broke), and he returned to Europe as a journalist. During the aftermath of the Dreyfus affair (1894-1896), he worked in Paris. This, together with his amazement about the American Anglophobia during the Venezuelean crisis (1895-1897) and his indignation over the excesses committed in the Boer War (1899-1902), turned him into an intellectual activist. As early as 1909, he tried, in vain, to reveal the irrealistic foundation of the policies pursued to the public and the members of parliament.[11]

From his youth onwards, Angell was a world citizen (albeit one with a strong European orientation). In comparison, Muir was quite a provincial. His world was too small for him to worry about processes which he later realized to be of fundamental importance, for this small world, too. The war in particular made this painfully clear.

But, though he was a late developer, Muir immediately succeeded in grasping this broader horizon. Already in 1914, he gave a public lecture in Manchester in which he described the war that had just begun as the culmination of modern history. In retrospect to this lecture, he wrote:

> "I was thrilled to realise how all the greatest movements in modern history — nationalism, internationalism, the growth of popular self-government and the expansion of European influence over the non-European world — seemed to have come to a culminating point in the war."[12]

Liberal in heart and soul

Muir's autobiography ends abruptly in the year 1917, when he got off to India once again, this time as a member of a commission that had to investigate the education at the University of Calcutta.[13] Regrettably, we therefore have to rely on secondary sources for the most interesting part of his life, his political career: the scanty facts from *Who was Who?* as well as those in memoriams by his close colleagues and friends, collected in Hodgson's volume, which are probably too positive about him (nothing but good about the dead).

The sober facts already reveal his liberalism: in 1923 and 1924 Muir was a member of parliament for the Liberals of Rochdale (accidentally, it happened that from 1859-1865 Rochdale had been represented by Richard Cobden); from 1930 to 1931 he was chairman of the Organization Committee of the Liberal Party; from 1931 to 1933 he chaired the National Liberal Federation, of which he was president between 1933 and 1936. In that year, he became vice-president of the Liberal Party Organization. He was then aged sixty-four. After his retirement he worked at the Ministry of Information as a voluntary worker. On May 4, 1941 Ramsay Muir died.

Muir's political activities flourished during the interbellum period. In that period he was in close contact with Sir Ernest Simon and Sir Walter Layton, who founded the Liberal Summer School. This school was run from 1922 to 1939 and was intended to educate a young generation of progressive liberals. Muir was directly involved in the organization and he did a great deal of lecturing at the Summerschool. These liberals were progressive in that they judged governmental interference in the economy to be essential. According to Layton, Muir stressed that intervention was needed to assure equal chances and real individual freedom.[14] Thus, Muir definitely did not belong to the "laissez-faire Whigs", who ascribed godly justice to the "invisible hand" that controls the market mechanism.

The doctrine of free trade was criticized, for instance, in his *Liberalism and Industry: Towards a Better Social Order* (1920). According to Ernest Simon, this study was the first attempt to formulate constructively and comprehensively the industrial policy of the Liberal Party.[15] This attempt was taken up and elaborated further by the Liberal Summer School. Of great importance was the concern with the school of Sir Lloyd George, who, in 1925, donated ten thousand pounds, by no means a small amount of money. This enabled the summerschool to set up a permanent office. One of the collaborators, besides Muir and others, was John Maynard Keynes (1883-1946), who in 1929 wrote the economic foundation of the election programme of the Liberal Party. The research at the summerschool culminated in the report "Britain's Industrial Future", which was adopted by the Liberal Party.[16]

The impact of this success, however, should not be overestimated. The Liberal Party was a small party, without real political power. The Conservatives and Labour continued to dominate the political spectrum.[17] But, obviously, during the second half of his life, Muir himself was completely under the spell of the ideas of the Liberal Summer School and of liberalism in general. According to Layton:

> "He was certain that liberalism was the only possible cure, and that if disaster was to be avoided, the twentieth century must become the Liberal Century."[18]

Muir, being a son of a clergyman, even spoke of a "liberal faith":

> "I describe this belief as a 'faith' because ultimately it has a religious character. ... it rests on the conviction that the Spirit who has guided man in his toilsome struggle out of the mire of animalism is perpetually working upon every mind, goading it by means of those insatiable aspirations ... after the rightness of form which is beauty, after the rightness of fact which is truth, and after the rightness of relations which is justice. ... This is the ultimate faith of Liberalism, a belief in the supreme value of individuality, because individuality is the medium through which God works; an eager welcome for variety of type, character and effort, because variety is fruitful and desirable in itself ..."[19]

A liberal-christian paradigm

This quotation shows the kind of undisputed axioms one must be aware of when evaluating Muir's ideas about interdependence. Other characteristics of this liberal-christian paradigm can be traced in Muir's work, too. Specifically liberal are the following axioms:

- The trust in individualism is translated politically into the conviction that a parliamentary, constitutional democracy (after British example) is the best form of social organization.
- Obedience to the laws that serve society (in contrast to the laws that serve only specific rulers) is a prerequisite to attain and to preserve individual freedom.

- In the economic sphere, progress is equated with the sum of economic growth and technological development and innovation.
- In the line of this economic logic, it is believed that large-scale developments (a product of growth) are better than small-scale tendencies.
- This, again, influences the political opinion about nationalist tendencies: if these work towards unification (compare the German and the Italian unifications in the nineteenth century) and thus towards a growth of geo-political social units, in principle nationalism is valued positively. If nationalist tendencies work towards the disintegration of societies into smaller geo-political units (for instance in the colonies) they are valued negatively.
- A last characteristic of this paradigm is that tariff walls and protectionism are unacceptable: they prevent economic growth and developments towards a larger scale, and therefore the progressive development of mankind.

So much for the liberal aspects of Muir's thinking. The christian aspects in Muir's thinking are not confined to liberalism only, but are also present in, for instance, marxism, socialism, fascism, and conservatism. First of all, we are dealing with a form of eurocentrism of quite an expansive nature. This is a derivative of the christian missionary spirit: the (West) European civilization is the best conceivable, and thus an example for the rest of the world. (Within this civilized world, Britain in its turn is, of course, seen as the "prima inter pares" and the cradle of all positive historical forces.)

The second christian aspect in Muir's paradigm is the combination of a linear conception of history (optimism about the final "destiny" of human evolution; the "good" will reign the "evil") with a cyclical conception of history (pessimism, because of the permanent threat of collapse, or, to put it more precise, a relapse into lower levels of civilization; the threat of the anti-Christ and the Armageddon). The societal development of humankind, from tribal life to world society, is predestined, according to Muir. At the same time, however, people can act contrary to their predestina-

tion, causing a relapse of civilization. Therefore, specific developments are valued "good" or "bad", depending on their contribution
to the "progress" of civilization. In Muir's case, this progress is
defined in terms of liberalism.[20]

Muir's work did not, of course, escape the spirit of the age. It is
illustrative for his thinking that, in 1916, he expected Turkey,
Austria and, less surely, Germany to be beaten not because they
were economically and militarily weaker but because "these
powers are trying to withstand the main stream of civilisation".[21]
He was less enthousiastic about the dissolution of the British
colonial empire.

It is, of course, useless and futile to condemn Muir for having
ideas that were trapped within the spirit of the age and his personal
religious convictions. However, in order to assess the contemporary value of his work it is necessary to strip his insights of these
axioms. The aim is to find out to what extent the contemporary
development of IR-theories can profit from points of view that, for
whatever reason, have sunk into oblivion. What is revealed is a
typical account of the evolution of global *systemic* interdependence,
a warning for the negative effects of this condition (the perils of
interdependence), an ode to the positive effects (the fruits of interdependence), and a plea to adapt governmental structures and
internatonal law to these new conditions, by means of increasing
integrative interdependence.

The world a single political system

Almost lyrically, Muir described the communication revolution of
the nineteenth century. First, the railways appeared on the scene,
"whereby a great part of the earth's surface has been woven
together ... with a network of steel rails". Second, the steamer came,
accompanied by the building of docks, shipyards, loaders and
unloaders, which affected the infrastructure along all coasts on
earth. The next step in this process was the telegraph, "a sort of
nervous system for the now unified world", followed by the
telephone at the end of the century. Then, early in the twentieth
century, the automobile was invented, as well as the aeroplane.

"The aeroplane makes nothing of frontiers", Muir wrote. The conquest of distance was completed by the wireless and the television ("as it would seem", Muir added in parentheses, not knowing that this precaution would refer to the television-programmes rather than the distribution of television sets). Now, satellite links, the fibreglass cable, computer networks, intercontinental missiles and space shuttles can be added to this impressive sequence.

"In peace as well as war", Muir concluded, "the annihilation of distance has transformed the relations of men."[22]

Shouldn't this be accompanied by changes in the thinking about these relations? Muir linked three conclusions to this development. The conquest of distance had forced the world into one political system, and, secondly, into one economic system (he did not worry about the order of these developments). Thirdly, the physical unification of the world gradually lead to cultural assimilation.

In Muir's description of the political world system, his liberal-christian paradigm plays a positive role; particularly because of its combined linear and cyclical conception of history.

On the one hand, he had a great admiration for the physical unification that took place. On the other hand, he feared that precisely this progress bore its own ruin. "In the Great War, the world-system ... almost committed suicide."[23]

The dualism resulted in a moderate point of view and kept Muir away from the naïeve opinion that, since global interdependence was achieved, cooperation had become inevitable. One of the main characteristics of the system was that it generated conflict: it was a "unity in disunity". Muir made a striking comparison with the political system of the Ancient Greeks "whose City-States were all alike affected by the great clash of the Peloponnesian war, yet all knew themselves parts of Hellas". In that sense, the first World War was the Peloponnesian war of this interdependent world and the conclusive evidence of this interdependence:

"The Great War was itself the final proof that the whole world had been brought within a single political system, for

101

every people on the face of the earth was directly or indirectly involved in it — even the Lamas of Tibet and the
Samoyedes of Kamschatka."

Muir continued with barely concealed admiration:

> "Amid all its horrors, the war had this august and tremen-
> dous aspect, that it was the first event in human history in
> which all peoples of the earth were not only involved, but
> knew that they were involved."

Muir regretted that lessons had to be so hard and he feared future
ones ("any repetition must mean the suicide of civilisation"), but
he did not become a doom-monger and put his trust in the process
of learning. Cynically speaking, disasters are beneficial if the sur-
vivors take effective measures to prevent repetition. According to
Muir, the League of Nations was such a measure:

> "However imperfect an instrument the League may be, and
> even if it should prove to be a total failure, its institution is
> a recognition of the established interdependence in the
> world; the establishment of the first organ ever created to
> serve the needs of the whole human race."

He continued, saying that the League should not be seen, as was so
often done, as a product of sheer sentiment and unpractical
idealism. First and foremost, the League was the result of a practical
necessity, recognized by cynics.

In other words, Muir asserted that in the present modern world
the political fate of every community or people is inevitably linked
to the fate of every other community or people, and that for that
reason there exists a political world system, whether one likes it or
not.

> "We are beginning to realise that, unless we can contrive to
> rise out of a system of conflict into a system of co-operation,
> a collapse like that of the Ancient Greek system, but far more
> fatal, and indeed irremediable, must ensue."

102

The combination of the first World War and the League of Nations (and its reoccurance in the combination of the second World War with the United Nations Organization) forms a credible confirmation and convincing support of Muir's pessimistic idealism.

Economic interdependence versus autarchy

If in the eigthteenth century the world had perished save France and Britain, this would have left the daily life of the majority of the French and British people undisturbed. In 1933, this had become utterly impossible, according to Muir, despite the size of the country or its richness of resources. Obviously, self-sufficiency and autarchy remain possible to the present day, but at what price and at what level of welfare?

Muir denounced President Hoover (1929-1933), who, during the Depression, maintained that the United States would come through because they were self-sufficient.

> "No doubt it is true that if the rest of the world were suddenly destroyed the United States could provide her people with a generous subsistence. But her whole economic system would have to be painfully reorganized before she could do so; and she could not provide them with many of the things which have to come appear essential in modern life."[24]

Moreover, under Hoover's Administration the American Ministry of War had made up a list of about thirty products that were deemed essential to modern warfare but that the USA did not produce at all or in sufficient quantities.

Muir's addition "modern" is essential: global interdependence is the herald of modernity. Even the import-dependency of "luxury products" should not be trivialized. There is, of course, an essential difference between primary and secondary needs, and obviously, a country can more easily do without tropical fruits than without wheat or rice. But "habituation" to luxury (addiction) is an important factor, which increases the sensitivity to the loss of luxury products to a height that is not to be expected if only criteria of survival are applied. Discussions about what should be called the poverty line in rich countries, reflect this point. In many countries radio and television sets and refrigerators, for instance, are not considered to be luxury products.[25] Illustrative, too, are the social problems that were caused by the American Prohibition during the thirties.[26]

In describing the economic global interdependence, Muir directed his arguments against the ideals of autarchy and against the allegation that economic independence was a fact. Here, Muir showed himself to be a politician rather than a historian.

> "If ruin is to be averted, either the interdependence of the world must be brought to an end ... or the sovereignty of the nations must somehow be limited, or its exercise restrained."[27]

The price of the first "solution" would be a return to the conditions of barbarism, Muir said. It would mean a deliberate abandonment of modern methods of production and communication. The price of ending global interdependence was a return to the Middle Ages. If people were unwilling to pay this price for their independence, they had to accept the price for their interdependence, i.e. a limitation of sovereignty.

Yet, many people want to have it both ways. Either they neglect or belittle their interdependence and consider themselves safe in political isolation, or they are only aware of their own dependence and consider expansionist policies necessary to make themselves less vulnerable. Both options are very dangerous. Its pursuers will become frustrated. Real independence cannot be combined with high material living standards. Wealth cannot be produced in isolation and the list of countries and centres of production that have to be controlled politically, in order to achieve independence through imperialism, has grown immeasurably long. Or, as Richard Rosecrance put it in 1981:

> "So many sources of dependency exist, even for the most independent countries, that the agenda of necessary conquests becomes implausibly long."[28]

Cultural assimilation (I): fewer barriers between people

In Muir's description of the cultural assimilation which he expected to take place, his liberal-christian paradigm played a negative role. According to Muir, humankind was on its way to a common civilization in a unifying world, and this common civilization would be dominated by the Western culture, which was a good thing. Local and racial variation would, of course, remain ("long may they survive!"), but the overall tendency was towards worldwide adoption of "the fashions of the dominant West in most external things".[29]

As in his description of the communication revolution, Muir lost himself in lyrical words when he was writing about the cultural unification of the world: The Olympic Games (which had been organized since the end of the nineteenth century) were a symbol of the unity in the world, "just as the Olympic Games were a token of the unity of Ancient Greece." Almost everywhere on earth people played the same sports, all but a few of which originated in England (soccer, tennis, bridge, billiards, golf); people organized "world" championships and kept "world"-records; the fashion houses of London and Paris dictated the clothing of the well-to-do classes, worldwide; worldwide the meals of these elites were prepared according to the principles of the French cuisine and the ingredients came from far and wide; grammophones played the same music everywhere; movies spoke a universal language (though Muir feared that this could change with the appearance of the "talkies"); the radio, "infant as it is", was one of the most essential factors that brought people together. Meanwhile, Muir did not neglect the influence of other cultures altogether: he mentioned art from China and Japan, the philosophy from India and the "barbaric music" from Africa.

In the eyes of a post-war generation born with the radio and television switched on, Muir's amazement is hardly conceivable. But that does not make his observations outdated. What has changed is that the processes are no longer exclusively eurocentric. Western culture is being penetrated as well: acupuncture, yoga and meditation, the Chinese, Indian and Mexican cuisine, folk dance, liberation theology, drugs other than alcohol, the ideas of Bhagwan,

105

the theories of Ghandi, etcetera. Meanwhile, since 1945 the Western culture has continued to spread around the world, especially from the USA: Coca Cola and the fast food culture, Western architecture, pop-music, blue jeans, the culture of commercials, the Hollywood world of glitter and glamour; all of this is experienced more and more universally. In 1988, A. de Swaan phrased it as follows:

> "Only in this century and especially since the second World War an international culture has evolved, which is massive and vulgar. Internationalism was always elitist, while public entertainment, popular food and the workman's clothing were restricted to a particular area. Now, a *vulgar international culture* has evolved under American hegemony."[30]

Muir expected these kinds of developments to pacify the world. Yet, this seemed to be prompted by his belief in human progress, rather than by criteria of a more objective nature. It must even be doubted whether "assimilation" is the right term to describe the overall cultural development: parallel to developments that broaden cultural horizons, sects and closed subcultures have come into being (including the westernized political and academic elites in the developing countries). This constitutes a disintegrating and alienating force in society. Even to the extent that one is justified in speaking of cultural assimilation, the political implications are far from clear. The cultural assimilation of the Ancient Greek, which Muir gave as an example, exceeded by far the present level of assimilation; but the Greeks did not fight less because of that. Similarly, the City States of Renaissance Italy were culturally definitely a unit, yet, they were quite belligerent.

Despite his enthusiasm about the foreseen process of cultural assimilation, Muir himself, too, seems to have had doubts about a proper assessment of its political implications. He stuck to the intuitive notion that people are brought together when they show more interest in one another's culture. This would increase the acceptance of interdependence, but to presuppose a direct causal relationship was a bit too simple.[31]

Cultural assimilation (II): the reign of law and human rights

Muir was more explicit about another aspect of assimilation: i.e. the worldwide acceptance of European principles of government. Actually, this is not a form of assimilation, but the export of European political culture. Identical, general ideas about human relations and about social organization are adopted worldwide. First of all, Muir pointed to matters that would nowadays be gathered under the heading "human rights". He observed that almost everywhere slavery was abolished, "though it has been the foundation of human organisation throughout the greater part of the world since organised society began."[32] Almost everywhere it is maintained that the concept of individual freedom of opinion and thought, of belief, of physical integrity, and of organization, under the protection of the law, is a fundamental, indefeasible right (though in many countries up to the present a hard battle is being fought against the traditions of castes and inherited privileges).

Secondly, he pointed at the polities which were set up in many countries after the European model. This was especially obvious in (a) the pursuit of representative self-government, based on parliamentary institutions, (b) an enormous increase of governmental interference on behalf of public welfare and well-being, and (c) the formation of powerful bureaucracies of government providing for these new tasks.

Thirdly, Muir pointed at a development that can be located at the borderline between polity and human rights: almost universally, the doctrine of the reign of law is accepted. The Reign of Law is "the doctrine that no man's liberties may be impaired otherwise than by process of law". Muir added to this his observation that Law is considered to be less and less a mandate of superior human or godly power and more and more an expression of the common will of the community.[33]

Obviously, in the thirties Muir could not possibly have had any knowledge of the post-war decolonization (which was itself a product of the principles of the reign of law and human rights just described) and he also underestimated the resilience of the Japanese and Chinese cultural traditions and of the islamic religions. But the fact is that throughout the world people are experimenting with the European model of polity and, worldwide, politicians pay at least lip service to the reign of law and human rights.

Such lip service, even if it is only that, does indeed point to a fundamental cultural change (which I would not contribute to the export of European values and norms only). The change is that rulers have greater difficulty in deriving a positively valued respect from the praxis of torture and corporal punishment. Virtually no government on earth is eager to show torturing on television in order to set an example for its subjects. The world press is seldom invited to report about public executions.[34] More illustrative for the common modern practice is the way the Securitate have worked in Rumania for many years: silently and underground, spreading fear and suspicion without displaying their crimes to humankind. Illustrative, too, is the suppression in Tibet by the Chinese government: each time they practise their medieval concept of maintaining order, they cut off the region from the rest of the world; tourists and journalists are sent away. For similar reasons the government of South Africa abolished the freedom of the press because the balanced reports about police actions under the state of emergency caused an international abhorrence and condemnation of the Apartheid Regime. The need to escape from the condemnation of world public opinion has become one of the complicating factors of all types of merciless policy and for any repressive regime. The mothers of the Plaza the Mayo or the anti-American sentiments during the Vietnam War are manifestations of public opinion that are feared worldwide by all governments. Should the veterans of Iran-Iraq war tell journalists proudly about the people they butchered, tortured and mutilated, eight years long, or should they bury these "heroic deeds" in the subconsciousness of their minds, and restrict their reports to lamentations about the crimes committed by the enemy?

Veterans of the Vietnam War (1964-1975), as well as Dutch veterans of the so-called police actions in Indonesia (1945-1950) are quite aware of this problem.[35] Terrorists struggle with it: violence attracts the attention of the public, but it seldom if ever leads to recognition or esteem. The PLO is only an exception thanks to its political skills. It is telling that the popularity of the Palestinian cause increased sharply after, in 1988, television news showed how Israeli soldiers cold-bloodedly broke the arms of Palestinians to prevent them from throwing stones.

The difference is not that there is less violence, but that it is harder to legitimize it to the rest of the world.[36]

The perils of interdependence

In summary, Muir's analysis of the world, as it has evolved since the sixteenth century, led to the following conclusions:

a)   the world, the globe, has become the macro dimension of politics;
b)   modern welfare demands cannot possibly be combined with autarchy and political independence;
c)   the political and economical unification of the different peoples on earth provokes a process of cultural assimilation, out of which new "rules of the game" will gradually grow that guide the social traffic in the world society.

A democratic polity, in which the reign of law serves human rights is the only possible outcome of this development, Muir claimed. This result, however, was long in coming. Muir, like Angell, saw the core of this problem in a misunderstanding of the conditions to which policies are subjected. In the face of this problem he developed two different scenarios for the nearby future.

The first scenario is the pessimistic one. If people refuse to recognize the conditions of interdependence, they will not be able to understand the scope of their own local and short-term policies, nor will they understand the impact of external developments. Muir described this situation in terms the "perils of interdependence" of which he mentioned five.

The first is the peril of war. Because in an interdependent world every part of the globe relies for its livelihood upon resources drawn from every other part, a great war dislocates normal life throughout the world. Moreover, modern weaponry has made the battlefield omnipresent. War can no longer serve civilization, since its only potential is its ability to destruct.

> "War, on any scale larger than mere police operations, has become a crime against civilization."[37]

The problem is that this must be recognized by *all* members of the interdependent world: the irresponsible action of any member endangers at least the very existence of a number of other nations, if not civilization as a whole.

The second peril concerns the spread of the principle of self-determination. Muir dealt with the phenomenon of nationalism at great length. He feared that peoples outside Europe would identify their justified claims for self-determination with claims for un-limited sovereignty and complete self-sufficiency. While recogniz-ing that this identification is no more than a mirror-image of the European development of nationalism, Muir pointed out that in an interdependent world these ideals have disastrous consequences (also within Europe), which go far beyond the negative effects of the nationalism of the relatively isolated world of sixteenth, seven-teenth and eighteenth century Europe. Rights of sovereignty must be limited or to some extent be pooled for there to exist any national freedom at all. Again the irresponsible behaviour of just one single member can upset the whole system.

The third and fourth perils are of an economic nature: tariff restrictions and the danger of monetary collapse. Here Muir was reflecting on the economic developments in Europe and the United States during the twenties, culminating in the Great Depression. Being a British liberal, Muir, of course, had an almost instinctive aversion from tariffs, but in this case there is little to be said against the instinct. After pointing out that you cannot have monetary stability if creditor countries obstruct the possibilities of debtor countries to pay in goods, that is through export; after pointing out how every nation strove to save itself at the expense of its neigh-bours by imposing tariffs; and after explaining the economic bad egg of the German war-reparation payments (something Angell had already warned against in 1910), he concluded that

"[though] all this tariff frenzy might have done comparative-
ly little harm a hundred years ago, when nearly all countries
really were almost self-sufficient, [it] was ruinous in the
post-war period, precisely because … interdependence had
become the dominant and ineluctable fact in the life of the
world."[38]

Muir was not pleading, however, for uncontrolled free trade. He
was strongly in favour of political interference in economic life,
albeit on an international scale. It is remarkable to hear a liberal say
that

"the vast industrial combines [multinational corporations]
must be subjected to some sort of regulation, if they are not
to be made the means of plundering consumers everywhere
in the interests of small groups of monopolists."[39]

Muir was less clear about the fifth peril than about the others. He
called it the peril of social revolution. By that he meant the breakdown of capitalism as propagated by communist theories. But
instead of explaining why interdependence enhances the chances
of social revolution, he started refuting what he thought was the
communist argument against capitalism. The mere fact, however,
that there was a Comintern with world communism as its stated
goal, that there was a worldwide Bolshevik scare in the twenties
and that people feared social revolution in their own countries, was
by itself ample proof of the global interdependence in this respect.
In his conclusions Muir summarized the perils of interdependence
as follows:

"It appears, then, that an interdependent world of sovereign
nations is a very dangerous and a very insecure world.
Interdependence makes war more difficult to avoid, and
more ruinous if it comes. It makes the extension of the
national spirit over the world — though in itself a fine thing
— the source of grim anticipations for the future. It makes
the long-established habit of the nations of striving after
economic self-sufficiency by way of tariffs a source of mere

111

ruin to them all. It makes the establishment of a sound monetary system more necessary than ever, but also more difficult than ever. It makes the problem of justly distributing the wealth which the world can now produce in unprecedented abundance more complex than ever."[40]

The myth of sovereignty

But even so, Muir remained optimistic. If people recognize the global dimension of politics, they will be able to adapt to that situation. If people are aware of the perils of interdependence, they can deal with them. Because of his deeply rooted belief — typical of the nineteenth century — in man's ultimate progress, Muir even called his optimistic scenario the "necessary consequences of interdependence". These consequences are:

a) limitation of state sovereignty;
b) abolition of war;
c) organized economic cooperation.

In the end, both the abolition of war and the organization of economic cooperation are a result of the limitation of state sovereignty or at least of a different attitude toward the idea of sovereignty. Muir therefore dealt with the problem of sovereignty at great length. He explained its historical roots and he questioned its empirical validity. How sovereign is the sovereign — and who is the sovereign, in the first place?

Particularly interesting is a psychological factor he mentioned. According to Muir it is an instinctive assumption of human beings that an absolute authority is responsible for everything that happens in the world. Many people create in their minds (or let others create for them) omnipotent Gods that are controlling the universe and in a similar way they envision ultimate authorities controlling their own earthly affairs. In the Middle Ages either the Pope or the Emperor, or both, were seen as supreme vicegerents of God on earth; not because they were able to exercise supreme power, but because there *must* be a vicegerent of God on earth. This belief was reinforced by Roman Law, which stated that the Emperor was the source of all law and, therefore, an absolute sovereign. In the Renaissance and the Reformation the Medieval concept of Godly vicegerents was abandoned in Europe, but the principles on which it was based lived on: both political and religious thinkers felt the need to define where the ultimate authority now lay. Muir referred to Machiavelli and Luther, who assigned this ultimate authority to the prince of the state, whose sovereignty included the right to determine the beliefs of his subjects. Similarly, in a more secularized world most people think in terms of sovereigns without questioning the empirical validity of these terms.

A related, psychological aspect is that in times of crisis and chaos there is always a strong search for mental anchorage. This explains, according to Muir, why Bodin (in the midst of the religious wars in France) and Hobbes (in the midst of civil disorder in England) concluded that a central sovereign power had to be present for there to be any law and order at all. With their work the doctrine of sovereignty as we still know it came into existence.

Muir's purpose was to explain that, from its very beginning, the Doctrine of Sovereignty had been a political myth.

> "[T]his respectable doctrine, which has wielded such unchallenged authority, is mere words, and has no relation to reality."[41]

But, like any myth or belief-system, this myth created a reality of its own.

> "[The Doctrine of Sovereignty] is drilled into the mind of every lawyer in every country, as one of the axioms of his science ... It is treated as an axiom in almost every treatise on political science, and implied in almost every history."[42]

The implicit assumption, however, that in the absence of a sovereign power there is anarchy, is empirically wrong and intellectually misleading. It makes people think that the only alternative for the (anarchical) state-system is a central World Government entrusted with global sovereignty. And, because this is a utopian

113

dream (if not a nightmare), it makes people stick to the myth of national sovereignty. The nation-state should guard and treasure its own sovereignty as best as possible, despite the interests of other states: the National Superiority Axiom once again.

If people come to see that there is no such thing as absolute sovereignty within and among states, they can start to realize that some governmental powers can be divided between states and some can be pooled for common exercise by a number of cooperating states without anarchy or chaos ensuing. Muir mentioned the federal structure of the USA and the British Commonwealth as examples.

As to the nature of these rights of sovereignty, he followed a functionalist reasoning: the State exists in order to render citizens certain essential services which they cannot supply for themselves. In an interdependent world, state-governments have to cooperate on all issues where they cannot render these services unilaterally. These issues vary from "trivial" things or "technical" matters, like the necessity of having a Universal Postal Union, to matters which governments have always regarded as vital prerogatives of national sovereignty: "the right of war, and of being the judges in their own cause; the right of coinage, and of exercising irresponsible control over their own monetary systems; the right of trade regulation, including tariffs."[43] People will discover this either by using their brains or by bitter experience.

In the end, therefore, the limitation of state-sovereignty is Muir's ultimate answer to the perils of interdependence. Awareness of the perils is the driving force, leading to the adjustment of governmental traditions and institutions in that direction.

In relation to the abolition of war this adjustment begins with the recognition of the fact that in an interdependent world there is collective security or no security. In relation to the economic perils of interdependence this adjustment begins with the recognition that the world will occasionally witness serious economic setbacks, that it will structurally maldistribute its costs and benefits and thus face social revolutions, unless governments decide to cooperate — or are forced to do so by their subjects.

The threat of the pessimistic scenario is meant to be the motor of the optimistic one. Muir — in the Idealist tradition — placed his trust in the learning process. Not every child has to be overrun by a car before it knows that crossing streets involves a degree of voluntary self-constraint.

5 Francis Delaisi (1873-1947): a Frenchman's view of global interdependence

"The world will only recover its equilibrium when, in the mind of each producer, the idea of interdependence has acquired the same value as that of salvation for the Christian, equality for the democrat, and the fatherland for the citizen. But how are the masses to acquire this consciousness? That is the vital problem which must be faced by all who can look beyond the surface of events."[1]

All roads lead to Rome. In contemporary literature it is generally assumed that interdependence theory has its roots in British liberalism, in Cobdenite pleas for free trade — the underlying thought being that this served British interests best in a period of hegemony. Delaisi was aware of this undertone: "Such was England's lead in the entire economic field that she could well afford to be liberal".[2] But one of the conclusions that can be drawn from his work is that interdependence theory is not ideologically bound to liberalism, nor to the Anglo-Saxon tradition in political thought.

Francis Delaisi was a Frenchman who belonged to extreme left-wing circles. Yet he analysed politics and economics in terms of global interdependence years before Ramsay Muir wrote his work on interdependence, and he developed the principle of functionalism years before David Mitrany started to work on it. Apart from being an enrichment in terms of ideological and international diversity, Delaisi's work deepens the insights in the cognitive dimension of global interdependence. The problem is psychological, he concluded in 1925: local life has internationalized, but the people are not aware of this. Political myth obscures economic reality. The essence of what he meant is clearly illustrated in the following fragment. The same fragment has also been quoted by Ramsay Muir, which makes it reasonable to assume that his thoughts about interdependence were influenced by Delaisi's work.

"M. Durand begins his day by washing himself with soap made from Congo nuts, and drying himself with a towel made in Lancashire from cotton grown in Texas. He puts on a skirt and collar of Russian linen, a suit made of wool from Australia or the Cape, a silk tie woven from Japanese cocoons, and shoes whose leather came from an Argentine ox, and has been tanned with German chemicals. In his dining-room, which is adorned with a Dutch sideboard made of wood from Hungarian forests, the table is furnished with spoons and forks of plated metal, made of Rio Tinto copper, tin from the Straits, and Australian silver. His fresh loaf is of wheat from the Beauce, Rumania or Canada, according to the season; he has a slice of chilled lamb from the Argentine, with tinned peas from California; his sweet includes English jam made of French fruit and Cuba sugar, and his excellent coffee comes from Brazil. He goes to his office in an American car; and after noting the quotations of the Liverpool, London, Amsterdam and Yokohama exchanges, he dictates his correspondance, which is taken down on an English typewriter, and signed with an American fountain-pen. In his factory fancy goods for Brazilian customers are being manufactured of materials of many origins, by

117

machinery made in Lorraine on a German patent, and fed with English coal; he gives instructions that they are to be sent to Rio by the first German boat sailing from Cherbourg. He then goes to his bank, to pay in a cheque in guilders from a Dutch client, and to buy sterling to pay for English goods. After a profitable day, he proposes to spend the evening at a show with his wife. She dons her blue fox fur from Siberia, and her diamonds from the Cape; they dine in an Italian restaurant, go to see the Russian ballet, and after supper at a Caucasian cabaret to the music of a negro jazz band, they return home. As M. Durand falls asleep under his quilt of Norwegian duckfeathers, he thinks with pride of the greatness of France, entirely self-supporting and able to snap her fingers at the whole world!"[3]

Extreme left-wing syndicalism

Francis Delaisi lived from 1873 to 1947. He did not leave any memoirs behind, but in the *Dictionnaire de biographie Française* (1965) the main facts of his life are summed up by A. Perrier.[4] His father was a cartwright in the village of Bazougers in the province of Mayenne. He attended grammer school in Laval and got his Bachelor's degree in history and geography at the university of Rennes. This allowed him to teach, and he worked at several grammar schools in the west of France. He never acquired his Master's degree, because in 1900 he went to Paris, hoping to start a career as a journalist.

By that time he had already developed extreme left-wing political ideas. Together with his college friend Gustave Hervé, he got involved in all kind of radical political movements. In this respect his career took a fundamentally different course from that of any of the other men discussed in this volume. In Paris he started to work with the journal *Pages libres*. Here he also published his first two books *L'Eglise et l'Empire romain* (1904) and *La force allemande* (1905). At the editorial staff of *Pages libres* he got in close contact with many militant workers and he became friends with Pierre Monatte and Alphonse Merrheim.

It is difficult to find out exactly to which particular socialist, communist or anarchist groups Delaisi belonged in his youth and after, but one thing is certain: he was a syndicalist. At the end of the nineteenth century the socialist struggle in France was dominated by anarchists and syndicalists. Syndicalists were anti-militaristic, not interested in political participation and they strongly opposed the state-system. They were against labour contracts, social reforms and parliaments. These were looked upon as sops to placate the public. In *La démocratie et les financiers* (1908) Delaisi remarked:

> "Once, someone compared politicians to wooden horses in a merry-go-round. They run and run and make a lot of noise; how fast they go! But when they stop, they are still at the same spot. In a democracy the politicians allow the public to ride on their backs."[5]

Instead, the syndicalists aimed at spontaneous revolts (general strikes, sabotage, direct action) to achieve a class-free society. These were the years of Georges Sorel (1847-1922) who wanted to form proletarian elite-groups to disturb the existing order. But it was not just revolution for the sake of revolution. "One thing the people must know", Domela Nieuwenhuis wrote in his translation of Delaisi's work:

> "the public is powerless as long as it is unable to confront the capitalist corps d'élite with a competent corps d'élite of its own. ... Before the capitalist society can be conquered by violence, it should be conquered by intelligence. Without that, any revolt, however successful, is doomed to end in defeat and contra-revolution."[6]

Actually, this period in history saw the birth of "pressure groups".

In practice, the syndicats were the French counterparts of the British trade unions. During the nineteenth century they developed into strong regional and national organizations and they gained regular political influence by the end of the century. In 1895 the syndicalists united themselves in the "Conféderaton Générale du Travail" (CGT), which was led by Léon Jouhaux (1879-1954). Delaisi

119

was a member of the CGT and belonged to its militant wing. In 1911 he became editor of its radical journal *La bataille syndicaliste*. Money, however, was a constant problem for journals like this, not in the least because the editors mistrusted anyone who had it. In *La démocratie et les financiers* Delaisi had pointed out the importance of creating a journal that was truly independent of any regular financial supporters. But that appeared to be a hard task: in 1908 he was editor of *Les Nouvelles*, but this newspaper, just as many like it, was short-lived and soon went bankrupt. In these years Delaisi started to study economics.

Apart from the CGT there were many other left-wing groups in France, moderate or radical, and it is unclear to what extent Delaisi supported them. In 1879 the French Labour party had been founded by Guesde (1845-1922) who was a marxist, but in 1882 the moderate "Possibilists" split off. In 1890 the so-called "Allemanists" did the same, together with Guesde himself. It is my impression that Delaisi's thinking was close to theirs. The "Parti Socialiste Révolutionnaire", founded in 1890 in the tradition of Louis Auguste Blanqui (1805-1881), was the most important counterpart of the labour party.

Jean Jaurès (born in 1859 and murdered in 1914) tried for a long time to unite all these separate movements and parties. He succeeded in 1905 when, under the pressure of the Second International, held in Amsterdam, the "Section Française de l'internationale ouvrière" (SFIO) was formed. In the Charter of Amiens (1906) the relations between the SFIO and the syndicalists were settled, too. But a few years later, round 1911, after a period of constant strikes and rebellions, the socialists split up again, this time in adherents of Aristide Briand (1862-1932) and adherents of Jaurès.

As a result of this split, the conservatives of Raymond Poincaré (1860-1934) got in power and Clémenceau agreed to pursue a policy of revanchism towards Germany. Delaisi strongly opposed such a policy. This is apparent for instance in his pamphlet *La guerre qui vient*, written in 1911. In his view, France was being misused by the British to destroy the competitive industrial power of the Germans, and, though he was no pacifist, he did not see any reason for the French people to fight the Germans. Perhaps his anti-war attitude influenced the "Féderation ouvrière des métaux", with which he had close contacts. In 1916 the metal workers went on strike in protest to the war, which provoked a mutiny in sixteen French army divisions. General Pétain restored the order.

Though Perrier argues that the first World War did not cause any discontinuity in Delaisi's political thought, he did become much more moderate. Perrier himself mentions that Delaisi took part in several reform movements — which implies that he left the revolutionary movements — and that he was a great admirer of the foreign policy of Briand — which implies that he had come close to accepting the political establishment.

Cooperation or collaboration?

During the interbellum France witnessed a coming and going of cabinets (only in the years 1925-1926, for instance, there were four) and Briand took part in many of them. Aristide Briand had formed a government in 1909, which held office to 1912, and he was prime-minister again from 1921 to 1922. After two attempts to form a cabinet in 1925-1926, he became Foreign Minister in Poincaré's government (1926-1929), and after Poincaré's retreat from politics he kept this post until 1932. All these years Briand tried to end the Franco-German rivalry, which made him support the Dawes-plan (1924) and the Pact of Locarno (1925).[7] He also proved to be a strong supporter of the initiative, put forward by the American Secretary of State Frank B. Kellogg, to rule out war as a legitimate means to settle conflicts. In fact, Kellogg's initiative was an extension of Briand's own proposal to draw up a pact between France and the USA renouncing war. Kellogg proposed that the whole world should be involved, and the plan was brought before the League of Nations and worked out in a treaty signed by fifteen nations in Paris in 1928: the famous Briand-Kellogg Pact (in 1929 another fifty-four states signed the Pact).

In Germany, these were the years of Gustav Stresemann (1878-1929). Stresemann, who had received the Nobel Peace Price in 1927, had signed the Briand-Kellogg Pact and, in 1929, also showed himself to be in favour of another ambitious plan that Briand put forward in the League: the proposal to bring about the "United

States of Europe". Obviously, the domestic circumstances in both Germany and France obstructed such far-going rapprochements. The plan hardly received any serious attention.

Important here, however, is that during the twenties Delaisi was thinking along the same lines. It is even possible that Briand's plan for a United States of Europe was influenced by his work. Delaisi strongly advocated the pan-European movement and in 1926 he wrote *Les bases économiques des états-unis d'Europe*. According to Perrier, he belonged to those who hoped to find an economic scenario that would guarantee the fragile peace in Europe. It was in this period of his life, that Delaisi wrote about interdependence. To be more precise, *Les contradictions du monde moderne*, the volume in which Delaisi developed his interdependence theory, was written in the period June 1924-October 1925, shortly before the conclusion of the Locarno treaty. Though he remained a syndicalist, during this period of his life Delaisi came very close to the ideas of the progressive liberals in Britain and the United States.

In 1932, when he was working for the "Comité fédéral de coopération européenne", he still seemed to be on that line. Hoping to find an answer to the immense unemployment problems that followed the Great Depression, Delaisi wrote a report about the financing of large public works. This *Projet de resolution relatif au financement du programme de grands travaux publics européens et à l'assurance-credit* even became known as "Plan Delaisi".[8] In the European context, plans like this one never had a chance to get even close to the success of similar plans in the United States that resulted in the New Deal; Europe was much too divided for that.

It would be interesting to know how Delaisi thought about his plan a year later, when Hitler was elected to power. For it seems that during the second World War he probably collaborated with the Germans. At least, Perrier mentions that from 1940 onwards Delaisi was a member of the editorial board of *L'Atelier*, a journal of syndicalist workers which went along with a policy of collaboration. Many of his former militant friends worked for this journal. Unfortunately, the biographical notes are scarce and Perrier does not spend a word on Delaisi's activities during the thirties, which, of course, is a critical period if one is to understand his attitude toward Hitler-Germany, nazism and fascism in general. Before the first World War and during the twenties, when Briand and Stresemann were in power, Delaisi clearly advocated the need of French-German rapprochement and economic cooperation. Perhaps this support found an echo in the fourties. It is hard to believe, however, that he turned to fascism or even had sympathies in this direction. This seems to be unlikely in particular because one of his books, *La Banque de France aux mains des 200 familles*, was published in 1936 by the "Comité de vigilance des intellectuels anti-fascistes". In the same year he wrote about the atrocities committed in the colonies; not a likely theme for a fascist.[9] On the other hand, his *La révolution européenne*, was published during the occupation and translated in German in 1943.[10]

Though additional research may yield evidence to the contrary, it is my opinion that the pro-German attitude of Delaisi was related to the domestic circumstances in France only: it was a reaction to popular revanchism and to extreme nationalism. In 1898 the "Action Française" was founded; a group which represented a radical French nationalism directed strongly against Germans, Jews, protestants and the Third Republic in general. In the mid-twenties Action Française was one of the main antagonists of the political left and in the thirties it developed into a fascist anti-parliamentary movement. In reaction to this the "Allemanists" and the socialists in general stressed the need of Franco-German cooperation, and in this they may have gone too far.

1911: "La guerre qui vient"

In 1911 Delaisi wrote a pamphlet "La guerre qui vient", the coming war.[11] It is a curious document, which to a large extent reads like an étude in writing war-scenarios for students at a military academy. But it is worth recalling it here, because, simultaneously, these aspects reveal the axioms on which his radical left-wing world view was based. His starting-point was that this war would essentially be an Anglo-German conflict. England feared the competitive power of Germany and aimed to destroy that power.

Delaisi started his analysis by looking closely at the economic infra-structural conditions that would be of central importance to both Britain and Germany in a coming war. The decisive factor would be the control of the sea and his war-scenario completely focused on that issue. The actual training manoeuvres of the British navy showed that their strategic objectives were to blockade ports and to destroy commercial ships. Britain followed two strategies: the first was to isolate Germany politically; the second was to beat it in an arms race.[12]

The political track bears upon the relations with France. France was in a remarkable position, according to Delaisi. Britain needed France because of its army and Germany needed France because of its money: Germany could not possibly finance a war against England, whereas England was in no position to fight Germany on land. France could profit from this situation, Delaisi argued, and even guarantee the peace if it remained neutral: by denying England its army and by denying Germany its money, war would be impossible. But France would not do this, because it was ruled by an elite and not by the people who had to do the actual fighting or to bring up the money.

The elite, aware of its role as arbiter of the world, Delaisi continued, would rather obtain a place in history by joining sides with either Germany or England, than stay neutral and remain unnoticed by doing nothing.[13]

"La guerre qui vient" shows a naïve belief in the intrinsic peacefulness of peoples (the elites excluded). If the people would really be in power, if they were the rulers of their own destiny, war would be unthinkable.[14] This is not explained but stated. Therefore, the only way to prevent war is by informing the people about what is really going on, to make them aware of the role played by the financiers. Then they would not be willing to fight.[15]

Foreign policy, however, was in the hands of only a small group of people, who (apparently) missed this intrinsic peacefulness. The press was in the hands of the financiers and was censored by the Foreign Office. The public was not correctly informed about what was going on in the world, and thus the elites were able to decide the fate of the masses.[16]

To understand his fixation on the role of banks and financiers, it should be realized, however, that France in these years was generally characterized as the world's banker: the capitalism of rentiers was dominant, which gave the banks indeed a big influence in politics. Large investments in the colonies and in Russia, for instance, were controlled by the banks.

According to Delaisi, the French rentiers had financed two years of Russian warfare against Japan, and the Germans hoped they would finance their war against England likewise (the costs of war with England would be about five billion marks a year, Delaisi said).[17] England, on the other hand, needed the French army in order to fight the Germans in Belgium, with the ultimate aim to occupy Antwerp.

Delaisi observed that Rotterdam and Antwerp were German cities in economic terms. But politically they belonged to foreign countries.[18] This fact would have enormous consequences for the war: German ships would immediately go under neutral flags, the moment England started to blockade Bremen and Hamburg. Thus England had to blockade Rotterdam and Antwerp as well. Holland was not the problem here, because it was completely dominated by Germany already, Delaisi thought, and the Germans would simply occupy Rotterdam without encountering any resistance. Belgium, however, was a neutral country and its neutrality had been guaranteed by other nations. This caused a problem for England (!) because now it could not blockade Antwerp. An additional problem was that the city of Vlissingen was being fortified by the Dutch, thus giving the Germans an ideal position to defend Antwerp against England.[19] Therefore the blockade could not work and Britain had to land in Belgium to keep the Germans out of Antwerp. If only the French army could do that job for them!

All this chessboard logic turned out to be quite meaningless, if only because Delaisi showed a complete neglect for the strategic problems of the war on two fronts that the Germans were expecting. In his pamphlet the Balkans and Russia were not considered. Neither did the United States enter his strategic considerations. But important is that he understood the economic basis of the war. He defined it as a hegemonic struggle:

> "Actually, all around the world, on the Balkans, in Turkey, in Persia, China, Central America, in Brazil, Argentine and

Chile a silent but bitter struggle is going on between the English and German banks, between the English and German merchants and between the English and German heavy industries. ... it is this rivalry between competing financial groups that leads the peoples into war."[20]

"The fate of the two Empires [Britain and Germany] will be decided by the possession of Antwerp, and the struggle for Belgium will decide which of the two industrialized peoples will get economic control of the old world."[21]

Also in his later work, he argued that at the end of the nineteenth century Germany had succeeded where France had failed: the German government had understood "that the aim of economic imperialism is not the conquest of territories, but the exploitation of markets."[22]

Delaisi versus Angell

One of Angell's main theses in his pamphlet *Europe's Optical Illusion* was that "conquest does not pay" — and he had to convince a lot of people who thought differently. The opposite axiom, that conquest added to the wealth of a nation, even came to dominate politics in the interbellum period, when "Blut und Boden" theories prevailed in Germany, Italy and Japan.

Beyond question Delaisi agreed with Angell that conquest had turned into a useless activity given the modern economic conditions in the world. But he did not think for a moment that this knowledge would prevent the nationalists or the capitalists from wanting a war. He defined the problem of war completely different than Angell did.

The aim of modern warfare was no longer the conquest of land, he said.[23] These goals were restricted to agrarian societies. Modern warfare was about markets, resources and the destruction of one another's competing power. Delaisi mentioned recent wars in support of this argument: In 1895 Japan and China struggled over the exploitation of Korea; in 1898 America struggled with Spain over the exploitaton of Cuba; in 1899 England wanted to chase the Boers away from the mines in South Africa; in 1900 Europe fought with China to force it to accept railway contracts; in 1904 Japan and Russia fought about the exploitation of Manchuria. None of these wars were about the extension of territory; they were all about economic gain. The money-oligarchies did not seek subjects but customers. Why, in other words, should economic competition exclude military means? Couldn't war be the continuation of economics by other means?

The practical answer to that question was given in the Versailles peace treaty in 1919. Here, Germany was brought to its knees and was stripped of every penny it owned or would earn; its competitive power was destroyed. Yet, no one profited from this, it only created economic and political instability. It did not return economic world hegemony to Great Britain or even improve its economic position on the continent. The reparation payments did not make France wealthier either. Neither did the United States need a temporary economic destruction of the old world in order to become a great power. It had already become a great power, economically and militarily, in the years preceding the war, but no one had been aware of it because it had not yet been tested.

In 1911 Delaisi looked at the economic factors, but he did not look at their reciprocity. This is the main difference with Angell's way of thinking. Delaisi looked at the egoism of the bankers and industrialists, which brought economic motives for war to the centre of his analysis, but he shared the logic of the bankers and industrialists: competition is the essence of economics and the survival of the fittest principle implied competition with all available means. War, in order to destruct the industrial potential of another country or in order to take possession of its resources, was the "ultima ratio" of modern economies, like plunder and conquest had been the "ultima ratio" of agrarian economies. Angell argued that, though this logic was indeed applied by the bankers, it did not serve their interests at all. It was in the interests of capitalists to make profit, not to have competition. Destruction of economic potential reduced the purchasing power on consumer markets and was therefore not a rational thing to do.

In the twenties Delaisi became aware of reciprocity in economic

127

activity and this fundamentally changed his analysis about the usefulness of war for economic gain.

1925: Is this the same man talking?

Delaisi was not blind to the fact that the causes and the results of the first World War were a bit different from what he had predicted. The victors had emerged hardly less ruined than the vanquished, "such is the essential lesson of the World War", he wrote in 1925.[24] That lesson changed his diagnosis of world politics fundamentally:

> "The old method [of] approaching economic and international problems by political and national means has had its day. Economic and political functions are now distinct, they should therefore dispose of different organs. More and more, economic negotiations will be taken out of the hands of the representatives of the old agrarian sovereignties. ... Let us leave territorial and military agreements to the diplomats, but business problems should be entrusted to business men."[25]

This thesis was quite different from his previous claim that all politics were secretly steered by the bankers and the industrialists. He went even further and suggested that

> "peace can only be finally established with the general introduction of free trade. ... It will mean a rapid return to general prosperity and the law of universal economic interdependence will operate along normal lines."[26]

Is this the same man talking? It is, and he actually remained loyal to many of the syndicalist principles. The syndicalists had mistrusted politics from the outset. Politicians were compared to wooden horses in a merry-go-round. Democracy was a myth and it was misused by the bankers and the industrialists who were controlling the press and the elections with their money. To abolish and ban politics had been the principle objective of syndicalists, socialists and anarchists throughout the nineteenth century. Economic forces were determining the course of history and therefore they had to be brought out into the open; politics was a derivative of economics; only historical materialism mattered. The ultimate objective of *La guerre qui vient* had been to explain to the people the real dynamics of economic life. The war had not changed that objective. The only, though not unimportant, matter the war had changed was Delaisi's own understanding of these economic dynamics. Global interdependence had become a material condition of life but this was obscured by politics and thus the separation of the economic from the political remained as important as before the war.[27] In his struggle against politics this socialist thus came to preach free trade.

The subtle change is, of course, that Delaisi now implicitly confirmed that politics was an independent social force — not completely determined and reigned by the economic elites. He now even argued that the main reason for separating politics from economics was that political myths clouded the eyes of the bankers and industrialists.

He seemed to sense his own uncertainty about the relationship between politics and economics, when he argued that the contradiction and opposition between the *homo politicus* and the *homo economicus* was living in each of us and was the key problem in the modern world.[28]

The homo economicus versus the homo politicus

The distinction between politics and economics puzzled Delaisi throughout his life. Before the war, he was sure about the conspiracy of bankers and financiers who misused political myths to pursue their selfish interests at the cost of the masses. With good reason Domela Nieuwenhuis summarized the essence of "Democracy and its Financiers" by saying that Delaisi had made clear once and for all that political and economic power could impossibly be separated, and that there was no use in conquering political power because parliaments, ministries and governments were only instruments of economic power; power which was in the hands of the bankers and the industrialists. "Who dares to argue with that?", the last line read.[29]

Apparently, Delaisi dared to, himself. In 1925 he maintained that the fundamental cause of the malady of Europe lay in the fusion of the economic and the political factors and that the remedy would be found in their separation.[30] This distinction had even been one of the aims of the French Revolution, he claimed: the principle of laissez-faire, laissez-passer expressed the ideal to keep economics out of the hands of the state.

In a footnote he tried to reduce the whole issue to a trivial affair: scientists worry a lot about the question what comes first, politics or economics, but

> "does the heart dominate the brain, or does the liver come before the lungs? A pretty subject for discussion for our modern scholastic pundits! ... Instead of opposing the organs of the same body, were it not better to point to their interdependence?"[31]

But the debate about "what comes first" is not as trivial as it looks. It reflects the fundamental debate about the balance between the material and the intellectual aspects of life: to what extent are ideas about reality enforced by reality? To what extent is reality created by ideas?

The social function of political myths

Les contradictions du monde moderne has been translated as *Political Myths and Economic Realities*. This translation calls the contradiction by name: the book is about the struggle between political myth and economic reality, about the struggle between the cognitive and the structural conditions of life, the struggle between reality and its perception.

Political myths are needed because reality is too complex to be understood in all its facets. Behind the most simple things in life — the bread you buy, the road you walk on, the book you read — incomprehensible complex structures are hidden. Myths help to "explain" their working or to cut short the endless string of "why"-questions (which we know from little children). In other words, a myth is a paradigm, a world view, and its first function is *to identify reality*.

Its second function is *to legitimize reality*. "A myth's essential function is to create willing obedience", Delaisi wrote.[32] The Papal Myth, for instance, says that the pope represents God on earth, which makes it logical to obey his command. The Democratic Myth says that parliaments represent the people. Whether this is true or not, it sanctions the authority of democratic government and the people will obey its laws.[33] Myths are the origin of authority.

A third function of a myth is *to preserve reality*. Once a myth has become "the prop and fulcrum of the group conscience", it is intolerant to change: it makes people deny or belittle change when it occurs and it makes people persecute the adherents of a different myth.[34] A myth consists of faith and hope; to disturb it means to shake the psychological fundaments of someone's existence. Yet, every myth will be challenged by new ones and by changing social structures, and will thus in due time be replaced.

Within European history Delaisi described a sequence from the polytheistic myth in Ancient Greece and the Roman Empire, via the christian myth, the feudal myth, the papal myth and the monarchical myth, to the democratic myth. He also mentioned the national myth, which made a mystical ideal of the unity of territory, language, race and culture.

Should facts give way to ideas or ideas to facts?

According to Delaisi, the Industrial Revolution had created a fundamental disruption within the age-old sequence of changing myths.

> "[D]uring twenty centuries of agricultural civilization, the nations were made up of autonomous economic units between which the exchange of products was only intermittent and, so to speak, accidental. Within three generations, machinery has revolutionized all this."[35]

131

The problem was that, since the mechanization and industrialization of the world, economic realities had been changing faster than the political myths that ought to reflect economic reality.

From the Agrarian Revolution up to the Industrial Revolution, the economic structure of life changed much more slowly than political structures. All economic changes were therefore more or less automatically incorporated when the political system changed. The political myths that legitimized the existing order changed more frequently than the economic base of that order; laws, regimes and constitutions changed faster than economic structures. This was no longer the case:

> "During the last hundred years ... the roles have been reversed; the basic structure has changed much more rapidly than the institutions it supports — and violent upheavals have been the result."[36]

As a consequence, the world is caught in a fundamental contradiction: the political myths are sanctioning a non-existing economic reality.

This made the distinction between politics and economics so important to Delaisi. To which information should people listen: to the reality that is sanctioned by their political institutions or to the reality that is determining their material well-being? Or, to use Delaisi's own words, should economic reality be subordinated to the myths or should the myth be adjusted to reality? Though the second would be the most logical thing to do, Delaisi observed that people were trying hard to do the first. He distinguished two dangerous ways in which people tried to adjust the economic reality to their political myths. The first was economic nationalism and the second was imperialism.

Rural ideals and industrial realities

State sovereignty is a political myth that was developed in agrarian societies. As long as agriculture was the "mother cell" of European society the rural ideal of self-support kept returning in all political myths. It was present in the ideal of the Roman "villa" and in the feudal estate. In an agrarian society state sovereignty did not impair economic life. Economic life was local. "The old monarchies never considered themselves as economic entities."[37] Internal customs were a normal phenomenon in France up to the French Revolution. The farmer or the land-owner lived on his own grain, he drank his own wine and dressed himself in clothes made of his own wool and flax. But this all changed with the rise of specialization, and finally even agriculture itself lost its autonomous character:

> "Today a farm is no longer self-supporting; it has become auxiliary to the flour and spinning trades, to sugar refiners and to oil wells. The peasant buys his wine, his clothes, even his bread as would any town dweller. He no longer consumes his own produce; he produces for sale. Exchange, from being accidental, becomes the rule. ... Society has thereby assumed an entirely new aspect. ... Interdependence has become the common law; autonomy no longer exists except in backward regions."[38]

One of the political consequences was that, during the nineteenth century, the sovereign nation evolved into an economic entity, and in the last quarter of that century political frontiers and economic frontiers were the same; "they were guarded by the customs officer no less than by the soldier", Delaisi remarked.[39] This turned the right to impose protective tariffs into an inherent part of the sovereignty myth, which hampered the further increase of economic interdependence.

This was aggravated by the fact that many countries achieved national sovereignty at the very moment that they lost their economic autonomy. "From that moment the political myth was flagrantly contradicted by the economic reality."[40] Politically, nations acted in conformity with the spirit of the age when they strove for independence and sovereignty; economically they acted in conformity with the spirit of the age when they strove for internationalization and interdependence.

These two contradictory forces led to a compromise.[41] Countries with a vulnerable industrial development pursued policies of economic nationalism, and the more developed countries, with a high level of industrialization, tried to get political control of the countries whose products were complementary to their own industry "in order to achieve economic interdependence within the framework of one political dominion".[42] This was imperialism.

Both economic nationalism and imperialism were the wrong political reactions to the increasing economic interdependence; they finally helped to cause the first World War.

Economic nationalism and imperialism

Economic nationalism reflected the increasing governmental control over economic life, which had led to notions like "national industry", "national trade", "national agriculture". Their protection became a "national interest". Here politics fused with economics.

But the division into national economies was rather arbitrary, because the political borders were formed under completely different economic conditions. This made the fusion of politics and economics a half-hearted one and the "law of interdependence" caused continuous political friction, for instance in the form of tariff wars.[43]

In his protest against protectionism, Delaisi's radicalism returned when he concluded that all this protectionism neglected the interests of the consumers, the people. It is the buyer who eventually pays the tariff, not the seller, he said: either the tariffs are on-charged expenses in the price of imported products or the consumer buys a domestic product which he could have bought cheaper from a foreign producer.[44] Yet, Delaisi also understood that, once a protective system had worked for a while, its abolishment would cause all kind of social problems and violent upheavals.[45]

Imperialism was the other way to fuse politics with economics. Delaisi's attitude to imperialism was inconsistent. On the one hand he praised Great Britain for "ingeneously welding together" the imperatives of industrial expansion and of securing the national unity:

"Great Britain was able for a century to enjoy all the advantages of economic interdependence without losing anything of its solidarity. ... The dominions enjoyed unhampered development, but were not able to free themselves from the hegemony of the mother country. The rigid formula of nationality had given way to a more flexible one, that of empire. But the spirit of domination lost nothing in the change."[46]

Liberalism had given the required elasticity to the national myth and British hegemonial power had been the result, as had been the prosperity during the Victorian age.

But, on the other hand, he looked upon imperialism as the unpleasant by-product of protectionism and economic nationalism. The protected industries needed markets, but because they could not compete with similar industries in other countries (for they even had to be protected against them in their home market) they needed artificial outlets. These were found in colonies, protectorates and spheres of influence; "the pursuit after outlets has degenerated into colonial expedition". Protectionism led to imperialistic wars.[47]

The classic solution — the classic mistake: a plea for free trade

This inconsistency with respect to imperialism had strange consequences. Delaisi called the year 1860 "the economic 1789".[48] In 1860 Cobden and Michel Chevalier had concluded an economic treaty, which made an end of many protectionist tariffs. This was followed by similar treaties with Belgium, Italy, Switzerland, Holland and the German Zollverein. In the same year the Suez canal was opened and there was a multiplication of steamer lines across the world. This way, Europe found its way to the rest of the world, "exploiting new and backward countries and preparing the economic unity of our planet". In one breath, he concluded:

"The principle of free trade, by turning the economic interdependence of nations into a reality, would eventually have

135

made for universal peace. ... It was not to be, however."[49]

Here, Delaisi showed a tendency to radicalism again, but this time of an extreme and naïve, liberal kind. In his analysis of the contradiction between political myth and economic reality he had come very close to the discovery of a vital factor in late-nineteenth century Europe, but he missed it: the problem was not one of free trade versus protectionism; the problem was that the scope of modern national economies was artificially confined to national borders that were established under fundamentally different economic conditions. The traditional territorial frontiers had become anachronistic in economic terms. Geo-politics clashed with geo-economics.

Free trade might have solved the problem with respect to the scope of economic traffic, but it could not possibly have solved the welfare and service issues that were also typical of this modern economy. These issues required political organization and political debate (how much money should go to the unemployed, how much should be invested in education, how much in industrial innovation — questions like that), and they had to be settled in an authoritative way.[50] Especially the "authoritative" part is hard to achieve by means of free trade.

Extreme advocacy of interdependence

In his anxiety to provide a substitute for the dominant political myths, Delaisi went far. Not everything he wrote about interdependence contributes to the development of a serious theory. Throughout his book he shows the tendency to personify interdependence; as if he were writing a Greek drama in which Virtue struggles with Evil and Interdependence deceives Autonomy. At the end of his book this tendency reaches a level of absurdity when he actually presents interdependence as an "unknown God". Four pages long he adresses his reader with texts that are inspired by the bible, especially the old testament. I include a fragment here, because it is so bizarre:

"By making us suffer, the unacknowledged God imposes himself upon our consciousness. ... he strikes down those who disregard him. The Great War was the first scourge inflicted upon them: instead of short campaigns, 'refreshing and joyous', restricted to a few people and merely affecting the political and administrative organism of the states, he imposed upon them general war, world-wide and without mercy. They still did not understand. ... The God then drove them into a senseless peace, as nefarious as the war itself. He spoke to them and said ...[two pages follow with condemnations of human shortcomings concluding:]... Such is the logical sequence of your blindness. ... Have you still to endure further disasters before you can convince yourselves of your errors? ... If reason and self-interest be not enough, the mere interplay of irresistable forces will compel you to see the light. Untill then, you will not be left in peace ... you will be scourged — until your discrowned nationalities bow down before the majesty of facts."[51]

His objective must have been to stress the need to fill the ideological no man's land that was created by the internationalization of human activity. Neither nationalism, nor marxism or bourgeois pacifism provided satisfactory myths to identify, legitimate and preserve the reality of interdependence.[52] And therefore, it seems, Delaisi tried to make a new myth of interdependence itself.

Much more interesting than such curious passages and much more relevant to contemporary interdependence theory, however, is his analysis of the way people adapted to the conditions of interdependence in practice.

The organs of interdependence: Delaisi's "working peace system"

In 1943 David Mitrany wrote a pamphlet entitled *A Working Peace System*. In it he elaborated upon his earlier work, especially *The Progress of International Government*, published in 1933. As a result he took the credit of being the brain behind the theory of functionalism (see chapter 7). He should share the credit for developing functionalism, however, with Delaisi. Five years before Mitrany made his first steps into the field of functionalism and about twenty-five years before he completed his walk, Delaisi had laid down the principle of functionalism.

> "If interdependence is to triumph, it must lean on permanent institutions, specially devised to keep in tow the forces which are ever diverging from it, and to conciliate contradictory interests."[53]

(These diverging forces were "the various imperialisms and nationalisms and jingo passions".) This was not just a remark but a prelude to pointing out that the germs of the organs of interdependence already existed. These were (a) the International Chamber of Commerce (ICC), (b) the International Labour Office (ILO) and (c) the League of Nations.

> "The economic field is covered by the International Chamber of Commerce; the social field by the International Labour Office; the political field by the League of Nations. The function of interdependence has found its organs. I.C.C. + I.L.O. + L.N. — such is the formula of the future. They are the three pillars which will serve as a basis for the joint reconstruction and peace of the world."[54]

This praise did not make him blind to the many short-comings of these organs.

a) The International Chamber of Commerce. The ICC was founded in 1919 on the initiative of a group of American businessmen. According to Delaisi the plan originated in their disappointment in the Versailles treaty and their scepticism about the League of Nations. Originally, the ICC was modelled after the US Chamber of Commerce. The idea was for business enterprises to be directly associated with both the local chambers and the central one. But finally, concessions were made so that the ICC came to reflect the national base of its members. The ICC started to deal with trade restrictions in a technical manner (as contrasted to a political approach) and it even created a court of arbitration. Delaisi hoped that in this way the ICC would become the supreme tribunal in business.[55]

b) The International Labour Office. While the ICC had to take care of the economic equilibrium in the world, the ILO aimed at a social equilibrium, in order to prevent the emergence of a "dictatorship of an international oligarchy which would substitute class war for business war".[56] In its design the ILO was "a courageous innovation", because the professional element was on equal footing with the political element. But in its result "national egoism" remained dominant, because of veto-rights and because its decisions were not binding. Delaisi recalled that in the period 1919-1924 only 157 out of 800 ILO-resolutions were ratified by the memberstates.[57]

c) The League of Nations. Though he put his faith in it, Delaisi knew that the League was mutilated. The treaty of Versailles had excluded the vanquished nations, the old imperialist powers obtained the strongest position within the League, the USA kept aloof, and its decisions had no executive consequences. Yet, in a historical perspective, it was the best thing ever tried.[58]

The need for international professional organizations

Delaisi developed his functionalism on the lines of syndicalism. His solution to the problem of war was to get rid of the nation-state system or at least to get rid of the political myths that stemmed from the agrarian era. This could be achieved by the formation of international professional associations, organized like trade unions (or syndicats). He extented the logic of socialism to all social classes, not just to the workers. This peace system was already working, it was not a far away Utopia. The increasing number of international conferences proved that professional groups were organizing themselves on a cross-border scale. Some of these conferences even resulted in permanent organizations, like the Institute of Metals in

London, the Petroleum Institute in New York and the International Institute of Agriculture in Rome.[59]

These institutions were "making for interdependence" and they would fundamentally change the perceptions of the world:

> "Thanks to these organizations, the heads of enterprise are growing accustomed to viewing their own affairs as part of a whole, and they have come to realize that world problems can only be solved by the collaboration of all. *Thus, little by little the consciousness of universal interdependence is growing.*"[60]

The professional organization would become the key organization in the era of economic interdependence. Just as the "city" and the "nation" had been the essential organs in previous phases of civilization, the professional organization would be "the most suitable instrument for bringing about the full realization of economic interdependence".[61]

This syndicalist conception of the professional organization did not deny the existence of nationalism, as socialist internationalism did, nor did it disown the existence of internationalism, as bourgeois pacifism did.[62] Instead, it combined socialist internationalism with bourgeois pacifism. The members of professional organizations would develop an awareness of both their national interests and their international interests. When these were in disharmony, the disharmony would be recognized. In this way a certain equilibrium would be achieved within both the professional group as a whole as within the individual minds of its members. This equilibrium is the main condition of peace, Delaisi argued.

Epilogue: "On taking one's bearings"

> "So it comes to this: Democracy has solved nothing; Soviet rule is bankrupt; Fascismo is an expedient that can only be provisional; and the whole world a prey to cross purposes, still-born solutions, hazardous improvisation, indecision and insecurity."[63]

This conclusion formed the starting point of *Les contradictions du monde moderne*. Delaisi compared the world at this juncture with a ship lost in a storm. What to do, he asked himself. Adrift in a storm, a captain is guided not by the waves, nor the winds (like politicians who only think about the next election), but by the stars. The most distant data provide the strongest grip. Therefore, to understand politics a historical perspective was essential.

> "In judging events of which we have been eye witnesses, we often appear to be inflicted by a curious shortsightedness. We look for the cause of a catastrophe in the immediately preceding circumstances. ... We usually gauge contemporary events on the scale of our own span of life. [but:] Each generation begins by accepting the institutions and ideas that have been handed down by its predecessor. It adapts itself to them to a greater extent than it adapts them. ... The soldiers who are slaughtering each other on the battlefield are sometimes performing the fifth act of a tragedy whose first act had been interpreted by their forbears."[64]

Only in a historical perspective can it become clear what structural changes have taken place and have to take place.

Delaisi set out with the challenge to determine the coordinates of politics. He discovered that economic interdependence was the loadstar of modern history and he judged the birth of professional organizations to be the first act in a play that might bring peace in its fifth act.

Meanwhile the storm persisted.[65]

6 Charles E. Merriam (1874-1953): civilized power in a pluralistic world

Merriam did not write about interdependence. At times he used the term, but by no means can one speak of a concept. Yet, there are good reasons to include an evaluation of his work in this study of interdependence theory from 1900-1950.

In the first place, it is remarkable how close his writings are to modern, late twentieth century theories of interdependence: He denied the state-as-actor axiom and subscribed to a multiple-actor paradigm, instead. He subscribed to the cobweb axiom of international relations as well, and he actually used this term. He adhered to the idea that democracies have the best value-system to create and maintain a world order, because democracy (in its true sense) inherently accepts the pluralistic nature of such an order.

Secondly, the complete neglect of Merriam's writings by modern scholars is remarkable, because he was by no means an obscure scientist who worked in isolation. Merriam institutionalized political science in the United States and created his own school. But this Chicago School, as it was called, found itself at a dead end in the second World War; a kind of collateral damage, which asks for clarification.

A third reason to save his work from oblivion is that it represents the American tradition in political science from 1900-1950, whereas the other authors included in this study all represent the European tradition. One of the most interesting differences between these two traditions is that people on the European continent were primarily concerned with sovereignty, nation-states, military power and territorial security, while people in the States (except the native Americans) were preoccupied with the management of an entire continent in terms of domestic politics. The absence of a feudal and an aristocratic tradition led to a political agenda that was dominated by issues unknown in Europe.

Fourthly, Merriam's work contains valuable points of view that, to my knowledge, have not reappeared in more recent literature on interdependence.

In this chapter the parts of Merriam's work that are directly relevant for interdependence theory are reviewed in the second section, starting at page 157. In the first section, his scientific and political careers are discussed in order (a) to cast new light on the old controversy between Idealism and Realism, and (b) to point out how much the political climate in the USA differed from the climate in Europe.

Behaviourism and the Chicago School

When Merriam is known by contemporary students of IR at all, it is because of the Chicago School which he founded. Even less is known about the views of the Chicago School. The Chicago School was the cradle of behaviourism in political science, though, generally, the development of this line of research is located in the late 1950s. Some textbooks describe the emergence of behaviourism in the study of international politics as the second great debate in IR-theory; assuming that the controversy between Idealism and Realism is the first one. Richard Little, for instance, argued in 1980:

"It was only in the mid-fifties that behaviouralists began to emerge in international relations. It was also to be expected

143

that because of the opposition by realists to behaviouralism that the behaviouralists should be seen as establishing a second school of thought in opposition to the realists (or 'traditionalists' as they later came to be called). At that time, the disjunction between the two schools of thought appeared to be absolute."[1]

The essence of this second debate was of a mainly methodological nature. The idea of Grand Theories that explain every aspect of political life was denounced as being too ambitious and empirically too inaccurate. Essentially, the debate reflected the emergence of sociologists in the study of IR. Human behaviour had to be recorded in detail and as objectively as possible, and this objectivity was sought in quantitative and statistical research in particular; let the figures speak for themselves.

In respect to the denial of grand theories this debate was indeed new, but in respect to its emphasis on empiricism it was a continuation of the Chicago School. Merriam's biographer, Barry D. Karl, even called him the father of the behaviourist movement.[2] This is not mentioned by Richard Little, though he noted that Merriam's work was an exception to the main stream of Idealism during the interbellum period.[3] Early in his career, Merriam urged the use of modern methods for collecting and processing data. With that he opposed the historical and comparative methods which were dominant in the USA between 1850 and 1900.[4]

It was not, however, his intention to depart from theorizing. In Merriam's view, empirical research, the "measurement" of behaviour, merely constituted one of the aspects essential to scientific knowledge. Intuition, observation and experience in practice were equally important.

"Ironically, Merriam himself would be credited with originating an American version of a value-free behaviorism but that had never been what he meant", Karl claimed without saying, though, of whom he received this credit. "His emphasis upon the necessity of an empirical approach to theory ... was intended rather to determine that theory be verified by continual empirical testing."[5] But, according to Crick, who, in 1959, wrote a devastating review of the Chicago School, Merriam's own work cannot stand such a test:

intuition dominated empirical verification by far. As a scientist, Merriam was even supposed to be a complete failure: he argued in favour of a kind of research that is hard to find in his own work. According to Crick, Merriam came closer to being a philosopher in the tradition of the eigthteenth century than to a behaviourist scientistand that was not meant to be a compliment.[6]

This criticism is not without reason, but Crick exaggerates. Merriam seriously attempted to improve the methods of studying political behaviour. In 1923, for instance, he founded the Social Science Research Council, mainly to supply social science workers with the necessary research equipment, for which the universities reserved hardly any funds.[7] In building up the Chicago School, he clearly preferred "men of facts" to "men of hunches". Merriam began his School by appointing Quincy Wright, who at that time had already earned some reputation in studying diplomacy and international law. Harold Gosnell conducted statistical research on voting behaviour; since 1920, Leonard White had been doing research on the mechanism of public administration and public service; in 1931, Albert Lepawsky analyzed the problems of urbanization; since 1923, Harold D. Lasswell had quite successfully studied the utility of psychology and psychopathology for the analysis of political behaviour. Frederic Schuman was recruited to explore "world politics" and "world order". With him Merriam even pulled in one of the predecessors of the Realists. During the late 1920s, Merriam also tried to set up an international, empirical research programme in which forms of public education in several countries would be compared systematically.[8] Equally ambitious were his attempts to make political science profit from biology, anthropology, sociology, economy and medicine.[9] This endeavour to establish interdisciplinary research is typical of behaviourism.

Moreover, the fact that Merriam was a generalist himself (the last one of a generation, according to Karl) explains the success of the Chicago School, rather than its ultimate failure. Merriam surveyed the entire puzzle of constituent studies. This kept the project marketable to the foundations that were essential for its financial continuity. Equally important, he was able to keep the different points of view of the researchers within limits. Under his guidance, research flourished as is indicated by the eighty dissertations in political science that were completed at the University of Chicago between 1920 and 1940, compared to thirteen between 1892 and 1920.[10]

Scientific empire

Outside Chicago, at the federal level, Merriam managed to make a name for himself as well. He obtained key positions in the complex structure of organizations that were engaged in social research and political science. Since 1904, he had been active in the American Political Science Association (APSA), of which he became president in 1925. (The APSA had split off from the American Historical Association to distinguish political science from history.) Through the Social Science Research Council, which he had founded himself in 1923, he acquired good contacts with philanthropical institutions, like the Rockefellor Foundation, the Spelman Fund and the Public Administration Clearing House. A great deal of the idealism in serious research projects stemmed directly from the philanthropical objectives of its financeers. In 1929, under president Hoover, Merriam became vice-chairman of the President's Research Committee on Social Trends, and under Roosevelt he got a seat in the National Resource Planning Board, a think-tank for the New Deal.

Yet, immediately after his retirement in 1940, Merriam's scientific empire fell apart. During the 1930s the specialized research at the Chicago School had already led to a fragmentation of interests, and the urge to generalize the results at a higher level of abstraction was slipping. Moreover, the opposition against the New Deal grew steadily. In 1941 — Merriam had hardly turned his back — a Committee on Social Thought was formed at the university by colleagues who looked upon "New Dealers", like Merriam, as "misguided provincials, caught in a naive interpretation of the nature of man".[11] They wanted to internationalize the discipline and were served hand and foot by the wave of intellectuals who had fled from Europe, Germany in particular. Kenneth Thompson about this movement:

"Among successive waves of migrations, one of considerable importance for international thought occurred in the
1930s and 1940s during the flight of intellectuals from
Hitler's Germany. Some were to find their way into positions
of government and others into science and business. ...
Younger men, such as Secretary of State Henry Kissinger and
national security advisor Zbigniew K. Brzezinski who came
to the United States as students, constitute second-genera-
tion thinkers who excelled in statecraft."[12]

The influence of the immigrants, among them also Hans J. Morgenthau who worked at the Chicago University from 1943 to 1971,
impeded the continuation of the Chicago School. Merriam watched
these developments with mixed feelings, not in the least because
he was concerned about the pessimism of the immigrant-refugees.

The new realism: singing the human blues

"The so-called Atlantic migrations produced upheavals in
the social sciences and the humanities as revolutionary ... as
those which rocked atomic physics ... threatening to the
system which two generations had produced."[13]

Firstly, the political refugees gave the study of politics an international context which had been lacking till then. Overall, their outlook remained very Eurocentric, but it still enriched the
"homegrown American political science"[14] of the Chicago School.
Crick used this argument to condemn Merriam's work once again:
in his opinion the Chicago School was more "an expression of
American political thought than of science".[15] He would surely
have agreed with the remark by Karl that "American internationalism would have to be purged of its Wilsonian naiveté and
its commitment to legalism".[16] But, here again, the baby was
thrown away with the bath water.

Though Merriam's understanding of politics was based on the
American context (which, of course, is a limitation), nobody seems
to ask why this limitation should be worse than that of the

Eurocentric political scientists. Why should the history of Europe be more crucial to politics than the history of North America?

After the Civil War (1861-1865) the Americans, except the native ones, started to experiment with a federal structure of separate states on a continental scale. Merriam's generation struggled with practical political questions with which the people in Europe will only start to struggle in 1992: How does local government relate to national and federal government? How should public education be adjusted in order to learn people think from a federal perspective, without lapsing into propaganda and indoctrination? How to achieve and maintain democratic control over a very mobile business community, without hampering business activity? How to manage an economic crisis on a continental scale? While people in Europe were literally struggling with the inheritance of centuries of feudalism and military-aristocratic rule and were preoccupied with the question how to separate countries into secure, independent social entities, people in North America struggled with the question how to integrate separate states into one society. From that perspective, it is not surprising that "real-politik" in the American context was interpreted in terms of functionalism.

The second big change was that the lessons drawn by the political refugees from their European experiences were far from optimistic. Obviously, the criticism on the unrestrained, christian belief in human progress, which is typical for Merriam's generation, meant an improvement of the discipline; the direction in which the world was evolving was no longer undisputed or seen as irreversable. But on the other hand, this generation had been right in contending that planning without a plan or policy-making without a vision is fruitless and cannot exist. Some positive expectations had to be present.

It is disputable, even, whether Merriam needed the Realists to make him aware of the nuance between unrestrained idealism and pragmatic planning. From the outset he rejected any mystical reliance upon fantasy and imagination, and he had built up his scientific empire precisely in order to make a science of politics. Meanwhile, he also rejected any glorification of pragmatism. In 1948, for instance, he accused Morgenthau, who had just published

148

Politics Among Nations, of making the "human blues" very evident.[17] Real realism does not reject Utopia, but looks for existing means to realize it.

> "The key lay in the continuous construction and reconstruction of that utopian image in accordance with the development of these tools."[18]

Morgenthau's justified criticism of the Chicago School

Merriam and "most of his hand-raised enfant terribles"[19] had left the stage, when Hans J. Morgenthau (1904-1980) came to Chicago in 1943. Therefore, they did not cross swords directly. Yet, the way in which Morgenthau pictured the Idealist School in *Politics Among Nations* clearly reveals that he was reacting against the preceding generation. Merriam belonged to that generation.

Against whom precisely Morgenthau reacted seems to be unknown. "In general, Morgenthau has defended his theory in a very abstract way and the utopianism he rejected was not specified by making reference to academic theories", Jaap Nobel argued in his study on the work of Morgenthau.[20] Morgenthau's protest, it is argued, would have concerned the spirit of the interbellum in general and it would not even have concerned Merriam's work at all.[21] This, however, must be doubted; in particular, because in many respects Merriam's work does show the very characteristics Morgenthau ascribed to the Idealists. But even when he did not mean to include Merriam explicitly or implicitly, the effect was the same: Merriam's work was quickly forgotten, because Political Realism stigmatized the scientists of the interbellum period as naive dreamers, illusionists.[22] In one of the most widely used textbooks, Holsti writes the following about the twenties:

> "[M]ost work in the field during this decade had a normative orientation: Writers were less concerned with the variables or conditions affecting government behavior in external relations than with judging the policies of states according to their own values."[23]

149

Like Morgenthau, Holsti mentions no one in specific; apparently, his remark concerns everyone. Nobel refers to Grayson Kirk, who in 1947 maintained that this unedifying start had discredited IR as a scientific discipline.[24] It appears, then, that the founders of the trade should not have done so!

Morgenthau formulated the differences between the axioms of the Idealist School and Political Realism as follows:[25]

Idealist School	Realist School
Human nature is essentially good and infinitely malleable.	The world, imperfect as it is from the rational point of view, is the result of forces inherent in human nature (historical precedent as an axiom).
A rational and moral political order, derived from universally valid abstract principles, can be achieved here and now.	Moral principles can never be fully realized, but can at best be approximated through the ever temporary balancing of interests and the ever precarious settlement of conflicts.
The failure of the social order to measure up to rational standards is due to a lack of knowledge, obsolescent social institutions, or the depravity of certain isolated individuals or groups.	Opposing interests and conflicts are inherent to the social order.
Trust in education, reform, and the sporadic use of force.	Trust in a system of checks and balances as a universal principle.

In their generality these distinctions cannot be applied. Phrases, like "conflicts are inherent to the social order", "trust in sporadic use of force" and "trust in checks and balances" can easily be placed under both headings. Likewise, trust in education and reform and the importance of a correct understanding of the social order are characteristics applicable to anyone who values the study of IR. The differences, therefore, concern the remaining points.[26]

Merriam's trust in the feasibility of a rational and moral political order, based on principles that are universally valid, is unmistakable. He had an everlasting belief in man's ultimate progress, which was based on a parochial, protestant value-system. "God hath made of one blood all nations of the earth." By birth, he had been endowed with the conviction that Capitalism, (American) Protestantism and (American) Democracy formed a triad that could not be meddled with. This did not embarrass him:

> "I am assuming the indefinite perfectibility of men. I am assuming the validity of continuing creative evolution of mankind in the direction of higher levels of the physical, intellectual, and spiritual. ... A long-time student of political power, I repudiate the conclusion that government is merely a struggle for power or a means of exploitation of the weak by the strong. It is not realistic or naturalistic, while observing the many personal and group battles for the power, to lose sight of the main end of the whole process, namely, the progressive development of associations in which human personalities may best live together. ... The characteristic of the struggle for survival is not alone the struggle as such but the survival and the evolution of survivors to loftier forms of human life."[27]

If all of Merriam's work had been written from this point of view, Morgenthau should have called him by name. But Merriam had too much practical experience in politics to be blind to either the "struggle as such" or the unknown content of the "loftier forms of human life".

Obviously, his high inspiration and his linear view of the historical process show their negative influence on occasion. It is typical, for instance, that, in sketching the linear evolution of political organization from tribal forms to world order, he did not know how to deal with the Egyptian, the Babylonian or the Roman Empire. Long before the Christian era, Egypt witnessed a higher level of development than Europe during the Middle Ages, but Merriam neglected this. Chinese, African or Middle- and South-American empires are not even mentioned, let alone that their function in the "progress of the human race" is explained.[28] In fact, in Merriam's work history starts with feudalism in Europe in the early Middle Ages.

In practice, on a lower level of abstraction, however, he showed more realism with respect to the concrete measures that were necessary to continue the progressive developments that had taken place since the early Middle Ages. The circumstances forced him to.

Political experience

In conformity with his father's wish, Merriam looked for a political career. The only sound basis for an experimental approach in the study of politics was to participate in politics, he argued. Around the turn of the century, political science mainly consisted of historical research and the study of constitutional law. The political process was not taken into account. By choosing a political career Merriam expected to be better able to fathom this process. On the other hand, one of the lessons he learned during the twenties was that party membership can harm the soundness of research. This dilemma was felt under Hoover, especially.[29]

Around the turn of the century, Merriam belonged to the Progressive Movement, though originally he was a Republican. This movement of liberal reformers was particularly concerned about the growing power of business, which developed outside democratic control. Industry controlled a large part of social life and became, so to speak, a form of "invisible government", a term coined by Theodore Roosevelt. "The function of reform is to make that government 'visible' by bringing it under public regulation", Merriam argued.[30]

His political career started in 1905, when he became chairman of the City Club of Chicago (by that time he was already working at the university). He got a seat in the City Council for the Republicans, in which position he spent most of his time combatting corruption. Merriam aspired to become mayor, and in the mayoralty campaign of 1911 he was elected candidate of the

Republicans. The people, however, gave a majority vote to Harrison, the candidate of the Democratic Party (177.977 votes, against 160.627 votes for Merriam). According to Merriam, this was due to electoral fraude, but, according to Karl, the loss was primarily a result of controversies within the Republican Party. The party had difficulty in accepting the progressive reformers, and vice versa.

As a result, Merriam did not succeed in becoming the Republican candidate again in 1915. That year he lost to William "Big Bill" Thompson, a corrupt demagogue, it seems, who took advantage of the elitist and "thus" undemocratic image of the universities. In his speeches he always sneered at Merriam by addressing him as "the professor". In those years, there was a general debate about the need for professionally trained politicians versus the danger that this would result in undemocratic government by elites. "Big Bill" became mayor and this victory of corruption and demagogy tempered Merriam's progressiveness.

Meanwhile, the first World War had started. Initially, Merriam, like many of his contemporaries, considered the war an exclusively European problem. The war was looked upon as a struggle of the people against "an industrially based military aristocracy in the process of decay"; a point of view which in respect to the Habsburg empire was accurate, indeed. "That America would involve itself in a war to defend any of the monarchies governing Europe seemed unthinkable."[31] It turned out otherwise: on February 1, 1917, Germany announced the unlimited submarine warfare, and, a month later, the British government published the Zimmermann telegram, which revealed that Germany tried to move Mexico to participate in the war. Subsequently, the United States declared war upon Germany on April 6, and on Austria-Hungary on December 7, 1917.

Merriam went to Italy as a Captain in the Signal Corps. Apart from a number of adventures with local beauties (his marriage, since 1901, with Hilda Doyle was no success), his work for the Committee on Public Information is especially worth mentioning. This bureau was founded in Rome in March 1918 in response to the Russian Revolution and the fear for a similar revolution in Italy. The bureau was headed by Merriam, and its task was to explain to the public the ends America was fighting for and to foster confidence in the cause of democracy in Europe.[32] In addition the

153

bureau was used for espionage (under the auspices of the Creel Commission). The bureau was constantly at odds with the American Embassy, because of overlapping activities. Perhaps Merriam did not write about "real-politik", but he certainly knew what it was. In Italy, he also came to know Franklin D. Roosevelt, who at that time was Assistant Secretary in the Navy.

Science, public education and society

The Russian Revolution gave the reform movement in America a hard time. The Red Scare during the twenties hampered attempts to increase public control of industrial capitalism. During the Palmer Raids suspect persons were arrested and deported. In *American Political Ideas: Studies in the Development of American Political Thought, 1865-1917*, Merriam, therefore, turned against socialism explicitly, but, in the meantime, he continued to oppose free enterprise. He wanted something in between: no control of industry, no uncontrolled free market mechanisms, but regulation and coordination.

> "Progressivism thus becomes a counter-revolutionary force against a usurpation of political power by nongovernmental groups hidden from public control."[33]

This field of tension between coordination and controla central theme in Merriam's workwas constantly fed by political developments. The Soviet planned economy, the rise to power of Mussolini in Italy and the Great Depression of 1929, which had started in the USA, had shown the bad to worse tendency of pure leftwing, rightwing and unguided directions. In the light of the social-economic crisis in the United States, and in the light of both the Russian and Italian examples of how things could go wrong, there was plenty of reason to call for scientific skill to evaluate plans of social reform. In that sense it is more honest to compare the Idealist School with the post-war scientific think-tanks of political parties and policy departments.

Roosevelt's New Deal was the culmination of this development.

154

An answer had to be found to an unemployment of fifteen million people (in the absence of any structural unemployment funds), to high inflation, to sharp declines in industrial productivity, to the fast spreading erosion and to overproduction of grain and cotton. One might say that the USA was in need of a kind of "perestroika", and science was called upon to create it. In such times no one is waiting for sharp-witted, critical accounts of how things go wrong; science, including political science has to be applied.

In the "Hundred Days", the first phase of the New Deal from March 9 to June 16, 1933, financially unsound banks were closed, hoarding or exporting gold was prohibited, the dollar was devaluated by fifty percent, agrarian reform was initiated (the Agricultural Adjustment Act), the Tennessee Valley Authority was set up (construction of hydropower stations, irrigation works and the suppression of erosion in the basin of the Tennessee river), and industry was given new impulses by coordinating the interests of employers and employees in the National Industrial Recovery Act (fixed prices, limits of production, minimum wages, maximum working hours). Some of these initiatives were suspended by the High Court on the ground that they were in conflict with the constitution.[34]

Merriam started to work for the New Deal on July 20, 1933, when he was appointed to the National Resources Planning Board. "If we cannot think of any better lines of social control", he wrote to his brother in September that year, "it is not unlikely that violence will settle the lines of social organization for a generation or so, and without being an alarmist there is a chance that the whole western civilisation will be pulled down."[35]

In the National Resources Planning Board the issue of coordination or control came up once again, and the Board chose for coordination. They urged for decentralization and regionalization of reform plans, albeit directed by a strong federal planning. This did not only link up well with the cultural and historical traditions of the USA, but, according to Merriam and his associates, "local politics [formed] the ultimate protection of democracy and the most effective vehicle for its continuity."[36] The Board continued to function until 1943, and its task was to gather and analyse data about public works and to coordinate the setting up of these works.

Merriam himself was primarily involved in the second main task of the Board: the development of bureaucratic mechanisms to enable governmental planning.

This idea of a strong federal planning created problems for the New Dealers similar to those of the Progressive Movement. Time and again they had to explain that the reorganizations would not turn Roosevelt into a dictator, nor did the Board aim to introduce communism in the United States. Yet, the opposition in Congres against the proposals by the Board remained strong and, in the end, the Board mainly functioned as a presidential think-tank.

The rise of totalitarianism in Europe had great influence on Merriam's thoughts about education, too. Faith in education was certainly typical of Morgenthau's idealists. It should be realized that education was an urgent social problem, because of the rising mass culture. As has been mentioned, there was an area of tension between the necessity of having a well educated professional elite of politicians and the necessity to represent public opinion. The intellectualist progressives "worked to return politics to the people", Crick wrote, but in the end they were confronted with "the fierce anti-intellectualism of the popular press in the early twenties".[37] This made trust in better education in fact the last straw for this generation of Progressives.

But the question what this education should look like brought Merriam from one dilemma into another: schools should not be used for propaganda and indoctrination, yet they should deliver "good" Americans.[38] Just as he did in dealing with the difference between coordination and control, Merriam moved between subtle margins here.

As a result of the Russian Revolution, in many places throughout the United States schoolbooks had been screened thoroughly "to assure proper indoctrination".[39] In the US, the relationship between ideology, education and indoctrination traditionally had a special dimension because of the large number of immigrants. The conditions of entrance included a course in American values and norms, a training in "good citizenship". Under the influence of the educational programmes in the Soviet-Union, Italy and, later on, Germany, this took on a new aspect.

Confronted with these developments, Merriam developed a very realistic view of the societal position of education. The one and only thing public education had to do, was to reflect the existing civilization. Primarily, education was a vehicle for handing over the "civic culture". Civilization was, and could only be, a product of the community, not something which could be imposed on the community by some ideological elite.[40] To enforce or forbid specific values and norms in conformity with the ideas and interests of one subgroup or another could not be called education but was indoctrination. The problem of Merriam's age was that exactly this line of thinking threatened to become a minority view.

Despite, or perhaps stimulated by, the opposition by both the macro developments in the world politics and the micro developments in Chicago politics, Merriam stubbornly continued to work out his own line of reasoning. In 1945 he published *Systematic Politics*, the crown on his work. In Crick's view it is the culmination of everything that is wrong with Merriam's scientific efforts. Crick typified *Systematic Politics* as "a return to something like a traditional level of political speculation ... a book unhappily loose and shallow ... a retreat from pure science of politics."[41] But Crick is overdoing it once again. *Systematic Politics* does indeed show all facets of Merriam's unrestrained faith in human progress, but it also contains sober insights in the complexity of world politics, some of which were not to be rediscovered until the 1970s or 1980s.

Pluralism I: the family of authority

In 1989, Peter Willetts worked out one of these insights. He argued in favour of a more correct use of the term nation-state in political science. Willetts noted that in the study of IR the concept of the state is used in the tradition of both philosophy and international law, without noticing the difference. In international law the state is a collective unit, characterized by a government which is sovereign in its control of a people within a given territory. "The concept is a holistic one, in which the system is coherent and has clear legal, political, social, economic and geographical boundaries. ... society and its citizens are an integral part of the state."[42] In philosophy, however, the state is distinguished from society. Here, the state refers to the authorities in the broadest sense (the legislative, executive and judicial powers, and governmental bureaucracies ranging from municipal administration to ministries), but the state does not necessarily represent the people, does not control the people in all respects, nor does it act in the people's interest by definition.

These two visions of the state are incompatible: "One encompasses society within the concept of the state, while the other separates society from the state."[43] Still, many scholars use the same term for the two concepts without being aware of it.

At the concrete level of daily events, this does not necessarily lead to confusion. The combination of sentences like "The United States has imposed a grain-embargo on the Soviet-Union" and "The United States ended the grain-embargo because of pressure from the domestic agricultural lobby" does not cause any confusion. But on a higher level of abstraction it does. The first sentence can be interpreted within a "state-as-actor" paradigm: state A imposes something on state B. The second sentence, however, cannot be interpreted in a "state-as-actor" paradigm because, apparently, the international interests of American farmers are in conflict with the embargo policy. The state (= the government) is not the sole actor in relation to the other state, and to understand its foreign policy one has to be aware of the different, contrasting interests of each group.

Confusing the two interpretations of the state leads to inaccuracies in theorizing. At first sight, this seems to be a level-of-analysis problem, but it is not. If one treats domestic politics as the micro-level of analysis and international relations as the macro-level, it is possible to use a "state-as-actor" paradigm for IR and a multiple-actor paradigm for internal affairs. The national society, then, is treated as a body: whereas in itself it is a complex compound system of cells, vessels, nerves, etcetera, externally it is working as an atomic system, a definable unit.[44] If this micro-macro distinction were empirically valid, one could perceive IR as the study of state behaviour within the world state-system. Since, however, many of the vessels, nerves and cells of the bodies called states have their own independent (meaning "selbständig" instead of "unabhängig") international or transnational relations, the problem

158

does not involve different levels of analysis.

In other words, the true discussion involved is the paradigm debate.[45] Willetts argued that the Pluralist theory would improve a lot if its adherents used the concept of the state only in its philosophical sense. Just as any society, the world society is characterized by the struggle between different actors for the support of other actors to achieve specific goals. The church, the government, the union, the family, the party, the army, etcetera, all appeal to both the public and the individual to achieve the desired priority in invidual and collective behaviour.

Merriam caught this multiple actor perspective under the heading "family of authority". The government is only one of the members. Religious groups, economic classes, ethnic and racial groups, "sex antagonisms and affinities", regional groups and cultural groups are, potentially, equally important to the understanding of a society.[46] The multiplicity of actors results in all kinds of cross-cutting relationships, which one has to be aware of to understand both the discord and the cohesion in a society. Members of conflicting economic classes can for instance also be members of the same church, which is why they remain on speaking terms longer than would be expected on the basis of their economic conflict only. In other cases, it might be possible that an economic conflict will escalate faster because the parties involved belong to different cultural or ethnic groups as well. William Fox went as far to call this even the Merriam paradigm:

> "'International Relations' ... in this perspective expanded to become 'world politics'. ... Nation-states, in this view, are only one class of associations to be related to each other and to various sub-, trans- and supranational associations."[47]

This idea of "cross-cutting solidarities" is quite well known in the study of domestic politics. Arend Lijphart, for instance, analysed them in the Dutch society of the sixties. But in his theoretical justification he makes no reference to Merriam's work.[48] In fact, the only resources from the interbellum period he mentioned are H.J. Laski, "The Pluralistic State" (1921) and Kung Chuan Hsiao, *Political Pluralism: A Study in Contemporary Political Theory* (1927). Lijphart added the remark that these works are strongly characterized by idealism. This seems to imply that they should not be taken too seriously.

But, if taken serious, Merriam's image of the family of authority is very useful to describe the pluralistic character of world politics and to explain its dynamics. The different members of the family all evolve in their own way and their political weight fluctuates. In *Systematic Politics*, Merrriam observed, for instance, that Science is taking an ever more important position within the family of authority:

> "In modern times, with the vast growth of science and the immense projection of education and of research, it may be said that science is accorded a seat at the table of government. ... In recent times it must be observed ... that science occupies a far more important position than in other periods of history."[49]

It is interesting to notice that in the 1980s attention was drawn again to this aspect of IR by James Rosenau. Without making reference to Merriam, Rosenau argued in 1989 that the value attached to the provision of *scientific* evidence in the management of political conflicts (in contrast to the value of physical strength as an powerful argument) was increasing slowly and silently.[50] This has, of course, important consequences for the conduct of "real-politik": whether one needs military or scientific skill to achieve one's ends makes quite a difference. Merriam pointed at this development. He stressed that the spreading of public education formed the growing power-base of this form of social authority.

So much for the first aspect of Merriam's pluralism. To sum it up: he argued that political analysis must be differentiated with respect to the multitude of individuals, groups and organizations in a given society that are seeking one anothers loyalty in order to achieve their specific objectives. This is not only true of domestic politics but of all politics.

Pluralism II: a world society

The second aspect of Merriam's pluralism, which would be redis-covered in post-war interdependence theories, is the cobweb image of international relations.

> "We observe that many of the local intrastate groups have extensions outside the boundaries of the political association (e.g. nationalities, linguistic groups, religions, etc.) and the web is correspondingly more involved as the number of possible interrelations increases. The task of political as-sociation is thus a manifold one of reconciling the interests of internal groups and at the same time of the external groups, and simultaneously of the internal projected into the external interrelationship."[51]

Frequently, also in the international arena, the carriers of governmental power are merely *mediators* between this multitude of societal groups, and, therefore, not the masters of these groups or the rulers of these relations. In this context Merriam referred to Toynbee, who in *A Study of History* (1934) enunciated how the cultural map of the world deviates from the statist map: some countries enclose several cultures, while some cultures enclose several countries.[52] With reference to the work of Quincy Wright, Alfred Vagts and Edward Mead Earle, Merriam concluded:

> "Commercial and cultural relations of many varying forms and types are found flourishing across state lines. Trading companies and modern cartels are sometimes more power-ful than the smaller states, while 'internationals' of many colors stretch through the network of politics."[53]

Moreover, Merriam pointed at the revolution in the means of communication and transport (Ramsay Muir's "conquest of dis-tance"), which had ended the physical character of state borders. Making use of Eugene Staley's *This Shrinking World* (1940), he addressed the big theoretical problem that "the unit of political aggregation" was extremely difficult to define.[54] What should theory start from? The State, the World or the local Community?

Take for instance Great Britain, Merriam said. On the one hand, the isolated, insular territorial location has decreased sharply as one of the most relevant factors determining social-political developments: British industrialization, starting with the cotton industry, was made possible only by using resources from, among others, India. The Commonwealth of Nations, which spans the whole globe, has become an important, if not an essential element of the British community. On the other hand, regionalism has remained an essential characteristic of the community as well. Northern Ireland is, up to the present, the most dramatic example of this.

> "Under present conditions it may easily happen that parts of different nations are in closer touch than parts of the same nation."[55]

Pluralism III: world order

The cobweb characteristic and the multiple actor characteristic are both descriptive in nature. A third aspect of Merriam's pluralism has a prescriptive character and addresses the question how this complex structure can be governed.

> "A prime difficulty in undertaking even a preliminary exploration of the possibilities of broader forms of association is that the vocabulary of politics, in its commonly accepted definitions, lags behind political events."[56]

Merriam had too much experience with the practical problems of federal government on a continental scale to lose himself in vague illusions about a world federation. But, in the absence of a highly developed political science, he also had to be careful with very concrete scenarios, of which the effects are unknown. Therefore, neither the development of detailed blueprints for world order, nor the development of highly abstract philosophies about the ideal of world order made much sense. The only reasonable thing Merriam could do was to steer a middle course.[57]

As a result, Merriam argued that the existing pluralism was the desired aim of society and that democratic principles of law were most suitable to serve and cultivate this end because these principles were based on the recognition of pluralism. This is a combination of pragmatism and idealism that is typical for all the pluralists reviewed in this study.

Merriam aimed at creating a central planning combined with a diffusion of power both functionally and geographically. The whole family of authority should be awarded a seat at the table; according to the idealist because the members of the family have a right to that; according to the pragmatist because they will run amock otherwise. Every group in society wants recognition and prestige, if possible domination, and tolerance at least. Recognition of this fact forces the parties to a certain division of power. This principle of "shared power" forms the political foundation of Merriam's jural world order.

He supposed democracies to have the greatest evolutionary adaptability to this end:

> "When democracies plan for a jural order of the world, they are in the line of the logic of their system."[58]

But why should democracies desire such an order? Merriam hardly raised that question. In *On the Agenda of Democracy* (1941), he stated that the drive for world order is "no longer merely the product of ethical hopes alone", but has become "the mechanical fiat of revolutionized transportation, intercommunication, and production". Yet, as a first reaction to this structural change, he expected a transition period in which countries would try to restrict cross-border mobility in order to preserve their exclusiveness. Why these limitations would pass away and would be replaced by "the social and economic and political recognition of the nature of the new world", Merriam did not say.[59] The mere fact that, on rational grounds, a world order is the most sensible system to create, was enough to convince him that sooner or later such an order indeed would emerge. At this point Merriam missed the concern and worry of his contemporary Norman Angell.

163

All his life, Angell struggled with the poor level of the "public mind", the media and the politicians. As a consequence of this underdevelopment, governments of truly representative democracies would only decide to strive for democratic internationalism the moment a majority vote asked them to. However, as long as the masses were caught, and were kept caught, in the myths that told them that their nation, their culture and their polity were superior to any other, politicians would be elected who thought the same, and the newspapers would be inclined to confirm this prejudice because of their sales.[60]

Often, equal rights have been obtained after a fierce struggle. Democracy is not only based on the awareness that freedom is the product of voluntary self-constraint. It is also based on a pragmatical acceptance of the impossibility to deny one another's right to exist; a wrested policy of tolerance.

The epitaph of war

"Few writers remain who now characterize war as desirable, although they may find warlike impulses inevitable and unavoidable even if undesirable. But the inevitability of war is no longer generally conceded as a fundamental fact in social relations. Violence is increasingly recognized as a lower form of organization, serving only as a substitute for the higher and possible types of organization ... With the increasing spread of intelligence in social affairs and with the rise of respect for the dignity of man, the resort to violence tends to lose its hold upon social adjustment."[61]

This observation points at the aspects of Merriam's work that are most valuable for the thesis about the causality between chances of war and levels of interdependence. It concerns the evolution of the role of violence in the community. This evolution involves two determinants: a) the relation between social objectives and the means to realize them, and b) the legitimacy of violence as one of these means. The correlation between both is that when social objectives, ends or values cannot be properly served by the use of

164

violence or when less demanding options promise a similar result, the legitimacy of violence will decrease. Conversely, a decline in the legitimacy of violence makes violence more costly (e.g. because greater effort is needed to explain its use), which leads to an increased competition from alternative means.

This logic, of course, has many pitfalls: which social objectives and whose objectives are we talking about? When is violence a means to something else, when is it an end in itself? Whose opinion is decisive in defining the legitimacy of both objectives and means? How do we know whether specific means are successful and, therefore, how do we know that the same result can be achieved by other means? Merriam's answers to these questions are anchored in his pluralistic world view and in his functionalist logic towards societal developments.

He described government as "a phenomenon of group cohesion and aggregation, a child of group necessity, a function of the social relations of men."[62] This does not only apply to government in the sense of the authorities, but to government in general, that is, to all members of the family of authority. The existence of churches, governments, families, political parties, etcetera, is the result of social needs, which makes them functional. The decisive criterion is whether the authoritative organization can or cannot perform the tasks it is supposed to perform. Here, Merriam, like David Mitrany, primarily had in mind the serviceability of every organization to the society. In the next chapter it is argued, however, that this should be extended to include the serviceability to only parts of the society, for example (and most common) to the staff and members of the organization itself.[63]

Every authoritative organization performs specific tasks within a given society which require specific means that have to be present within that society. Merriam called this the "ends and tools of government". He distinguished the following ones:

Ends of government	*Tools of government*
external security	custom
order	violence
justice	symbolism and ceremonialism
welfare	rational consent and participation
freedom	strategy
	leadership

It is of the utmost importance to understand that both the ends of government and the tools can vary with time, place and member in the family of authority. In Ancient Times, for instance, slavery was not seen as injustice and, therefore, the servitude of the slave to the welfare of the master rooted as strongly in "custom" as in "violence". Slave-trade was a normal, legal business. Through the ages, however, its legitimacy declined so much that no government can use slavery as an official instrument to increase the welfare level of its society any longer. The legitimate use of such human resources has become a scornful, illegal abuse. Such a process involves the evolution of our collective intelligence, our social values and norms and the material foundation of the society. Once again, both a cognitive and a structural dimension is at stake. (It is not without reason that people in the South of the United States believed that slavery was part of the nature of things longer than people in the North. On the plantations in the South, slavery had an economic, structural function that it did not have in the more industrialized North.)

That slavery was abolished does not mean that large-scale and officially recognized slavery can never return, but it does mean that this is very unlikely. It is unlikely because both the social values and norms, and the social structure have to change fundamentally to enable this return. Phrased differently: slavery is culture-bound.

According to Merriam, a similar evolution can be detected with respect to "violence" as a the tool of government, notably warfare. The conduct of war is equally culture-bound. The development from tribal life to world order has affected the social role of violence. The power derived from the use or threat of violence is not a constant but a variable, and the overall tendency is, still according to Merriam, for this power to diminish. To test this hypothesis, research is needed into the development of a) the ends of government through the ages, b) the tools of government through the ages and c) the utility of each tool to each end through the ages. Here, however, Crick's criticism is correct: Merriam pointed in the right direction, but took another track himself.

As he lived in the midst of wars, obviously, proof was a bit harder to give than in the case of slavery, which had been abolished already. But these wars, especially the coming second World War, strengthened Merriam's resistance against fatalistic views of the future, rather than tempering it. In 1942, he proudly — or is it desperately? — quoted from his *Prologue to Politics,* a book that had been published in 1939:

> "But in a moment when the world rushes forward perhaps to its most terrible, titanic, and destructive war, I see somehow an end of violence. I see an epitaph written large — an epitaph not of civilization but of war."[64]

Of interest is, of course, the "somehow", and not Merriam's prophetic gift, his overstrained distress or his doggedness: the idea that the society could lapse back to a lower level of civilization was simply out of the question and had to stay out of the question, otherwise it had all been for nothing. In other words, Merriam's expectation of the end of war was evidently influenced by his provincial, protestant moral views.

Two other elements of his thinking about the end of war, however, deserve further attention. These are the relation between violence and levels of civilization and the changeability of the essence of power.

Civilized power: a neglected aspect of pluralism

Probably Merriam was too optimistic when he observed an "increasing spread of intelligence in social affairs" (see note 61), but in doing this he pointed at a causality which is in fact recognized by anyone who claims that education and schoolingboth rationally and emotionallyare a basic need for social development to proceed along an orderly course.

> "[T]he conditioning factor of government is the whole complex of customs, institutions, ideas and ideals, acting and reacting upon each other and upon the going concern of government. The political association must adapt its policies and programs to these networks of social custom and thought. ... Back of all is the culture pattern of the time in which government and other institutions are set."[65]

Decisive, therefore, for the role of political violence is its place in social "custom" and "thought". That place, in its turn, is partly determined by material conditions.

One of the conditions for the abolition of war, which Merriam mentioned, is "the economy of abundance". When the cake is too small or when the distribution of its parts is inadequate, "haves and have-nots" emerge, "outsiders and insiders", which is a potential cause of war.[66] Again, we are faced here with a combination of cognitive and structural dimensions.

The evolution of the networks of social custom and social thought touches upon the nature of power. According to Merriam, power consists of four elements: force, obedience, persuasion and participation. The fourth pillar is especially interesting, as its relation to the first pillar is strained. If force, violence, is needed to enforce obedience or to support persuasion, the community spirit, the wish to participate, is put under pressure. Drill and discipline take the place of education and schooling; fear and servility take the place of appreciation and esteem; apathy and resignation take the place of creativity and spontaneity. The fourth pillar of power is, in fact, synonymous with constructional interdependence (see page 24-25).

Merriam's thesis is that simple forms of social organization can almost do without the fourth pillar, while complicated forms of social organization rest on it almost completely. The nature of power thus moves from the use of force to participation in proportion to the level of civilization. The higher the level of social development, the less important is the power-pillar of force and the more important is the power-pillar of participation or construction-al interdependence.

As an example of a simple social organizational structure Mer-riam mentioned the army. The command structure of an army is the archetype of order: there is a clear-cut division of labour based on sharp distinctions of authority and responsibility.[67] Police states, dictatorships, military regimes, and the like, are the large scale translations of this principle. The other extreme is democracy. A true democracy (not every democracy is a true democracy) is the most complicated form of social organization. The chance of disor-der and situations in which no one knows what to do or whom to listen to is far larger than in the ant-society of militarism.

In a democracy, power primarily rests on participation. Merriam called this the *community nature of power*.[68] According to him, the community nature of power leads to the situation that in democracies "the so-called 'struggle for power', which is cynically held up [by the Realists -jdw] as the mark of the political, may in reality become a struggle for rendering service."[69] The use of force, political violence, remains one of the pillars of power but its role declines.

"Violence is not the climax of organization but its very lowest form. Peace is not essentially passivity but the highest organization of the highest activities and energies on the highest levels. ... Peace is not the end of struggle but the finer organization of it."[70]

7   David Mitrany (1888-1977): functionalism as statecraft and revolt

"If functionalism does not work, no other approach will."
Hans J. Morgenthau, *Times Literary Supplement*, July 1974[1]

David Mitrany has been called the father of functionalism. Functionalism is a theory of international organization and can be characterized as an issue-specific approach to politics. The idea is to deal with social problems by looking first at their so-called technical aspects. The purpose of this is to sidestep the obstacles formed by nationalistic ideologies and by anachronistic governmental mechanisms. "Our time has produced a wholly new factor that is fundamental and inescapable", Mitrany wrote in his memoir, "the emergence for the first time of world problems and world activities which escape the range and control of any existing political sovereignties, or of any partial combination of them."[2] Functionalism is a reaction to the emergence of global interdependence, and its emphasis on the technical management of issues is an attempt to go beyond political boundaries and divisions without disputing them.

Functionalism is also a strategy of international organization:

when you neglect cultural, religious and ideological differences by respecting them, it is possible to organize your business on whatever scale required. Ultimately, this strategy serves a normative end, to create a "working peace system":

"The historical task of our time is not to keep the nations peacefully apart but to bring them actively together."[3]

This chapter falls into three parts. First, Mitrany's functionalism is discussed (pp. 171-182). Secondly, the position of functionalism within the paradigm debate is worked out (pp. 182-191). Then the discussion on functionalism is picked up again and Mitrany's ideas about interdependence are explained (pp. 191-202).

Bridging the second World War

David Mitrany's life and work spans and connects the pre-war phase of Pluralism and the Pluralism of the 1950s and 1960s. Therefore, the study of the development of interdependence theory in the first half of the twentieth century comes to a logical close with a review of his contribution to interdependence theory. Obviously, Mitrany is not the only scientist in the Pluralist tradition who remained active after the war (Eugene Staley is another), but in his work especially the spark of Pluralism kept on burning: in the fifties and the early sixties, functionalism was studied and developed further by several scholars, Ernst B. Haas and James Sewell in particular. Mitrany's theory influenced the work of Karl Deutsch and Inis Claude, and was admired even by Hans J. Morgenthau. Integration theory and, of course, neo-functionalism are the immediate consequences of Mitrany's work. Policy initiatives, such as the foundation of the European Coal and Steel Community (ECSC) in 1951, were defended politically with rhetoric based on functionalism.[4] Indirectly, even the theory of interdependence that was developed by Robert Keohane and Joseph Nye in the seventies can be traced back to Mitrany. In 1987 they acknowledged the (neo)functional roots of their thinking.

171

"As we now see the matter, we were seeking in part to broaden the neofunctional strand of liberalism that had been developed by Ernst B. Haas and others in the 1950s and 1960s, but that had been largely limited to the analysis of regional integration."[5]

In 1975 Paul Taylor pointed at similar roots in the special issue of the journal *International Organization* about Transnational Relations and World Politics, which was also edited by Keohane and Nye.[6]

But time moves in circles. One of my conclusions about Mitrany's writings in the thirties is that his functionalism should be considered a sub-theory of the then prevailing insights in interdependence.

A plea for functionalism followed logically from the general ideas about global interdependence that were developed during the twenties and thirties. Norman Angell's plea for a protective union of the Western democracies, the general debate about world government and world federalism, Ramsay Muir's warnings against the perils of interdependence, Francis Delaisi's plea for international non-governmental professional associations, and the general debate about nationalism versus internationalism all pointed at the necessity to adjust government to the conditions of world politics. In his early works Mitrany recognized that necessity, and his functionalism is based on that awareness.

A British Rumanian with an American accent

Mitrany was born in Rumania in 1888. After an early military service he left that country at the age of twenty. Most young Rumanians were attracted by Paris in these years, but Mitrany settled in London after a three year's stay in Hamburg. In his short autobiography, which he wrote in 1969, he did not motivate his emigration but perhaps his characterization of Rumania is telling enough:

"Born and educated in Romania, I had seen the mass of the people of a naturally rich country living in worse conditions than in the much-decried period of Turkish domination. A country with compulsary state education which still had some 70 percent of illiterates; a country with an advanced suffrage, and the great mass of the people living on the land, which did not have a single real peasant in Parliament ... a country in which a most liberal written Constitution and endless patriotic incense-burning proved no embarrassment at all to the most ill-found ways of government."[7]

Though he wrote a lot about the Balkans, the influence of his Rumanian background on the creation of functionalism should not be exaggerated. It influenced his thoughts about socialism and marxism (in his opinion the marxists underestimated peasants as an independent political factor), it stimulated his aversion to excessive claims of absolute sovereignty, and probably his emigration also explained part of his international orientation in politics, but functionalism had other roots.

In 1912 Mitrany entered the London School of Economics and Political Science (LSE), where he studied sociology and politics. During the first World War ("the outbreak of war in 1914 changed my outlook and purpose violently") he got involved in intelligence work for the Foreign Office and the War Office related to South-East European issues. This lasted until April 1919.

In 1916, he joined the League of Nations Society, for which he lectured throughout England, especially on the topic "Small states and a League of Nations". From 1918 to 1931 he was a member of the Labour Party's Advisory Committee on International Affairs, without being or ever becoming a member of this party (or of any other party or ideological group for that matter). The only ideological groups he had close contacts with, both in England and in the United States, were the Quakers, "though I was neither a Christian nor a pacifist".[8]

It is interesting that in the committee he worked together with people like Norman Angell, G.D.H. Cole, J. Ramsay MacDonald, Arnold Toynbee and Leonard Woolf. "Norman Angellism", therefore, must have influenced him in some way, though he did not mention it. The only influence Mitrany revealed is that of the Fabians. Cole belonged to the Fabians and Graham Wallas, one of

Mitrany's teachers at the LSE, had been one of the founders of the Fabian Society (1883). L.T. Hobhouse, his second teacher, was a Liberal.

From 1919 to 1922 Mitrany was on the editorial staff of the Manchester *Guardian*, which kept him in close contact with European politics. Of more direct importance for the development of functionalism, however, was his work as assistant European editor of the *Economic and Social History of the World War*, a project of the Carnegie Endowment for International Peace. He held this post from 1922 to 1929 and in this position he read manuscripts from many countries. These included records about the different reactions to the unforeseen character of the war. Economic and industrial factors appeared to be decisive and every country, friend and foe, had to react to that situation. It turned out that the reactions were not different at all: all belligerents had made similar arrangements to deal with problems of supply and production and distribution. "A rare thing in social experience", Mitrany noticed.

> "It showed that no matter how great the historical, constitutional and social variations, similar problems under similar conditions led to similar ways and means for dealing with them ..."[9]

The second event which played an important role in shaping functionalism was the great depression of 1929, which started in the United States, and especially the reaction to it: the New Deal. Mitrany was not involved in the New Deal in the way Merriam was, but he happened to be at Harvard, Yale and Princeton during this period. What he found attractive in FDR's New Deal was that it "was a question of saving a situation rather than of enthroning an ideology".[10]

The Tennessee Valley Authority (TVA) in particular appealed to him. Directed by David E. Lilienthal, the TVA started irrigation works, canalization, industrialization and reafforestation in the basin of Tennessee River, combined with social measures like the extra taxing of high incomes, loans to people with mounted mortgages and house-building in suburbs. The Tennessee River crosses several states but the TVA was able to surpass most of the

local juridical barriers because of its technical, issue-specific definition.[11]

What he actually observed was an approach to politics that in the
eighties was known as "no nonsense politics" (at least, that is the
label used in the Netherlands): no ideology or religion, no regard
for bureaucratic interests, but optimal efficiency by dealing directly
with the technical aspects of a given problem. In this context John
Burton's definition of functionalism is quite accurate:

> "Functionalism is decision-making within a specialised area
> by persons skilled in that area, whose self-esteem and loyal-
> ties relate to their specialisation."[12]

Global service networks or balance of power?

Other sources of inspiration to Mitrany were the public international unions that were founded at the end of the nineteenth century
for the purpose of managing "technical" issues. Despite the international confrontations in terms of power politics and despite all
ideological or nationalistic differences, these Unions were created
for the simple reason that there was an international need for them.

The Universal Postal Union (UPU) is the best-known example:
the UPU, first called General Postal Union, was founded in 1875 by
twenty European countries, Egypt and the USA. Its work extended
to the colonies of these countries as well, which made it one of the
first global service networks. The UPU still exists and has 158
members since 1980. The International Telegraph Union (1865),
predecessor of the International Telecommunications Union (ITU),
developed similarly. In 1919 the technical committees of the League
of Nations were formed, and Mitrany was impressed most by the
International Labour Organization (ILO). The ILO was a unique
body because it consisted of both governmental and non-
governmental actors. Moreover, it was the only institution of the
League that would survive the second World War. "Experience
with such institutions suggested a new approach to international
peace and integration."[13]

In 1932 Mitrany formulated his first thoughts about functionalism in the Dodge Lectures at Yale Univerisity. They were published in 1933 in *The Progress of International Government*. The same year he got a chair at the Institute for Advanced Study in Princeton, New Jersey. But the years he spent there were not specifically significant for the development of functionalism.

"The need and the opportunity to expand the functional idea came early in the Second World War."[14] As has been described in the previous chapter, the second World War was a turning-point in the theorizing about the essence of world politics, especially in the United States. The Chicago School and its Pluralism did not survive the war but were pushed aside by Political Realists and strategic thinkers who accepted the interstate struggle for power as a cut-and-dried principle of politics and who seemed to put a premium on worst-case analyses. The effect of the war on the intellectual development of Mitrany was completely different.

Mitrany still had connections at the British Foreign Office and in 1938 he was asked to work "with an academic intelligence group (camouflaged as 'The Foreign Research and Press Service')".[15] In 1941 he wrote two papers for this group that would culminate in the pamphlet *A Working Peace System*. But, as the papers were badly received, he resigned from the Foreign Office in the meantime. His superiors were not interested in any post-war scenarios that included an active role for the Soviet-Union. According to Mitrany the diplomats put too much emphasis on balance-of-power interests.[16]

A Working Peace System: An Argument for the Functional Development of International Organization was published in 1943 and was an immediate success (except perhaps in diplomatic circles). In this pamphlet Mitrany urged a peaceful approach to the need to achieve unity in diversity. The objective of that approach was not to win or to contain, to limit or to freeze the interstate struggle for power, but to end it by making it meaningless.

The essence of functionalism was to achieve the erosion of territorially based power. The war did by no means affect Mitrany's confidence in the feasibility of this end. But the war sharpened his view of the way in which this erosion could be achieved. The failure of the League of Nations occupied his mind and strengthened his

176

criticism of the idea of world federalism. State borders could not be made meaningless by laying down which powers should be exercised on the federal level and which on the state level. In some areas this would surely diminish the importance of state borders, but it other areas this importance would be emphasized.

The one and only way to make territorial borders truly irrelevant is "through the continuous development of common activities and interests across them."[17] In that way, it would become possible to create security in terms of an "undisturbed social life" instead of security in terms of an "adequately guarded territory". Mitrany thus formulated the thesis that increasing interdependence is essential to abolish war among states. Increasing interdependence forms the starting-point for functionalism.

The remaining part of Mitrany's career did not really influence his basic assumptions about politics. Yet, it is worth mentioning that he became a policy adviser of Unilever and Lever Brothers, Ltd. in 1944. He kept that post until his retirement in 1960. This appointment appears to have been without precedent in the business world, not only because Unilever took the risk to work with "a fairly left-of-centre professor"[18] but especially because it meant a recognition of the relevance of political expertise for economic enterprise. In this context, it is curious that Mitrany paid little attention to the role of multinational firms in terms of functionalism. He concentrated on non-profit INGOs only.[19]

Two principles of functionalism: form-follows-function and spill-over

a) Form follows function: Functionalism is both a theory and a strategy. It is a combination of descriptive and prescriptive aspects: there exists a *working* peace system and the challenge is to develop it further.[20] This combination reflects Mitrany's disapproval of organizational blueprints. He stressed the so-called virtue of "technical self-determination". The approach to a problem should be determined by the characteristics of the issue in question and not by bureaucratic, political or ideological interests. "Scope and purpose" must determine the line of action. This principle of functionalism is called "form follows function".[21]

But one of the problems is, of course, that a clear-cut distinction between the "technical" and the "political" aspects of an issue is often hard to find. In practice Mitrany distinguished between ser-vice- issues and order-issues, between welfare-issues and sovereignty-issues, between the requirements of interdependence and the requirements of independence, between community inter-ests and egocentrism. In all these distinctions, however, he favoured the first category and what he labelled the "technical" solution always appeared to support that preference.

Even apart from these subjective preferences the entire logic of dividing issues in technical and political aspects is rather ques-tionable and has been criticized by many scholars.[22] This criticism, however, should be nuanced. At an abstract, theoretical level dis-tinctions between technical and political matters can indeed hardly be made. But it may be doubted whether Mitrany had a high level of abstraction in mind. *A Working Peace System* has a low level of abstraction. It was a pamphlet, and as such it dealt with concrete, practical matters. At such a practical level it is much easier to distinguish different aspects of a social problem. Functionalism is both a theory and a strategy and *A Working Peace System* reflects more of the strategy, while *The Progress of International Government* primarily reflects theory.

b) Spill-over: Mitrany expected that cooperaton in technical fields would exert a certain de-escalating influence on power politics and nationalist conflicts. This principle has become known as the spill-over effect: when actors A and B cooperate on issue X, why, then, should they be after one another's blood on other issues? In 1936, Sir Alfred Zimmern characterized this aspect of functionalism as follows:

> "Little by little, so it began to be believed, the morass of 'high politics' would dry up along its edges, as one issue after another was rained off to Geneva [the seat of many interna-tional organizations]. Thus eventually there would be a world-wide co-operative system held together by a network

of contacts between government departments (other than Foreign Offices), professional organisations and individual experts. ... a curious combination of Fabianism and Cobdenism."[23]

Zimmern's rather cynical sketch may be too simple, but the essence is clear: functionalism shares with interdependence theory the thesis that the causes of war and the conditions of peace are located in the *structure* of society:

"Man goes to war because his social environment encourages him ... and his social environment can equally restrain him from going to war."[24]

Mitrany could be quite explicit about what this meant:

"I have always fought shy of suggestions for a 'functionalist society' to propagate this particular approach. ... But if we are ever to pump some measure of sanity into relations in the Middle East, or between India and Pakistan, or between the two parts of Ireland, and in general between East and West, it could only be through the growth of joint functional arrangements, and not for a very long time through any kind of political union."[25]

It was mainly in economic spheres that Mitrany looked for societal restraints. Given the welfarism of the twentieth century, national authorities had to yield to the tendency of forming international organizations. International organizations are more capable of making the changed economic conditions serviceable to welfare ends. National authorities can no longer look after the material requirements of modern society on their own. In due time welfarism would overrule nationalism or at least diminish its extremist forms.[26] It is remarkable that E.H. Carr, the founder of modern Realism, reached similar conclusions during the second World War. In *Conditions of Peace* (1942) he wrote that interdependence had become an inescapable fact of survival.

"[T]he political right of national self-determination must be reconciled with the exigencies of economic interdependence."[27]

And looking ahead, at the peace treaty negotiations that would follow the war, he warned for the neglect of interdependence:

"There is indeed a real danger that — as happened to some extent in 1919 and after — legalistic discussions about sovereignties, leagues and federations may serve as a red herring to divert public opinion from those practical issues of cooperation and interdependence, military and economic, on which the future depends. ... At the present stage interdependence is a practical, not a constitutonal, problem. ... What we are required in fact to surrender is not a mythical attribute called sovereignty, but the habit of framing our military and economic policy without regard for the needs and interests of other countries."[28]

Carr defined interdependence as a constraint on the arbitrariness of state power; a positive constraint upon the exercise of the national right to self-determination.

But how and why exactly does this constraint work? The "how" concerns questions about the future role of the nation-state in a functionalist working peace system. Mitrany was very inconsistent with respect to this matter. And as to the "when", his expectations of a positive spill-over and his thrust in the axiom that form would follow function was far too optimistic.

The social function of swindle and extortion

The axiom that form follows function can be read also as "function determines form". Thompson was right when he proposed to amend this to "function ought to determine form", because this does not happen automatically.[29]

Mitrany's implicit determinism is the consequence of a naïve axiom. He adhered to the thesis, which he attributed to Aristotle, that "the permanent end of any political community is to make its members happy".[30] If only this would be true. Here, Mitrany neglected the principle of what could be called "functional extortion"; the logic of insurance swindle: When someone refuses to conclude an expensive fire insurance, his house is burnt down by the insurer. Based on a cost/benefit analysis this perspective makes it more sensible to pay the high insurance premium; fire is worse. You buy protection against your protector. Indirectly and on the long run, however, the swindler may be accepted or even recognized in his role of insurer, especially when he is clever enough to reimburse the costs of accidental fires. (S)he charges too much, but is also behaving functionally. In other words: governments never serve the interests of the political community only, but always serve their own interests to a certain extent as well; and, inversely, any selfish government will to some extent serve the wider interests of the political community.

This explains why a specific social system can survive itself and become an anachronism. What is actually meant when a regime is called anachronistic is that the regime has become disfunctional in relation to the rest of society. But as long as the regime survives, one is allowed to assume (on the basis of Aristotle's thesis!) that there are enough persons who profit from its existence to guarantee its survival. By applying the principle of functional extortion, a priviliged group can keep itself in the saddle for a long time: fire is worse. In a number of cases revolutions have been necessary to restore the balance between the needs of a society and the needs of the authorities. The fate of the Ancien Regime, of tsarist Russia, of colonial rule worldwide and, recently, of elitist party-rule in Eastern Europe and the Soviet-Union is illustrative; the Apartheid system may come next.

An important enrichment of functionalism would therefore be to specify always *for whom* something is functional and *to what purpose*. Functionalism should be more actor-specific and value-specific. In all the literature I have consulted, functionalism is equalled with "in service of humanity" or "instrumental to the solution of a social problem" and not "in service of a ruling elite" or "instrumental to a specific organization and its bureaucracy". Functionalists and their critics have neglected the social functions of swindle and extortion.

Where do national governments fit in?

The second main issue concerning the expectation of peace among nations as a result of positive spill-over effects involves the question about the future role of nation-states. What is Mitrany's axiom here? Should nation-states disappear in order to abolish war or can they be reformed to that end?

The central question is how flexibly the state-system can react to changing circumstances. On the one hand, functionalism concentrates on the notion of the "self-contradiction of the state"; the notion that nation-states have become an anachronism in a functional sense. This easily leads to the conclusion that the only sensible thing to do is to get rid of the nation-state. Indeed, Mitrany came close to that conclusion several times, especially in the postwar context of European integration. "The state is almost become an organisation for the prevention of international intercourse", Mitrany wrote in 1948.[31] In the introduction to Mitrany's final discourse on functionalism, *The Functional Theory of Politics* (1975), Paul Taylor even listed the decline of the nation-state among the major principles of functionalism:

> "The major principles of functionalism are that man can be weaned away from his loyalty to the nation state by the experience of fruitful international co-operaton; that international organization ... could increase welfare rewards to individuals beyond the level obtainable within the state ... Individuals and groups could begin to learn the benefits of co-operation and would be increasingly involved in an international co-operative ethos, creating interdependencies, pushing for further integration, undermining the most important bases of the nation state."[32]

When the integration of states is looked upon as the ultimate solution of the war-problem, functionalism is treated as the best strategy to achieve that solution.

Unfortunately, however, sound though this logic may be (without states interstate warfare is impossible), it is irrealistic to expect states to disappear. The disappearance of states is not even a desirable thing by definition. The conclusion that the state should or will disappear neglects an important part of reality: up to the present the state (that is, the authorities) clearly performs many functions which are indispensable for society. (In countries where the authorities fail to do so, part of their legitimacy stems from the attempt or the proclaimed attempt to improve this record.) These functions include many new ones derived from the realm of business. In countries like the Netherlands the state is one of the biggest employers, an important consumer of goods and services and the main subsidizer of public education, science, social security and culture. Japan is another obvious example of a country actually functioning like a multinational corporation. The service state, the welfare state and the business state are twentieth century realities without any mark of anachronism. Moreover, a number of functions traditionally performed in the legislative, executive and juridical realms remain of unimpaired interest and are in no need of replacement. What has changed is the context within which authorities have to perform these functions and the extent to which domestic problems have an international or even a global dimension. In that respect the problem of war is a problem of public awareness and of the adaptation of governments to these conditions; not a problem of abolishing the state.

Mitrany was ambivalent with respect to the role of state authorities. He was consistent in his plea concerning the necessity to replace territorially based political organizations (by which he meant the nation-state) by functional political organizations (by which he meant international issue-specific, specialized organizations). But he could also write in admiration about the "massive functional concentration in central government" leading to a "managerial state".[33]

With a little good will, this could imply that several scenarios were left open by Mitrany. Nation-states had to disappear, unless governments could be transformed into functional political organizations, leaving state borders meaningless. That interpretation is supported by Charles Pentland:

> "Structurally, the minimal result might be something like a pluralistic community of states whose sovereign power is reduced and controlled by international functional linkages. A more extreme and less likely possibility is the eventual disappearance of the nation-states as political units, and their replacement by a global administrative system whose organisational pattern is determined by criteria of functional rationality."[34]

Strangely enough, this radical scenario was picked up by Morgenthau.

Morgenthau and functionalism: the State is dead — long live the State!

A Working Peace System (1943) has become a classic thanks to a republication in 1966. Hans J. Morgenthau, one of the champions of contemporary Realism, wrote a preface to this edition in which he matched Mitrany as a true Pluralist:

> "Modern technology has rendered the nation state obsolete as a principle of political organisation ... If national states acted in accord with the rational requirements of the age, they would strive, as it were, to make themselves super-fluous."[35]

Here, Morgenthau filled in his remark from *Politics Among Nations* (1948) that the nation-state, as a unit of social organization, is finally doomed to disappear because states are a product of history and not an elementary part of nature.[36] But his reasoning behind this statement is dubious.

Partly, Morgenthau's assertion that the state had become obsolete reflected the realism of people like Angell:

> "[T]he nation state is no longer able to perform what is the

elementary function of any political organization: to protect the lives of its members and their way of life."[37]

Already in 1918 Angell had written that the values of Western democracy could not be protected by the nation-states in isolation.[38] Given the physical unification of the world, the national interest could no longer be defined and served in isolation. Apparently, Morgenthau was convinced of this, too. He even maintained that the atrophy of the nation-state had been one of the key issues in *Politics Among Nations*.

Yet, it apparently was necessary to repeat this claim time and again. In the foreword to the second edition of *Politics Among Nations* (1954) he wrote that, from the very beginning, he had stressed "the obsolescence of the sovereign national states". In the third edition (1960) he lamented again about his critics who wrongly attributed to him the thesis of "the permanence of the international system based upon the nation state".[39]

Despite these lamentations, however, both *Politics Among Nations* and the preface to *A Working Peace System* show an unimpaired state-centric thinking and, more seriously, a strong fixation on the "ultima ratio" of military power in international affairs.

According to Morgenthau (as well as many other scholars), the atom bomb caused the watershed between a world in which nation-states are the logic, self-contained units of political analysis, and a world in which nation-states are forced open. The nuclear revolution was seen as the decisive turning-point in history: "in the *pre-atomic age* a nation state could count upon its physical ability to defend itself ..."[40] In other words: up to Hiroshima the billiard ball model of IR had been realistic, since then it had been outdated.

It took nuclear weapons to make Morgenthau aware of the friction between the "ultima ratio" and the "self-destructiveness" of military force. That friction, however, has been present throughout the twentieth century. Even without nuclear weapons wars could already escalate to global proportions and — if continued long enough — probably bring to an end complete civilizations, too. Nuclear armament has concentrated destructive power in time, but it has not caused the irrationality of war, it has merely confirmed it.

There is no reason, even, to call the beginning of the atomic age in 1945 a turning-point in warfare. Nuclear weapons are the superlative of an ongoing development towards absolute warfare, not the starting signal of that development. In fact, the intrinsic logic of war preparation, its dynamics towards all-out destruction and its concentration in time, were brilliantly described as far back as 1830 by Carl von Clausewitz in *Vom Kriege*.[41] The only way in which the atom bomb can be called a turning-point in history is in a cognitive sense: it made the world come to itself. Suddenly a host of people became aware of facts they could have been aware of long before.

It is characteristic of Political Realism that Morgenthau's solution to the nuclear friction was as state-centric as ever. The only way out was to scale up the nation-state to supranational proportions; "the amalgation of nation states into larger supra-national entities".[42] A variant of the king is dead — long live the king!

Politics Among Nations is indeed a plea for this supranational solution. The most important instrument to this end was diplomacy. Yet, one of Morgenthau's theses about the basic principles of diplomacy is that "The Objectives of Foreign Policy Must Be Defined in Terms of the National Interest and Must Be Supported with Adequate Power". Additionally, he wrote that "national interest ... can only be defined in terms of national security", while "national security must be defined as *integrity of the national territory and of its institutions*".[43] That brings us back to the beginning: the mine and thine of nation-states should always be clearly defined in terms of territorially based power. After all, the integrity of the state is synonymous with national security, which is, in Morgenthau's mind, the power base of diplomacy.

This even brings the "ultima ratio" of military power back into the picture, because behind the diplomat always stands the military. In Morgenthau's words:

"The dependence of national power upon military preparedness is too obvious to need much elaboration. Military preparedness requires a military establishment capable of supporting the foreign policies pursued."[44]

186

This creates the paradox that the formation of supranational organizations is to be aimed for by nation-states, which are better able to do so, the better they can protect their own territory and their institutional integrity. Meanwhile the only need for supranational organization is caused by the atrophy of the state, that is, its inability to preserve its territorial and institutional integrity. Realism can be quite confusing.

Mitrany versus Morgenthau?

"Of contemporary international relations theories functionalism is perhaps the main alternative to theories of power politics." That was stated by John Groom and Paul Taylor in their volume on functionalism to which also Mitrany himself contributed (at the age of eigthy-seven).[45] It should be assumed therefore that Mitrany agreed with Groom and Taylor.

> "The billiard ball analogy of international society is rejected; greater significance is attached to the emergence of an increasing range of inter-, cross- and trans-national systems of inter-dependence; the term 'world politics' or 'world society' is preferred to 'international politics' ... peace and security are to be guaranteed by the efficient provision of essential services to fulfill commonly-felt needs rather than 'non-war' being induced by fear of threat systems and sanctions."[46]

Thus, Groom and Taylor claimed that functionalism is entirely at odds with the tradition of Realism. Mitrany's work ought to be related, instead, to the work of Leonard Woolf (author of *The Framework of a Lasting Peace*, 1917), Norman Angell (!) and G.D.H. Cole (author of *Guild Socialism*, 1920 and *The Intelligent Man's Guide Through World Chaos*, 1932) and is rooted in the tradition of the Fabians (1883) and Kropotkin's anarchism.[47]

It is remarkable, therefore, that, in 1985, John Eastby came to the diametrically opposite conclusion. According to him "the analysis offered by functionalism [is] basically in harmony with Morgenthau's".[48] He devoted a full chapter to Morgenthau's interpretation of functionalism, but gave no sign whatever of any surprise at this marriage of two paradigms. Actually, Eastby simply denied the problem. He introduced Morgenthau as a "primary exponent of realism" and continued to say, without giving any further explanation, that Realism "is now mistakenly identified with state-centrism".[49] The previous paragraph showed differently: Morgenthau's theory is state-centric to a high degree.

But, assuming that Taylor and Groom are right and Eastby wrong, why, then, was Morgenthau attracted to functionalism and did he write a preface in Mitrany's volume? And what brought Mitrany close to Morgenthau? These questions are not raised by Taylor and Groom, nor in the other literature about functionalism that I consulted. No one seems to be surprised by the cooperation between exponents of essentially different paradigms. There are several reasons for this cooperation.

The flirtations of functionalism and Realism

The first reason is trivial, but mentioned so infrequently that it is worth pointing at: the paradigm debate is less fundamental than is often assumed. The differences between Realism and Pluralism are big and essential (let there be no misunderstanding about that) but simultaneously they relate to one another like a brother and a sister within one family. Both paradigms are rooted in European scientific traditions, both are the product of a christian culture, and both are abstractions and generalizations of European history. Despite their differences Realism and Pluralism speak in related languages (just as Norwegian and Swedish are both Scandivian languages). Mitrany and Morgenthau shared similar concerns (the crisis of the state system), similar ideals (peace, welfare and well-being in a democratic world) and also the same scientific criteria (reasoning in terms of causalities and a detached commitment to politics). This congeniality explains why Morgenthau already in 1948 honoured Mitrany for his "brilliance and persuasiveness".

The second reason is that, because of this congeniality, Morgenthau could make use of Mitrany's points of view in a dialectical manner. Morgenthau followed Mitrany's reasoning quite a while, but then he drew opposite conclusions (in *Politics Among Nations*, at least). He fully agreed with Mitrany that societies and governments were products of common activities and common administrative organs. He also subscribed to the view that the *loyalty* of the people to these managerial structures is the decisive criterion for stability. Furthermore, he recognized that internationally oriented loyalties can emerge, as had happened during the second World War in the allied camp. But, having arrived at this point, Morgenthau made an about turn and used the same argumentation to show that it is irrealistic to seek for world peace along these lines.

International loyalty during the second World War was based on the binding factor of a common enemy. In times of peace that factor is absent. Since 1945 the loyalty of the individual citizen has once again been completely national in focus, Morgenthau said, because the national government is the only actor with a direct and visible influence on the individual's life. Who on earth is thinking about the Universal Postal Union when he or she is sending a letter abroad? Despite the real existence of a global community of interests,[50] the individual continues to direct his or her attention to the national government only. Therefore, Morgenthau even turned the logic of Mitrany's working peace system upside down:

> "More particularly, the conflicts of power which separate nations and the insecurity they create make identification with the nation the overriding concern of most members of all nations. The nation offers the individual protection, vicarious gratification of power drives, and immediate satisfaction of material needs."[51]

In other words: because of the malfunctioning of the state system, the demand for a strong state will increase — causing the state system to function even worse.

In contrast to his Pluralist colleagues Morgenthau did not make any effort to expose the irrationality of that thesis; apparently he considered it a fait accompli, a "realistic" fact of life. Logically, he therefore did not believe in the possibility that a world community would be brought about by the development of grass-root functionalism.

But Morgenthau, too, was ambivalent, because at the same time he realized that "modern technology has rendered the nation state obsolete as a principle of political organisation" (see note 33). For that reason he put his money on functionalism. When there is a way to bridge the gap between state anarchy and a world community, it will be functionalism. But this strategy could only be imposed on the public from above; from the supranational level, from international politics with diplomacy as the instrument. The state favouring that solution, has to be a strong one.

With his trust in a supranational solution Morgenthau closed ranks again with Mitrany, because the latter also did not exclude supranational cooperation. The League of Nations received his warm support, as did the European Coal and Steal Commission (ECSC) and the European Economic Community (EEC). With respect to international organization, he also saw a positive development in the sequence that ran from the The Hague conferences in 1899 and 1907, via the the League of Nations in 1919, to the United Nations Organization in 1945.[52] During the war he also stressed the necessity to have some kind of supranational authority in the military sphere.

> "There can be no real transfer of sovereignty until defense is entrusted to a common authority, because national means of defense are also means of offense and also of possible resistance to that common authority."[53]

Here, as well as in their regard for supranational developments in general, Realism and Pluralism obviously share common ground. This is also the point Eastby concentrated on when explaining that Mitrany and Morgenthau were complementary.

The final reason that made functionalism attractive to Realists lies in the strategic character of functionalism. "Functionalism is not bound to any ideology or dogma", Thompson remarked.[54] A maxim like form follows function, or function determines form, may serve many purposes. Mitrany consciously kept functionalism as neutral as possible, but, because of that, functionalism lends itself easily to the support of any ideology, dogma or political theory, including Realism.

Illustrative in this context is that in 1966 Morgenthau had great difficulty to handle the paradox of increasing nationalism in a "shrinking" world. In his judgment the revival and spread of nationalism to the colonies was a threat to peace and order, and to the survival of the world as such. Nationalism was "at odds with the rational requirements of the age", he wrote.[55] Functionalism offered a trump in the struggle against the irrationality of nationalism: the nation-state had to merge in a supranational structure; separatism was disfunctional. Mitrany was capable of greater nuances with respect to this struggle, because he defined the problem differently:

> "The problem of our generation, put very broadly, is how to weld together the common interests of all without interfering unduly with the particular ways of each."[56]

Though extremist nationalism troubled him, too, he was not puzzled by the paradox of increasing nationalism in a shrinking world.

Sovereignty as a solution

All his life, Mitrany argued that the fundamental problem of world politics in the twentieth century was that two contrasting historical developments were merging:

> "[I]n its material life, the world has moved far toward a common unity ... but politically our outlook is bound to a mosaic of separate units."[58]

The material unification is explained by the growing division of labour. Historically, this development meant that the self-sufficiency of individuals and local communities gradually eroded. The material interdependence between local communities has been growing steadily through the ages.

The political disintegration of the world into a mosaic of separate national units is explained by another process, the disintegration of the medieval spiritual unity. In 1933, in *The Progress of International Government*, Mitrany wrote about this more extensively than he did after the war. During the Middle Ages, Europe was a cosmopolitan unity, symbolized by pope and emperor; an echo of the West Roman Empire. But that medieval unity was quite arbitrary: "[It was] dispensed from above upon a world that was generally unconscious of it."[58] Medieval cosmopolitism could exist only because daily life was not or hardly affected by it; it was only a varnish.

Mitrany did not explain exactly why cosmopolitism disintegrated, but it boils down to the following. On the one hand, the technological and infra-structural means to exert power improved. Direct interference of the privileged with the remainder of society increased. On the other hand, there was a steady development and emancipation of new sections of the population (starting with the bourgeoisie). The combination of these two developments made it hard for people to keep up their faith in the unity of God's creation if this implied acceptance of the view that the secular authorities should reflect this unity. The cosmopolitan paradigm mainly served the old privileged classes and hampered the development of the rest. Local development therefore implied resistance to central government, and the increased interference in the life of the ordinary people aroused protest which stimulated local development.

The more the central government's claim to exert God's will on earth was felt, the stronger the resistance became. Moreover, the development of the monetary economy also increased the resistance against feudal practices. Both the secular power and its spiritual legitimization were contested.

The Netherlands, for instance, appears to be a product of these developments: the eighty years' war (1568-1648) started as a conservative rebellion of the local aristocracy (Stadhouders) against the centralization policies of Philip II of Spain. Dutch nationalism was born out of this struggle.

According to Mitrany the Peace of Westphalia (1648) finally put an end to the notion of the universal earthly power of pope and emperor. The actual fragmentation of Europe was recognized. In this context, Mitrany referred to Ernest Nys, who recorded that in the sixteenth century Europe consisted of about 2,000 sovereigns. Monaco, Andorra and Luxembourg are the curious remnants of that age.[59]

In 1648 in Europe, the artificial cosmopolitan unity was replaced by the universal recognition of actual fragmentation: the principle of state sovereignty. The pacification of Westphalia was achieved by recognizing European pluralism. This was caused by an increase of interdependence in Europe.

Given the measure of social intertwinement in the seventeenth century, the principle of sovereignty actually brought relief. The states were still independent enough to regulate international affairs sufficiently through regular diplomatic and consular channels. But the process of material unification and the conquest of distance continued. Mitrany made a very important observation, when he concluded that this increasing interdependence was causing further political fragmentation:

> "[D]uring the nineteenth century the opening of new lands, the discovery of new materials, the tremendous development in communications made the peoples of the world truly inter-dependent. While these developments unified the world materially they also divided it politically into a growing number of independent sovereign states, and the working of these two opposite trends complicated as much as it enriched the content of international relations."[60]

This view is so important because it makes clear that two contrasting developments can be explained by one key variable: the measure of interdependence. Unification and fragmentation are both a result of interdependence. This is in conformity with my definition of interdependence as a condition between independent social actors, who wish to preserve their identity, but who are also structurally affected by one another's behaviour.[61]

On the basis of this observation it can be hypothesized that the development from medieval cosmopolitism to the late-twentieth century individualist age, with its emphasis on human rights (individual sovereignty), is inextricably tied to the development from

193

medieval local isolationism and parochial autarchy to the late-twentieth century world politics and world economy. This would mean that the development from cosmopolitism via state sovereignty and national sovereignty to human rights closely relates to the development towards global interdependence.

The "state fixation" of political writers

In 1648 the principle of sovereignty brought peace. It meant a pragmatic solution for the thirty years' war and, more generally, for one and a half century of religious wars. But it also introduced a distinction between domestic and foreign affairs in politics. That distinction was as artificial as medieval cosmopolitism had been: one myth replaced the other. The mere fact that a political compromise was needed to limit the power of the kings and princes is ample proof that sovereignty was based on pure arbitrary criteria.

The artificial distinction between domestic and international politics, however, became a social reality in law and an abstract reality in the minds of the people, including scientists. It got a life of its own, and, according to Mitrany, this is one of the main causes of a general misconception in political science.

> "It is my general thesis ... that the crisis through which our institutions of government are passing springs precisely from that divorce between the two fields of municipal and international political theory and practice."[62]

In 1933 Mitrany made a serious attack on what now is called the state-as-actor paradigm and what he called the "State fixation of political writers".[63] He had a long list of "victims" of this fixation. Gumplowitz, Tarde, Ratzel and Giddings were misled by this fixation when they thought to observe an evolution toward ever greater political units (Morgenthau's supranationalism!). Comte, Le Play and Vaccaro were concentrating on small states. They believed that these were the motors of civilization. Even Cobden was accused of having a state fixation: his cosmopolitan doctrine about free-trade would have been dictated by his concern that the state tried to

194

extend its power over economy. Actually, Mitrany reproached all economic and political theorists, from Machiavelli to Treitschke, for having "all regarded the State as the most fit and proper vessel for the social and political life of a community."[64] He accused them of dogmatic narrow-mindedness.

Because of this state fixation it was impossible to come up with more than only two alternatives in international politics: a world state or a league of states. The negative consequence has been that, since both options were irrealistic, the best thing to do for governments was to strive for superiority or, if necessary, to accept a balance of power. "Most of our present difficulties are caused by that conceptual stagnation."[65]

Since 1933 Mitrany had pleaded for the recognition of a different reality. The entire conception of Foreign Politics, defined as an articulated set of principles which are consistently executed by the Foreign Office during a period of government, had become a complete fiction. Without using the term Mitrany pointed at the existence of transgovernmental relations to prove his point:

> "The strands of modern international relations spread to every nook and cranny of the governmental machine and weave a pattern as complex as that of domestic administration."[66]

In support of his argument Mitrany referred to the work of experts in international law, like Novicov, De Greef, Alfred von Verdross and, from the Austrian School, Hans Kelsen.

> "It has long been argued, especially by Nowicow and De Greef, that the doctrine of sovereignty cannot for a moment be upheld in the face of the actual interdependence of States, of the treaties, conventions, and other acts through which they allow their will and actions to be bound."[67]

On the other hand, Mitrany did not go so far as to deny the actual existence of states in the way this was done in the marxist and anarchist traditions. As has been said before, his attitude towards the state was ambivalent. States have indeed developed their own identities; this also gives them a certain right of "self-expression". Peoples have their own identity, governments have their own identity, countries have their own identity and theoretically all these identities can converge or correspond. In those cases it would be right to speak of a nation-state, defined as a country inhabited by people of one nationality and governed by a native government according to native values and norms.

Of course, little of this is to be found in practice: peoples are divided over several countries, countries are populated with several nationalities and, apart from their countries, governments especially represent themselves. The notion of the nation-state, therefore, rests almost without any exception on an illusion, on political myths.

But political myths are a part of reality, too, as deceit and lies are a part of reality, and this makes nation-states real political entities. History has given peoples, governments and countries their own identities with their own loyalties and group interests. Mitrany recognized these identities, though he was not very happy about them: "we should renounce the pagan worship of political frontiers."[68]

This might be one of the reasons why he called attention to the material, the physical relativity of these frontiers. Here, the concept of interdependence played a major part: the material interdependence between the countries "has grown to the point where it turns their formal separation into a myth".[69]

> "State individualism ... took root in theory and practice long before the change in economic and other conditions created a real interdependence between peoples."[70]

During the nineteenth century, Europe had developed itself into an "intimate organic unity", mainly because of economic developments. That created the fascinating historical paradox which has been discussed before: thanks to the principle of sovereignty, Europe escaped from the artificial cosmopolitism of the Middle Ages, but, because of the continued growth of interdependence, pressures from below forced a functional universalism that confronted the principle of sovereignty straightforwardly.

From "order state" to "service state"

The process of state formation, the integration of smaller sovereign units into larger ones, had an obvious functional aspect. But dynastic and national fragmentation had gone too far to be completely absorbed by state formation. A return to arbitrary forms of centralized secular and spiritual power was impossible. This had, in fact, already been proved by Napoleon, but politicians, up to and including Mussolini and Hitler kept trying nevertheless. It should be recognized, however, that these attempts had a certain logic of their own. The limits of pacification-by-conquest were of course not known beforehand, and within its limits its successes have been quite considerable.[71] The countless sovereign units of the sixteenth century were reduced to about twenty-five in 1815.[72] Since that time integrative and disintegrative tendencies in state formation have seemed to balance one another in Europe.[73] Since 1815, the method of pacification-by-conquest has been slowly replaced by the method of pacification by international organization. Mitrany made this method a general principle and goal.

> "The functional approach ... seeks, by linking authority to a specific activity, to break away from the traditional link between authority and a definite territory (perpetuated by either an association or a federation of nations) [and by] building up authorities which would be comprehensive and solid, in selected fields of common life."[74]

Organization at an international level meant a historic break with territorially based power politics. International organization was not enforced but the result of willing compliance. That principle was known from domestic politics, but because the legitimate use of violence was a government monopoly, this had always been interpreted as a product of the established order. International organization on the basis of willing compliance, however, was not the result of order, but its beginning.

The rise of the welfare state had changed the political agenda. But this development was hampered by the traditional agenda of the

197

"order state". On that agenda military power and prestige, the flags of sovereignty, scored high. The myth of national sovereignty had become dangerous, because it stimulated the wrong reactions to the costly effects of interdependence, making these effects still more costly. (Here the enhanced chance of war is the criterion for "wrong".) Governments reacted with either an ostrich policy of isolationism or a muscle showing policy of imperialism. Mitrany said it thus:

> "Pan-Europa, Imperial Crusade, American isolation — they all and equally are the last ditch of the old doctrine of sovereignty ..."[75]

Here again, he used the concept of interdependence to point to the alternatives that followed from another world view. The frontiers of states as shown on the world map had hardly any relevance to economic and social life. In a negative sense, Mitrany saw this demonstrated in the economic depression of 1929; in a positive sense, he pointed at the conquest of distance during the nineteenth century.[76] According to Mitrany, the social-economic map of the world grew more important by the day.

But because this did not imply the disappearance of the map of states, the notion of interdependence exactly caught the essence of what was going on: more and more the state units in the world related to one another like cities, provinces and parochial units in a country and the material significance of state borders declined, just as town-walls and provincial borders had lost their function. The awareness of this changed structure had to be translated politically, but the traditional agenda of politics hindered this development, especially at the governmental level.

As a result new organizational structures developed; new types of concerted action, mostly outside the official channels of the foreign offices. These new types of cooperation developed only because there was a need for them: they were functional. They reflected the issues of the new political agenda and undermined the traditional issues of national power and prestige. This was one of the reasons for Mitrany to conclude that these functional relations were benificial to peace and formed a working peace system.

Sovereignty bypassed — the threat-system surpassed

Important in functionalism, therefore, are the International Non-Governmental Organizations (INGOs): developing them is structuring the world society. The question how and to what extent the INGO-framework is indeed a "working peace system" has been addressed since the seventies by more scholars than can be mentioned here. Not all conclusions are unanimous but so much is known that it is safe to assume that, once a network of INGOs is formed, it has a de-escalating influence on conflicts between governments.[77]

The most impressive aspect of the development of INGOs is that it has got round the issue of sovereignty. But Mitrany showed himself unable to explain exactly why and how. Again his ambivalence about the future of the state created problems.

On the one hand, he observed that the nation-state was undermined by an INGO-framework and surpassed by a network of IGOs simultaneously. This led him to the following conclusion: *The end of the state drew near*, because of that the international threat-system would disappear and because of that war would vanish.

On the other hand, he observed a metamorphosis of the state: "the State is becoming increasingly a service State — an instrument of life and not merely of order."[78] The welfare state reduced the distinctions between private and public life; economics and politics merged. The authorities were faced with the impossible task to pursue both the interests of power politics and the interests of service politics at the same time. Governments sensible to the welfare demands of the population would more and more come to prefer service politics. This led to Mitrany's second conclusion: *The metamorphosis of the state drew near*, because of that the international threat-system would disappear and because of that war would vanish.

Mitrany shifted randomly from the first to the second thesis. He treated national governments as beacons that had broken from their moorings.

Grass-root functionalism

Because of his emphasis on the development of international functional forms of cooperation, Mitrany's thesis about the mischievous distinction between internal and external politics fell into the background. So much even that John Burton in 1975 criticized the functionalists for their neglect of domestic forms of functionalism. Burton pleaded for the analysis of these relations and their spill-over to the macro-level of the world society.

The underlying thought was that many international conflicts are the result of national conflicts and that, for that reason, the quality of "decision-making *within* the state" is as important as the quality of "decision-making *among* them".[79] According to Burton, this aspect had been neglected: functional cooperation on the international level left the national hotbeds of conflict undisturbed; functionalism was presented too much as a solution of interstate conflict (conflicts between governments), without even noticing the intrastate causes of these conflicts. The other way round, Burton also argued that many existing and successful forms of functional cooperation were neglected because they were characterized as domestic affairs.[80]

It would be wrong, however, to apply this criticism to Mitrany's work. He consistently argued that, though official pacts and treaties between governments have more than just a ceremonial function, they cannot create unity. Treaties can contribute to cooperation and integration, be the crown upon it or clear the way to it, but they cannot enforce actual integration of different groups of people. Therefore, Mitrany took care not to neglect domestic politics. Characteristic is his statement about the American federalization:

> "It has been said that Benjamin Franklin did more toward unifying the country by creating a national postal service than did constitutional rules."[81]

The micro-political example was even taken as a macro-political goal:

"The only sound sense of peaceful change is to do internationally what it does nationally: to make changes of frontiers unnecessary by making frontiers meaningless through the continuous development of common activities and interests across them. ... one might say indeed that the true task of peaceful change is to remove the need and the wish for changes of frontiers."[82]

This might be typical of Mitrany's functionalism, it does not characterize its further development after the war. Here, Burton's criticism is more relevant.

The problem of war is defined the wrong way

During the fifties the interest in supranational tendencies was growing, which affected Mitrany too. Especially in the European context it was hoped that the integration of the nation-states could be achieved through supranational cooperation on specific issues, like coal and steel and, later on, economics in general. But the spill-over effects were disappointing: initially, England refused to join the European integration process, while France, under De Gaulle, withdrew its "force de frappe" from the allied command.

"The states, particularly the France of de Gaulle, seemed impervious to the logic of spill-over and remained as adamantly sovereign as ever."[83]

Functionalism had not developed a time-scale, but it was not expected that it would take to 1992 before the integration process would enter a decisive political phase. Even up to the present (1990) there remains a lot of resistance against and public debate about actual integration.

This development is, of course, extremely crucial and interesting by itself, but with respect to the problem of war and peace in Europe it is only of secondary interest. Though integration has so far proven to be an illusion, the actual abolition of war has not. The West-European countries have done away with the military component of diplomacy in their mutual relations. *Internally,* Western Europe has been close to a true "security community" (a concept developed by Karl Deutsch) for four decades; security, not in terms of an "adequately guarded territory", but in terms of an "undisturbed social life".

Simultaneously, however, the most persistent internal threats to the *military* security are posed by separatist nationalist movements (like the IRA and the ETA), by groups of people who fear that their own specific character and culture will be lost in the endeavour to build superstructures. The idea that the integration of national groups is a precondition for the abolition of war is, therefore, disputable; integration dynamics can themselves be a cause of war.[84] Political differentiation is of course a problem, but is it a key variable in the causes of war? That question has fallen into the background, but will be answered negatively by any true democrat.

Under the influence of attempts to integrate the European nation-states, functionalism came closer and closer to the ideals of Political Realism: the ideal of world government and all its regional variants. The idea to manage interdependence by creating a centralized government in Europe, however, obscures the basic pluralism that developed further because of the same increasing interdependence. There is no use in building a new Rome in Brussels — and probably that is why European integration took this long.

Only in the seventies the non-Realist aspects of functionalism were taken up again. The research of transnationalism, regime-change, issue-structures and complex interdependence, in the way it was initiated in the United States in the early seventies, picked up the ends Mitrany had dropped before the second World War.[85]

8   Saved from oblivion: "new" insights in interdependence[1]

The background and the challenge

In the seventies, interdependence theory was portrayed as a new phase in the study of IR: a moderate version of functionalism, formulated in reaction to the dominant Realist paradigm and also in reaction to the political setbacks which signalled the hegemonic decline of the United States.

The criticism which interdependence theory received to some extent confirmed its originality: it was claimed that interdependence theory was a form of academic modernism.[2] At the same time, however, the criticism denied the originality of interdependence theory. It was claimed that the authors of interdependence were re-inventing the wheel. In defence of Realism it was argued that the new interdependence theories were reflecting the utopian phase in the study of IR. The idea that governments would not consider the use of military force against one another when the peoples which they represented were involved in a complex network of relationships, was interpreted as a repetition of an old, disproven "war-does-not-pay" theory.[3]

Interdependence theory was criticized for being outdated and for being modernistic at the same time. This may seem a strange combination, but in a sense both criticisms were right. Interdependence theory has a long tradition, but the contemporary writers about it seemed not to be aware of this or not to see the need for considering it.

The challenge, therefore, was, first of all, to trace this tradition and take it seriously. This would answer the criticism that interdependence theory is mere modernism. Next, the tradition of interdependence theory should be evaluated to find out to what extent the other type of criticism holds true. For the critical comparisons with pre-war literature have so far not been based on a profound analysis of this literature but on the assumption that the political science of the interbellum has been correctly identified as the utopian phase of the discipline. Neither the critics nor the authors of interdependence theory have worried much about the actual content of the presumed idealism or the kind of observations about interdependence that lay at its basis.[4]

The reasons for this neglect may vary individually, but some general aspects are involved, too. First of all, most of the scientists that started to write about interdependence in the seventies belonged to a generation that had been educated in the study of IR during its postwar phase, which was dominated by the Realist paradigm on the one hand, and by sociology on the other. Due to the sociological approach to IR less value was attributed to traditional forms of theorizing in general and, as a result of the victory of Realism over pre-war Idealism, the value given to the first fifty years of political science diminished likewise.

Secondly, in 1945 the world entered the nuclear age. Especially the nuclear weapons had a strong effect on people's imagination, and, worldwide, people started to argue that the pragmatic logic of waging war had lost its ground. The traditional logic concerning national security interests was even turned upside down when it was realized that national security required high-tech development on the part of the enemy. An example of this was the delivery of the PAL-system by the Kennedy Administration to the Soviet-Union. This electronic system could seal nuclear weapons, thus preventing the Soviets from launching through a technical mistake or the military from launching an attack without political approval.[5] To reduce the risk of mutual assured destruction, the enemies decided to install a "hotline" to better understand one another. Step by step it was recognized that the "ultima ratio" of good statesmanship was to strive for détente or peaceful coexistence. This revolutionized political thinking so fundamentally that there seemed few reasons left to study the interbellum period except for the sake of doing historical research.

A third reason, why attention for pre-war literature slipped, concerned the fundamentally changed structure in Europe after the second World War. In so far as the Pluralist tradition was picked up again it concentrated on the Western European prospects of integration. The end of the nation-state seemed to be close. Europe was divided into two blocs and each of these blocs, especially the western one, might integrate into a security community. Europe, bi-polarity and the Cold War provided a new research agenda, and, apparently, E.H. Carr's *The Twenty Year's Crisis, 1919-1939* provided the student of IR with a sufficient background to the politics of the interbellum period.[6]

A fourth reason for the neglect of the past concerned the authors of interdependence only: when interdependence theory reappeared on the scene, this had little to do with normative considerations about peace or with the kind of prescriptive idealism that had been characteristic for political science during the interbellum. On the contrary, the concept re-entered political science in the 1970s in order to express the need to change the dominant concepts of the basic forces, relations and actors in world politics. This need was not provoked by idealism, but by the experience that the state-centric theories of power-politics had become too simplistic to be of assistance in understanding the complexity of the contemporary world. Interdependence was used essentially as a descriptive concept.

In general, interdependence was used to point out the irrelevance or relativity of demarcations that were accepted as more or less absolute. Relevant for the study of IR were the following:

First of all, interdependence performed an eye-opening function in regard to the decline of the political relevance of territorial state borders. States were no longer the closed entities they were once perceived to be. This was expressed in the "global village" studies, the Reports to the "Club of Rome", and became evident through ecological and economic problems. Economic imperialism as a substitute for traditional colonialism on the one hand, and economic integration on the other, showed the declining role of state borders. Transgovernmental relations, international regimes and international organizations were playing their own roles within the "autonomous" domestic policy-making process, also outside the economic realm.

Moreover, the issues had changed. The demands of the welfare-state had, through the years, captured a dominant position on the foreign policy agenda. This even held true for countries with a relatively high autarchic potential (such as the United States and the Soviet-Union). One result of this development has been that the presumed primacy of military security issues ("high" politics) over economic welfare issues ("low" politics) have became empirically untenable, or at least dubious.

Also the continuous technological developments that led to an ever further "shrinking world" raised a lot of new issues on the foreign policy agenda; the crises they provoked could not be managed on a domestic level. In the military realm, the realm of communication, culture and science, in the economic realm, and in the realm of environmental decline and climate change, the word interdependence was used to express the *community of fate* which had come into being. Serious government could no longer afford to neglect policies made at the other end of the globe, as in previous centuries it could not neglect the social developments in neighbouring countries or cities. The natural, geographical frontiers of human societies were in space, not on earth. In this respect, the distinction between domestic and foreign issues had become blurred. Put differently: in many respects the *world society* had replaced the *nation-state* as the macro-dimension of political analysis (just as the tribe, the family or the city had lost that position in the past).

Fourthly, the word interdependence was used to describe the inversion of power-relations. This was stimulated by the Vietnam War, as well as the breakdown of the Bretton Woods system, the oil-crises and, later, the debt-crises. In this respect interdependence theory was a reaction to the decline of American hegemony. By conceiving dominance and dependence as the net result of an interdependent relationship, the net dependent actor might discover a certain margin for manipulation, as the net dominant actor might discover specific sensitivities or even vulnerabilities beyond its control. Both might discover that complete independence, however, is unattainable. It is in this realm that the relevance for North-South relations was most obvious.

In short, the concept of interdependence worked as an eye-opener in laying bare the anomalies inherent in the dominant traditional theories on international relations. The concept of interdependence re-entered political analysis in the first place to improve the diagnosis of the present world.

However, the way in which a problem is analysed greatly affects the conception of its solution. A change in the "diagnosis" greatly influences the strategies for change, the "therapies" (compare the difference between regular medicine and homoeopathy). Consequently, the concept of interdependence got more than just an explanatory function. In the words of Ernst Haas:

> "Complexity and interdependence are concepts designed to 'catch' the logic underlying links. Whatever we mean by interdependence is used to describe what the whole *is*, what the whole *ought to be*, and what the whole will *become*."[7]

Normative ends and expectations about the influence of increasing interdependence on the chances of war also re-entered the discussion. Here, in defence of the conventional "therapies", the criticism that referred to pre-war Idealism made sense. And here, in search of better "therapies" than the conventional ones, the challenge to analyse this pre-war Idealism makes sense, too. The challenge was, therefore, to separate the wheat from the chaff and to save from oblivion those aspects of fifty years of political science that were still relevant.

The chaff: a liberal-christian, eurocentric paradigm

A few things are characteristic for all the authors discussed in this volume. Their work displays the general characteristics of the pre-war period of political science. Muir, Merriam, Delaisi, Mitrany and Angell shared a number of values which reflect the idealist spirit of the age.

In the first place, they shared a faith in the ultimate progress of humanity. This faith was based on a spiral or even a linear conception of history. That conception was Eurocentric: history started in Europe, either with the Ancient Greeks or with Medieval feudalism. (Though Merriam was American, his historical awareness was likewise Eurocentric. His outlook on contemporary politics, however, was American.) This world view made them latently idealistic: the ultimate progress of humanity implied that mankind was inherently good; sooner or later eternal peace on earth would be a fact. History had a purpose and an end.

The progress of humanity was interpreted in the terms of classic liberalism. (Though Delaisi was a syndicalist, he shared this liberal axiom, too.) They observed the progress of civilization in economic growth, expansionism and the missionary spirit. Western values were the best on earth and should "thus" be spread. In short, all the authors fall within a *liberal-christian, eurocentric paradigm*.[8]

This paradigm is one of the keys to understand the normative considerations of the authors and the contradictions within their points of view. Nationalism, for instance, was disproved of when it led to fragmentation, while it was valued positively when it united people into larger political organizations. More consistent was the rejection of protectionism, on the ground that it hampered the "natural" growth of economies.

The christian aspects of this paradigm worked in two directions. On the one hand, they were the origin of idealism: the unshaken faith that humanity will progress. On the other hand, this expectation was tempered by the constant threat of an Armageddon. Christian culture consists of both a linear and a cyclical conception of history. Societies can drop down the ladder of civilization; the turmoil of barbarism can return, but, when one is doing the right works, paradise can be reached. This constant conflict between fatalism and idealism resulted in a practical attitude to life which should not be called naïve. When Mitrany, Angell, Merriam, Delaisi and Muir put their trust in the League of Nations, for instance, this did not merely demonstrate their idealism but also their cynicism about what might happen without a global approach to politics.

Intrinsic confrontations within this paradigm are also present with respect to development issues. Obviously, European and white American literature in these days was weak on what nowadays is known as a North-South perspective. Decolonization was not yet the issue it became after the second World War.

The christian-eurocentric contribution was that colonies should be Westernized, because the "barbarians" would eventually find out that this was exactly what they wanted themselves (and as long as they did not find out, this proved they were still barbarians). The liberal-economic contribution was that nationalism in the colonies was a worrying development, because this might lead to an artificial fragmentation of the world economy. The christian-liberal contribution, on the other hand, also implied that individual development was seen as important, schooling was seen as essential and that slavery was regarded as inhumane.

Relevant to the issue of development was Angell's remark that in human relations the *quality* of the mutually performed service is of great importance. Simple forms of service, requiring unskilled labour, can be asked from people by the mere use of force, while for services that can only be performed by well-trained specialists in a specific field subtler methods, or, in Merriam's terminology, more civilized methods are required. In other words, development and specialization weaken the possibility of using force effectively. The quality of mutually performed services has an influence on the likelihood of violence.

A link to the development issues can also be found in Ramsay Muir's work, when he claimed that the maldistribution of welfare would lead to social revolutions that, because of the global systemic interdependence, would spread worldwide, affecting the old world as well.

On an abstract level of reasoning, thoughts like this are a first step towards the construction of a development theory of interdependence. But the specific statements about the countries of the South belong to the chaff.[9]

Change has become a constant in the 20th century

Angell, Muir, Delaisi, Merriam and Mitrany agreed with one another on several points. In the first place they agreed on the character of the main problems in politics. They observed that on the one hand the world had changed fundamentally by becoming interdependent (in its systemic sense), while on the other hand the development of instruments to control social processes had not kept pace with these changes. The institutions to coordinate social processes were still based on the requirements of a past reality. They observed a discrepancy between the political institutions of society and the political needs of society. The organizational structures had to be adapted in order to prevent the political agenda from continuously being overtaken by the events. Moreover, the political institutions hampered social developments and thus caused more political problems than they solved.

This diagnoses, that the world has fundamentally changed over the past decades while governmental mechanisms have remained unaltered, is typical of all interdependence literature throughout the twentieth century. (Examples are given in chapter 2.) What does it mean?

Perhaps it reflects the human tendency to exaggerate the importance of one's own life span: it may be hard to distinguish between events we experience as dramatic and events that are dramatic for the course of history. Perhaps it reflects political rhetorics: when someone desires a change in government, it is useful to call that government disfunctional and outdated. But, apart from these two aspects, the returning observation that the world had changed fundamentally over the last decades also points at a more important aspect of modern life, that is, the fact that rapid change has become characteristic for this era.

Social life in the twentieth century is much more dynamic than it was in the heyday of the agricultural civilization. This was demonstrated by Francis Delaisi in particular. In agricultural societies, the material conditions of life were more or less constant: grandparents taught their grandchildren how to work the land, how to sell its products, how to feed and dress their families, and how to think about the world around them. It was sensible for the grandchildren to act correspondingly. In the era of global interdependence, however, material conditions change faster than generations. Ramsay Muir was impressed by the invention of the wireless and the aeroplane in the same way his grandchildren (if he has any) may be impressed by the telefax and the space shuttle. The grandparents' traditional wisdom about practical matters has in general become almost completely useless for the next generation. This was true for Muir's generation, as it is true for his grandchildren's generation. Rapid change in the realm of technology affects the structure of society, and a rapid innovation of technology is characteristic for the present age.

What this exactly means for conventional wisdom about *non-material* human affairs is difficult to say, because there is no linear causal relation between social change and cognitive change. But it does mean that people are right when they claim that the structure of political organization ought to be dynamic. The best attempt to incorporate this dynamics in political theory has been Mitrany's theory of functionalism. Functionalism has taught us that the technical imperative should be the decisive factor in social organization.

Understanding the continuity of change, requires a historical context. The authors discussed in this volume made similar analyses of the origins of the change in structure. European expansionism, starting in the sixteenth century, the era of discoveries, together with the increase of specialization and the decrease of self-sufficiency and autarchy of individuals and local communities, and accelerated by the Industrial Revolution of the late eighteenth and early nineteenth century, resulted in a "conquest of distance" that made all peoples of the world dependent on one another.

This global interdependence meant that decisions made in one part of the world could influence politics in remote other parts and that events taking place in remote places could be experienced as

211

if they were happening in a neighbour country.[10] Specialization and industrialization made the European countries dependent on resources from all around the world and the peoples in what were called colonies were dependent on policies that were decided on in countries they had never heard of by people they did not know.

When did global interdependence become an inescapable fact of life? The authors agreed that the final proof of global interdependence was given by the first World War. Ramsay Muir regarded this war as the first event in human history that was worldwide in scope and that it was the first event that was recognized as such. Proof of this recognition was given by the foundation of the League of Nations, the first attempt in human history to deal with world politics. The impact of 1914-1919 also stimulated the institutionalization of political science: scientists wanted to know why they had been blind to developments that were so obvious in retrospect — a scientific study of the causes of war and the conditions for peace was necessary. For it began to be realized that war was becoming a menace to society.[11]

The neglect of global interdependence and its results

Though the conquest of distance is an impressive process, as the first man on the moon was an impressive event, its result, global systemic interdependence, is not necessarily a praiseworthy affair. The observation that the peoples of the world have become interdependent is first of all an observation about the macro dimension of politics. The concept of global interdependence, in the way the authors used it to describe the conditions of world politics, says something about the geographical scale on which politics should be analyzed to understand the dynamics of political behaviour. All geographical boundaries have lost their absolute character, in the sense that they are no longer able to guarantee absolute political independence or isolation. Geographical boundaries have lost their traditional political meaning, because local events, decisions, policies or developments (at home or abroad) can have worldwide consequences.

This observation about global interdependence refers to the sys-

212

temic type: two or more actors are structurally affected by one another because they are part of the same system. The fate of every actor in the system is linked to the fate of the system as a whole and through that to all individual behaviour that might or actually does affect the whole.

According to the five authors, the neglect of these conditions has negative consequences. If global interdependence was recognized as such and correctly understood, its political impact would be positive: people would profit from the opportunity to accumulate knowledge, power, wealth and welfare on an unprecedented scale, while being aware of the risks involved. But when global inter-dependence is not recognized or not fully understood its political impact will be negative. It will cause all kinds of unwanted and unforeseen conflicts. When you don't see a wall, you may run into it. But, though the wall forms the problem, it is failing to perceive it that causes the collision.

These normative considerations are at the heart of all pre-war literature on interdependence. Norman Angell frequently used the metaphor that the traffic in international relations had increased, while the rules of the road remained the same. The obvious result is an increase of accidents and death rates; an increase of international conflict. Ramsay Muir pointed at the "perils of interdependence"; the increased risks of war and economic instability caused by blind nationalism, blind protectionism and an unnecessary mal-distribution of welfare. These perils would flourish when people neglected or belittled the actual unification of the world into one single political system, he argued. Delaisi stressed the need to adjust the existing political myths to the realities of global economic interdependence. Merriam addressed the problem that the build-up of a world order was hardly possible as long as the cobweb nature of international relations was not correctly understood; when the decisive unit of political aggregation was not clearly identified. Mitrany stated that the "state fixation" of political writers had provoked the crisis through which the institutions of government were passing during the 1920s and 1930s. Systemic interdependence may seem to cause problems in case people are blind to it, the real cause is that they are blind. "Naughty table", said the little child after it had bumped its head.

213

This leads to an important thesis in respect to the question how global interdependence relates to the chances of war. Unwanted and unforeseen wars can be the result of increased systemic interdependence but they are caused by the failure to perceive this systemic interdependence. Popularly formulated: interdependence means trouble but only as long as it is neglected. In support of this thesis one could mention the first World War: its escalation was unforeseen and probably unwanted by all who were affected by it. The mere fact that a conflict in the Balkans could take on global proportions simply was not realized. Therefore no attempts were made or could have been made in advance to avoid such an escalation.

Learning interdependence

"Interdependence means trouble but only when it is neglected." This thesis places the cognitive dimension of interdependence in the heart of the analysis. To recall chapter 2: the two most important dimensions of interdependence are the cognitive dimension and the structural dimension. The structural dimension of interdependence refers to specific relational conditions among actors; the cognitive dimension refers to the awareness of these conditions.

Apart from the theoretical insights they developed, the experiences of the authors show the importance of the cognitive factor. It is illuminating, for instance, to compare in how far they expected a world war. Norman Angell predicted war, Francis Delaisi expected war, Merriam ignored the problem, Muir and Mitrany were taken by surprise.

Merriam lived in the United States and was occupied too much with Chicago-politics to worry much about Europe. He, like many of his contemporaries, considered the war an exclusively European problem. That America would involve itself in this war seemed unthinkable; the possibility of worldwide escalation did not come to his mind. Yet, a few years later he was sent to Italy as a Captain in the Signal Corps.

Delaisi was a syndicalist and as such convinced of the dominance of economics over politics. This made him see that Britain was losing its hegemonic position in the world. In that process war was likely. But he predicted the wrong war: he thought the war would essentially be one between England and Germany, initiated by England in order to destroy the economic competitive power of the Germans. He even thought that the destruction of German industrial power would indeed be to the advantage of England (especially when France did the fighting). Only after the war did he develop an understanding of the reciprocity of economic processes. This changed his view about the dominance of economics over politics: politics was not dominated by economics but by myths and the most dangerous aspect of contemporary politics was that people tried to adapt the economic reality to these myths.

In chapter 4, the lifes of Angell and Muir have been compared to illustrate the influence of experience on world views. Angell received his education in England, France and Switzerland, emigrated to the USA when he was seventeen and returned to Paris in 1897, to work as a journalist. From his youth onwards, Angell had been a world citizen. He had actually experienced that a world society existed and this made him aware of the illusions (Delaisi spoke of myths) that dominated political thinking. It enabled him to see that these illusions made war unavoidable. Muir, who typified his own life as the typical story of a middle class man, however, was completely surprised by the first World War. The question how he, a professor in modern history, could have been so blind to developments that were so obvious in retrospect, became a major concern in his work. Muir, like Angell, saw the core of the problem in a misunderstanding of the conditions to which policies are subjected, but the learning processes involved differed essentially.

These experiences point at one of most important unsolved controversies concerning the thesis that interstate violence is not employed in situations of complex interdependence. The first World War showed that the structural conditions of interdependence are by themself not enough to prevent governments from using military force for political reasons, a certain measure of "awareness" has to be present as well. Apparently, the presence of interdependence is not obvious enough by itself to make people

215

aware of it. When a professor in modern history failed to notice "global interdependence", what reason is there to expect that a policy of increasing interdependence will bring people closer to one another?

To put it differently: how long does it take before the cognitive dimension of interdependence emerges from the structural dimension? How many times do you have to run into a wall before you realize that it is there? How long can you go on blaming the wall for the collisions? When do you start to reconsider your own perception? Because mere facts do not shape political conduct, the (mis)perception of facts is an integrated part of reality.

If there is indeed a causal relationship between levels of interdependence and the chances of war, this relationship is complicated by a process of social learning and experience. Social learning starts with becoming aware of interdependence. This process means that social pressures against the use of violence will increase when interdependence increases, and that, if violence is applied after all, the conclusion (the "lesson") will be that it resulted in a lot of unforeseen and unwanted damage. Social learning here consists of a circular process of structural conditions, interpretations of these conditions and normative considerations about them.

But what lessons should be drawn from what experience? What structural conditions should lead to what kind of normative considerations? No absolute answers exist here, but the relation between the growth of structural interdependence and the development of cognitive interdependence can be studied in its historical context.

When 1914-1919 is taken as the beginning of the era of global interdependence, this means that the analysis should include the entire twentieth century. That century can be characterized by the struggle to come to terms with the dynamics of world politics (whereby world politics is defined as the global dimension of local challenges and the local dimension of global challenges). This struggle is the process of social learning referred to above.

Awareness is crucial but not enough

That the present global challenges should be analysed within a continuum running from 1919 up to the present does not apply to concrete issues like problems with nuclear waste or acid rain, which are new indeed, but it does apply to their general political dimension, to the general problems of management and control. For instance, the question how to deal with the economic world crisis of 1929 is not essentially different from the question how to deal with the debt crisis of the early eighties. These are global problems with local dimensions and the problem is how to come to terms with both aspects at the same time. Another example would be to link the experience with a programme like the New Deal to the experiment with perestroika. Both programmes tried and try to address several social problems simultaneously, on a continental scale, while seeking at the same time to create a working-balance between local governmental tasks and continental governmental tasks. The New Deal should not merely be studied for its historical value but because it sheds light on the contemporary interplay between the macro and micro dimensions of political issues. Within such an historical perspective, one can observe many different reactions to the problems posed by global systemic interdependence.

The first aspect of social learning concerns the process of becoming aware of global systemic interdependence. According to the authors discussed the main problem was the neglect of interdependence. This is certainly an important problem. When actors are not aware of interdependent relations, or when they neglect and belittle their importance, they will occasionally be confronted with unexpected crises. In reaction to these, isolationist or imperialist tendencies are very likely to occur, because, in crises, one will be especially aware of one's own dependence. Only the costs of dependence will be apparent and the primary reaction will be to end the dependence. Crises, furthermore, require immediate action and this stimulates short-track solutions that may make new crises unavoidable in the longer run.

To Angell, for instance, it was quite clear that the existence of economic and ideological interdependence was not enough by itself; it had to be recognized. As long as governments and their voters stuck to ethnocentric policies, stressing their independence and sovereignty, the idea that war could be abolished was a great illusion. As has been concluded before, the "material" conditions of interdependence do not necessarily make for peace by themselves. The "immaterial" conditions must be present as well.

But this psychological factor involves more than the awareness of interdependence as such. According to Angell and his contemporaries the main problem lay in the misunderstanding of reality. A proper analysis, leading to the awareness of mutual dependence in economic, political and military affairs, would automatically imply the acceptance of a democratic attitude toward the management of interdependence. This, though, is a bit too simple. Awareness of the reciprocity in political behaviour does, of course, strongly strengthen the structural constraints on the use of military force, and a proper understanding of politics is, of course, the best protection against unwanted violence, but violence may be wanted anyway and the reciprocity costs might be judged an acceptable price.

When global interdependence is recognized, this merely means that the price of an ethnocentric policy is better understood in advance. Whether this price will be a decisive constraint on adventurous or isolationist policies does not only depend on the existing structure, but also on the presence of alternative policies, and the price of these.

This leads to the second step in the process of social learning. How to manage interdependence when one is aware of it? Here, one leaves the descriptive level and enters the prescriptive one.

This shift has consequences for how interdependence is to be understood. In chapter 1 a typology of interdependence has been given: the structural dimension of interdependence consists of systemic, functionalist and integrative interdependence, and these types can be characterized by confrontational and constructional qualities. At the descriptive level this typology is meant to analyse existing (or past) social structures. When an appropriate operationalization is found, the various levels and measures of interdependence can be identified. The different types of inter-dependence are structural proporties and they are meant to be neutral in a normative sense, meaning that they can be observed.

When the analysis shifts to the prescriptive level, this neutrality is lost. Now, the different types of interdependence are political properties. They are not observed but imagined. Functionalist and integrative interdependence are strategies that deal with the exist-ing structure of interdependence. They are policy options that should be compared to other options that try to avert the problems with the existing levels of interdependence.[12]

But when functionalist and integrative interdependence have actually been applied as strategies for the management of systemic interdependence, these newly created types of interdependence will then be part of tomorrow's structural conditions and therefore should be analyzed again from a politically neutral point of view. In other words, the optional interdependence of today is the "natural" interdependence of tomorrow. This "natural" inter-dependence (which is not nature-given, but a product of civiliza-tion) presents itself as a given, the outcome of an historical process. To give an example: in 1949, the plan to create the North Atlantic Treaty Organization (NATO) was a form of optional interdepen-dence; governments could decide to do so or not. More than fourty years later, in 1990, NATO has since long become a structural condition: a form of functionalist political interdependence and of integrative military interdependence.

Policies of interdependence

A problem that affects all scenarios that are meant to cope with global interdependence is that they do not solve the discrepancy between parochialism and globalism. Somehow both interests have to be served simultaneously, but the "somehow" has not yet been discovered.

World history in the twentieth century seems to be one big struggle with this rift. Isolationism or imperialism, aloofness or world government and world federalism, protectionism or free trade, regional integration or containment and decolonization; all these policies can be seen as attempts to deal with either global interdependence or local independence.

The problem is that these policy options are based either on the world as a whole (a global perspective) or on topographic detail (a local perspective). Either the world is balkanized politically, territorially, economically and culturally — hampering the development of world order — or it is forced into artificial superstructures, hampering the development of local political, economic and cultural identities.

Is it possible to analyse and explain both the micro and the macro level of social developments from one perspective? Is it possible to develop a theory of world politics that can be used like a satellite with a zoom lens, analyzing both the globe and the topographic map from one perspective? The early interdependence theories provide some (though certainly not all) clues.

The authors dealt with in this volume formulated policies of interdependence that were directed against the conventional knowledge of statecraft.

As was argued by Delaisi in particular, the governmental wisdom was based on the logic that belonged to a completely different social structure, especially in the economic sphere. Up to the Industrial Revolution, political structures changed more frequently than economic ones and thus politics adapted more or less automatically to the economic changes. After the Industrial Revolution this order was reversed. In the nineteenth and early twentieth century the economic foundations of society changed faster than the political structures, Delaisi argued. Politics remained state-centric and ethno-centric, despite the emergence of a world economy. Within the logic of state-centrism, colonialism, imperialism and protectionism were the logical answers to the awareness of global interdependence: "conquer every territory you need for production and sales, and protect yourself against the rest of the world."

How this conventional wisdom could be tackled and replaced was the main concern of the five authors. Angell put his trust in "reason". He continually explained the logic of "democratic internationalism" and the resulting need for a "protective union of the democracies". This internationalism had to be based on "collective security" and on the principle that physical power should not be allowed to be the final judge in international relations. Because he put his trust in reason, his main problem was "the public mind", the quality of public opinion and, related to it, the quality of the politicians and the newspapers.[13]

Charles Merriam likewise emphasized "reason" when it came to the question how to achieve world order. He looked at the cobweb image of IR and the multiplicity of political actors and concluded that, given this pluralism, the only world order to be acceptable to all its participants would be a democratic one, because democratic rule was the only system that was based on pluralism and that was meant to express it. How to get there remained unclear. Merriam did not share Angell's concern about its effectuation. Apparently, pluralism would enforce its own emergence.

Ramsay Muir was not very articulate about policies of interdependence either. He directed his criticism mainly against the concept of state sovereignty, which in his opinion was being interpreted too strictly. He argued that sovereignty rights could be pooled or divided among cooperating governments, without falling into anarchy or chaos; and he pointed to the federal structure of the USA and the British Commonwealth as examples of these possibilities. Especially within well-functioning democracies state-sovereignty was a myth, he argued, because no single political actor possessed it; it was shared. Yet, it did not cause chaos. He did not, however, have a clear strategy as to how to limit state-sovereignty or the claims for it. He relied on the learning process: the awareness and experience of the "perils of interdependence" would change perceptions and political practice.

Francis Delaisi was more outspoken on strategies. He formulated a true policy of functionalist interdependence when he argued in favour of the deliberate propagation of "international professional organizations". Not just the workers or the elites of financiers should organize themselves internationally, but every profession should do so. These networks would bring about the full realization of global interdependence. The members would develop an awareness of both their local interests and the international ones and, in case of friction, this would create an equilibrium, a balance, between both types of interests.

This is an important key to bridging the gap between parochialism and globalism. When individuals experience a double perspective, this might create the kind of "reason" Angell, Merriam and Muir were waiting for. But, again, this is a solution that, in the first place, only ends the unawareness of global interdependence. Once this unawareness has gone, there is no reason to expect that the friction between local and global interests will automatically result in an equilibrium. The only, though not unimportant, gain would be that the price for serving either one of the interests would be better known in advance.

On a more general level, David Mitrany took up this principle and developed it into his theory of functionalism. Beyond doubt this is the best worked out strategy of the period (see chapter 7 for its details). Yet, it has fallen victim to a one-sided interpretation, also by Mitrany himself. In the sixties, functionalism was not seen as a goal as such, but as a strategy for the integration of nation-states. The whole idea of state-integration, however, is a product of state-centric thinking; it seeks a solution of interstate conflict by ending interstate relations. It seeks a solution for warfare by blowing up the scale of the territory in which the power of a single government can be effected. In other words: functionalism has mainly been worked out in the service of macro-interests; the micro-interests have been neglected. Therefore, Mitrany's functionalism, as it became known after 1945, turned out a failure.

When, however, functionalism is not presented as an instrument of integration, but as an end in itself, it provides a useful answer to the friction between micro and macro interests. Functionalism is an approach to deal with specific, tangible issues. To the extent that the characteristics of these issues have transnational aspects, the approach will require international organization (with or without the participation of governmental departments). To the extent that the characteristics are local, the approach will be local.

Why this combination of respect for local and global interests at one and the same time is so crucial, is demonstrated by the view on interdependence that Mitrany developed in the early thirties.

From cosmopolitism to individualism and from parochial autarchy to world economy: two sides of the same coin

Mitrany argued that the increase of interdependence led to two contrasting developments: on the one hand it led to an increased collectivization, and on the other hand to an increased individualization.

This thesis was based on his observation that, historically speaking, the principle of sovereignty had been a positive reaction to the slow increase of social-economic interdependence in Europe. At first sight this looked contradictory (and many scholars treat it as such): during the Middle Ages, Europe was a cosmopolitan unity — why did this unity disintegrate the moment the material interconnectedness among the local communities of Europe increased? If the growth of interdependence stimulated political integration, as was believed after the second World War, the spiritual unity of Europe should have been strengthened by the improved infrastructure and the improved means of communication. Why did the opposite happen?

According to Mitrany, the medieval political-religious myth of cosmopolitism was accepted by the people because the absolute sovereign power that was ascribed to pope or emperor hardly affected daily life. Moreover, this myth fulfilled a positive psychological function, as had been explained by Muir: pope or emperor were seen as vicegerents of God on earth, not because they were able to exercise supreme power, but because there *must* be a vicegerent of God on earth.

But, with the ongoing technological and infra-structural developments, the means to interfere and the ability to exercise power increased. This aroused protest. The actual fragmentation of the rural society became apparent and people started to fight for their independence. According to Mitrany, the peace of Westphalia (1648) meant the recognition of the actual fragmentation of Europe. This recognition was embodied in the principle of sovereignty and it was the result of a process of growing interdependence. The closer people come to one another, the harder they have to reinforce their own identity if they are not to be enslaved.

In the European context this gives rise to the hypothesis that the

223

development from medieval cosmopolitism to the late-twentieth century individualist age, with its emphasis on human rights (the sovereignty of the individual), is inextricably tied to the development from medieval local isolationism and parochial autarchy to the late-twentieth century world society, characterized by economic and political interdependence.

This implies that individual and national development are hampered by seeking isolation, parochial autarchy and stressing absolute national sovereignty (the Albanian model). Social self-development, in the Western meaning of the word, requires specialization of specific skills. Specialization, however, is a typical example of one actor becoming dependent on other actors; it is the basis of constructional interdependence.

Constructional interdependence changes the nature of power

Politics is a struggle for power. This seems to be a law of nature. But it is not a law in the sense of physical science, like Newton's law of gravity. The nature of power is culture-bound. Political leadership in a feudal society, for instance, requires other qualities than the ones needed in a high-tech society. When a king in an agrarian society conquered or plundered his neighbour's land, he thereby immediately increased his power. But how to conquer the present economic wealth of e.g. Japan? Whatever the answer, it is certainly not by conquering or plundering the Japanese Isles and enslaving the population to make them work for the invader the way they now work for themselves.

This, in fact, was the main thesis of Norman Angell in 1909, when he published *Europe's Optical Illusion*. The international economic order had changed in such a way that the relationship between the conquest of a piece of land and the economic surplus value of this new property had become less direct than in pre-industrial times. The wealth of a modern economy cannot be conquered, it can only be destroyed. In 1911 Delaisi expected that destruction would indeed be the only goal of war. Angell was blind to that motive, but it does not alter his message that he wanted people and politicians to be a bit more explicit about what can and what cannot be achieved by use of military means.

Apparently, power in 1990 is not the same thing as power in 990 and, probably, not the same thing as power in 2990. But how does it change and why?

According to Merriam, power is composed of force, obedience, persuasion and participation. Though power is always based on a combination of these factors, their mutual weight can differ. Of special interest is the friction between the input of force and the input of participation in the formation of power. For, the relation between force and participation is not complementary but contradictory. When force, violence, is needed to enforce obedience or to support persuasion, the community spirit, the wish to participate, is put under pressure. Drill and discipline take the place of education and schooling; fear and servility take the place of appreciation and esteem; apathy and resignation take the place of creativity and spontaneity. Too much force destroys the participatory nature of power and, inversely, participation, willing compliance makes the use of force futile.

In chapter 1 it has been argued that there are two major qualifications of interdependence: confrontational interdependence and constructional interdependence. Constructional interdependence has been described as a resource of power; there is a mutually perceived necessity of cooperation because two can achieve more than one. Constructional interdependence is a result of specialization and development. The participatory nature of power, as defined by Merriam, seems to be synonymous with constructional interdependence.

Merriam's thesis is that simple forms of social organization can almost do without the fourth pillar of power, while complicated forms of social organization rest on it almost completely. This thesis is consistent with the previous one, which said that individualism is a result of growing interdependence. Individualized societies are complex by definition, and their organization has to rest mainly on the power-pillar of participation. This means that though politics remains a struggle for power, the objects of the struggle have changed fundamentally. The use of force, political violence, remains an aspect of power but its share in the formation of political power declines as constructional forms of interdependence increase.

This, again, was also stated by Norman Angell when he claimed that our physical power over someone is limited by the degree to which we are really dependent on that person. When the service that is demanded from someone requires knowledge, tools and freedom of movement, the exercise of force will contribute little to the correct execution of the service.

What about the future?

These insights from the first fifty years of interdependence theory do not provide a complete answer to the main questions that inspired this study. They do not provide an ultimate answer to the question whether increasing interdependence eliminates the military component from diplomacy, and, if it does, how long it takes before it does. They do not provide an ultimate solution to the discrepancy between parochialism and globalism; they do not provide an operationalization of interdependence that can be measured statistically. But they do give partial answers.

a) the existence of a tradition: The tradition of interdependence literature has been taken seriously and its existence alone proves that it is not a passing fashion but has been a returning issue throughout the twentieth century. This volume reviews the work of Angell, Muir, Delaisi, Merriam and Mitrany, but it does not cover the tradition of the first half of this century entirely. The economist Eugene Staley and the sociologist Norbert Elias for instance deserve separate treatment. Elias, because he, like Mitrany, wrote about interdependence as a social force that worked towards unification and diversification at the same time.[14] Staley, because it was with his work that the empirical approach of interdependence started. He tried to measure the conquest of distance and he used economic data to express the economic involvement of countries in one anothers affairs.[15] Additionally, a review of the work of E.H. Carr from the Pluralist perspective would also contribute to the further development of a theory of interdependence. In *Conditions of Peace*

(1942) Carr wrote about interdependence as an inescapable fact of life and *The New Society* (1951) also contains passages which are typical of a Pluralist paradigm. Alongside these three scientists, there are many scholars who at times used the word interdependence in their works or who described affairs that fall within the definitions of interdependence. It might be worth looking at the early literature about International Law, for instance, in which the discrepancy between national sovereignty and the social need for new "traffic rules" in order to manage the increased number of transnational activities leads to a concrete conflict.[16] It is worth looking at these works, though they are certainly not all equally relevant.

Apart from deepening further the knowledge about the development of interdependence theory in the period 1900-1950, research should, of course, be extended to the second half of the century. Over the last five years, I have come across about 250 publications of which I am sure that they are of primary interest to the study of global interdependence, about 160 publications which appear to be of primary interest but which have to be checked further, and over 200 publications which are of secondary importance, meaning that they refer to theoretical aspects of interdependence occasionally. Though this list is far from complete, it indicates that a survey of the tradition in the period 1950-2000 should be subdivided either by decade, by theme or by selecting "landmarks" in the intellectual history of the development of interdependence theory. Whatever method is chosen, it is worthwhile to try to summarize the scattered knowledge about global interdependence in one comprehensive theory.

b) the value of the tradition: That a tradition of interdependence literature dating back to the beginning of this century exists is obvious, but how to value it? Are the critics right when they disprove of interdependence by pointing to the past? Though no ultimate answers can be given, the early writings about interdependence can be positively linked to contemporary literature in at least the following respects:

• The general world view that emerges from the early writings on interdependence enforces the thesis that the study of IR should focus on transnational relations rather than on interstate relations only. The world is characterized by a constant discrepancy between the political institutions of society and the political needs of society. This discrepancy has been caused by "the conquest of distance" and by the transition from an agricultural civilization to an industrial one. As a result geographical boundaries have lost their traditional political meaning. Rapid change, especially in the technological/infrastructural realm, has become a constant.

• To understand the contemporary political problems, the study of IR should adopt a more historical perspective that goes back to at least the period 1914-1919. This turning-point has not the character of a revolution, but is a pinnacle in an ongoing process that started in sixteenth century Europe. The era of global interdependence started in 1914-1919, because since that period, in the realm of communication, economics and warfare, social behaviour can have a global impact and social actors can also be aware of that possibility. It makes sense to characterize the history of politics from the first World War up to the present as an attempt to come to terms with global systemic interdependence. There are global challenges, and slowly people get to know them.

The history of the twentieth century shows a dramatic sequence of disasters and fruitless attempts to deal with global interdependence within the cognitive frameworks of nineteenth century nationalism. Policies of aloofness and isolationism on the one hand and policies of imperialism and dreams about world government on the other have been the result.

• Parallel to that, however, this history is also characterized by attempts to develop functionalist and integrative answers to global challenges. Here the early ideas about interdependence are most directly related to the question whether war can be abolished (like slavery, the duel or — in many countries — corporal punishment) by a policy of increasing interdependence.

When actors find out, by sound reasoning and bitter experience, that they cannot avoid dealing with one another and cannot end one another's existence, there is a chance that they start to apply an "interdependence calculus" to one another.[17] Motivated by pragmatic considerations, actors may conclude that they need the support of one another to achieve a desired political objective or to solve a social problem that goes beyond their own reach. Uniting for joint action to tackle shared problems is the principle of functionalism. This perceived need of support with respect to a specific issue implies that, at least against *some* actors, the use of military force is not preferred. The tension between "power based on force" and "power based on participation" is temporarily resolved in favour of the latter. People can grow accustomed to that.

Synopsis

1. THE CONCEPT OF INTERDEPENDENCE IN POLITICAL SCIENCE

The main incentive to study interdependence theory is formed by the hypothesis that governments will not use military force toward one another if they and the people they represent are involved in a complex network of interdependent relations. Support for this thesis can be found in West-West and East-West relations. It is challenged, however, by the relations that exist in a North-South context, while the manner in which politicians appeal to inter-dependence at times conceals the traditional, nationalistic and ethnocentric motives behind the foreign policy proposals they make. Apart from the need to analyse these problems concerning the interdependence thesis, another strong incentive to study the subject concerns its descriptive value as a central concept in IR-theory. Its relevance is particularly obvious in respect to the so-called global challenges, which can be summarized under the headings disarmament, development and environmental preserva-tion.

In general, interdependence refers to independent social actors, who wish to preserve their identity, but who are also structurally affected by one another's behaviour.

Interdependence is a structural condition which can be divided into three types: a) *systemic interdependence*; b) *functionalist interdependence*; c) *integrative interdependence*. The first type is primarily explained in terms of system dynamics; the second and third types are primarily explained in terms of the consequences of specific behaviour.

These structural conditions can be operationalized into a three-dimensional concept, which further qualifies the way in which given actors are mutually affected by one another's behaviour. The first dimension concerns the *degree* of mutual influence (the measure of existential value of the interdependence). The second dimension concerns the *character* of the mutual influence (confrontational and constructional aspects). The third dimension concerns the *(a)symmetry* of the mutual influence (the distribution of costs and benefits).

In this study, this definition is taken as a framework within which the different early contributions to the development of a theory of interdependence are placed.

These early contributions should also be related to the three dominant paradigms in contemporary IR-theory: Realism, Pluralism and Structuralism. Interdependence theory fits in the Pluralist paradigm. This means that the basic unit of analysis is the *world society*; the main subject is *world politics*. (World politics should be defined as the global dimension of local issues and the local dimension of global issues.) The normative goal is to develop an interdependence theory with the characteristics of a satellite with a zoom lens: both the globe and the topographic map should be sketched and analysed from one perspective. The present volume contributes, though only moderately, to this end by discussing the ancestors of interdependence theory; thus revealing an intellectual history which is generally neglected in the IR-literature.

231

2. THE ERA OF GLOBAL INTERDEPENDENCE: WHEN DID IT START?

In order to understand the emergence of global interdependence it is necessary the distinguish *structural interdependence* from *cognitive interdependence*. Structural interdependence refers to the conditions as defined in chapter 1. Cognitive interdependence refers to the awareness of these conditions. The cognitive dimension implies that externalities are internalized and politicized. The distinction is important, because it is open to debate to what extent political conduct is shaped by structural conditions or by the perception of these conditions. This problem is not a matter of either/or but concerns the balance between both aspects. The intermediary force may be that of social learning.

The history of the awareness of global interdependence starts at the beginning of the twentieth century. Since then, scientists and politicians discovered and rediscovered the conditions of global interdependence and debated their consequences for politics. The statements about the emergence of global interdependence share four arguments: 1. (descriptive) the world has fundamentally changed over the past decades; 2. (explanatory) the reason for this is that the communities in the world have become increasingly interdependent; 3. (prescriptive) as a result "old", traditional world views should be put aside; 4. (predictive) if not, disasters will occur, some of them on an unprecedented scale.

The observation that the world is at a crucial turning point, is typical of all literature on interdependence. Partly, this may be due to rhetorical motives, partly, it may be the result of a "natural" inclination to experience one's own life-time as a crucial period in human history. But in part it may also point to the fact that rapid change is characteristic for the twentieth century. Change has become a constant.

The origin of the processes leading to the era of global interdependence lies in the European expansionism of the sixteenth century. This process resulted in what nowadays is called the global village or the world society. The Industrial Revolution, that is, the rise of mechanization and of specialization, and the disintegration of self-sufficiency and parochial autarchy, is of major importance for this process.

Critical in this development has been the period 1914-1919. The first World War proved that the world had become the ultimate unit of politics, and the foundation of the League of Nations proved that the establishment of global interdependence was also *realized* worldwide: for the first time in history, humanity tried to devise a governmental mechanism on a global basis. Therefore, *the era of global interdependence started in 1914-1919.*

An important implication of this is that contemporary world politics should be understood as a continuum running from 1919 up to the present. Since 1919 people can be aware of global systemic interdependence and since then political history is about the struggle to come to terms with these conditions, both intellectually and practically. This struggle is characterized by many different types of policy, including isolationism, imperialism, integrationism and functionalism.

By accepting that current global problems are less unique than people generally like to think, we may detect processes of social learning that span several generations. In this context, it is a challenge to examine the extent to which contemporary theories on interdependence can profit from the contributions to this paradigm from 1900-1950.

3. NORMAN ANGELL (1872-1967): ANCESTOR OF INTERDEPENDENCE THEORY

Angell is generally considered to belong to the Idealist School of international relations. He is said to be a utopian because he considered it possible to "abolish" war, because he was an advocate of the League of Nations, because he trusted in the power of education to reform and believed in the ability of economic interdependence to promote conditions of peace. Part of this image also stems from misinterpretations of his work.

233

From the publication of the pamphlet *Europe's Optical Illusion* in 1909 up to his autobiography *After All* in 1951, Angell criticized the "conquest pays" axiom and the "national superiority" axiom. Instead, he argued for "democratic internationalism" and "collective security" based on a proper understanding of self-interest under conditions of economic and political interdependence.

His criticism of the "conquest pays" axiom was based on observations concerning the conditions of modern economies. Because the assets responsible for prosperity in a modern economy are largely intangible, annexations are economically futile. But, he did not specify in how far this criticism is valid with respect to the relations between countries with modern economies and those with undeveloped, traditional agricultural economies or among countries with both modern and traditional economic sectors.

The "national superiority" axiom is partly rebutted on logical grounds: when all countries live up to the principle "si vis pacem, para bellum" arms races, explosive situations and, finally, wars are inevitable.

The other part of his criticism results from his observation that an international order should be formed in order to manage the increased cross-border activities. Normative was his view that this order would have to be a democratic one.

In defence of democratic values and norms, Angell stressed the need of solidarity with small democracies and the need to form a military alliance, especially in face of the rising totalitarianism in Europe and Japan. Here the principle "si vis pacem, para bellum" re-entered his thinking, though he stressed the political (non-military) nature of deterrence. Moreover, he argued that to be effective, a peace policy should always be a dual track policy: combining resistance to aggressive behaviour with offering equal economic and political rights and opportunities.

According to Angell, war could be abolished because its fundamental causes lay (a) in social circumstances and (b) in (mis)perceptions of self-interest. If the social circumstances are such that war serves no self-interest but only harms it, war becomes futile.

In relation to the problem of defining self-interest, Angell concentrated on the poor quality of public opinion, of the politicians who had the duty to represent it and of the newspapers who, for commercial reasons, tended to confirm popular misconceptions. Angell did not succeed in incorporating irrationality as a given in his optimistic future scenarios.

Angell wrote about interdependence in relation to the question what kind of social conditions would make possible the eventual disappearance of warfare. For Angell, interdependence referred to a community of fates which is characterized by an intertwining of interests and mutual influence, and which is qualified by (a) the intensity of contact (density and speed of communication), (b) the geographical spread of contact and (c) the quality of mutually required performances or services. High scores on these qualifications should lead to the recognition that "external" factors play a direct role in the effectiveness of "autonomous" policy-making and that, therefore, these external factors should be internalized by means of international organization; if not, war will be inevitable.

4. RAMSAY MUIR (1872-1941) AND THE LESSONS OF THE FIRST WORLD WAR

Muir was a typical man of the British middle class and a confirmed liberal. Up to 1914 he was a provincial who lived in too small a world to worry about political problems of which he later realized the fundamental importance, for this small world, too. Though he was a professor of contemporary history, he was blind to the processes that culminated in the war and that made it a *world* war. This experience illustrates the importance of cognitive interdependence: Muir lived in an interdependent world, but it did not influence his thinking about politics because he was completely unaware of this condition.

Muir's *The Interdependent World and Its Problems* (1933) reflects the revolution in his thinking. He developed a cryptic thesis: world war is one of the risks of global interdependence, yet the end of war is its necessary consequence.

This thesis is based on the observation that the global infra-structure had changed fundamentally because of the "conquest of distance" by technological means and by economic and social impetus. The world had become the macro dimension of politics; modern welfare demands could not possibly be combined with autarchy and political independence. The political and economical unification of the different peoples on earth also provoked a process of cultural assimilation out of which, Muir hoped, new "rules of the game" would gradually grow that would guide the social traffic in the world society.

The price of ending global interdependence would be a return to the social, economic and political conditions of the Middle Ages; it would mean a deliberate abandonment of modern methods of production and communication.

The price of accepting global interdependence would be the surrender of the ideals of unlimited sovereignty and economic autarchy, including autonomous economic decision-making. This would result in growing economic prosperity, the abolition of war and worldwide cultural assimilation. Muir called this the fruits of interdependence, which he contrasted with the so-called perils of interdependence.

The perils of interdependence are directly related to the problem of perception. If people refuse to recognize the conditions of interdependence, they will not be able to understand the scope of their own local and short-term policies, nor will they understand the impact of external developments. This results in five perils: global interdependence (a) makes war more difficult to avoid, and more ruinous if it comes; (b) it makes for a growth of nationalism which will be a source of future conflict; (c) it makes the pursuit of national economic self-sufficiency by means of tariffs a source of economic loss to all people; (d) it enhances the risks and the severity of monetary instability; (e) it enhances the risk of social revolutions because it increases the complexities of justly distributing the wealth which can now be produced in unprecedented abundance.

Because of his belief in human's ultimate progress, he was sure that people would come to understand these perils and that mankind would survive the learning process. But he developed no time table for this process, while his definition of the fruits of interdependence primarily reflected his liberal-christian way of thinking.

5. FRANCIS DELAISI (1873-1947): A FRENCHMAN'S VIEW OF GLOBAL INTERDEPENDENCE

Delaisi was a French syndicalist and as such convinced of the dominance of economics over politics. This enabled him to see that Britain was losing its hegemonic position in the world. In that process war was likely, and in 1911 he predicted such in his pamphlet *La guerre qui vient*. But he predicted the wrong war: he thought the war would essentially be one between England and Germany, initiated by England in order to destroy the economic competitive power of the Germans. He even thought that the destruction of German industrial power would indeed be to the advantage of England, especially if France did the fighting. Only after the war did he develop an understanding of the reciprocity of economic processes. This changed his view about the dominance of economics over politics: politics was dominated by myths and the most dangerous aspect of contemporary politics was that people tried to adapt the economic reality to these myths.

The root of the problem was that, since the Industrial Revolution, the economic structure of life changed faster than political structures. In the agricultural, rural economies, economic changes were more or less automatically incorporated when the political system changed. The political myths that legitimized the existing order changed more frequently than the economic base of that order; laws, regimes and constitutions changed faster than economic structures. This order had been reversed.

Taken by itself, myths fulfilled the positive functions of identifying, legitimizing and preserving reality but, since global economic interdependence had been established, the myths reflected an outdated reality. The sovereignty concept, for instance, had been developed in agrarian societies. Neither economic nationalism nor imperialism were the right political reactions to the increasing economic interdependence; they finally helped to cause the first World War.

Delaisi's solution constitutes the weakest part of his book on interdependence, *Les contradictions du monde moderne* (1925): a classic plea for free trade and a bizarre attempt to create a new political myth based on an extreme advocacy of interdependence.

More relevant to contemporary interdependence theory is his observation about the silent development of the *organs of interdependence*. His is the first theory of functionalist interdependence. In the foundation of the International Chamber of Commerce, the International Labour Office and the League of Nations he recognized the beginnings of what David Mitrany in 1943 would come to call a *working peace system*.

Delaisi developed his functionalism on the lines of syndicalism. His solution to the problem of war was to get rid of the political myths that stemmed from the agrarian era. This could be achieved by the formation of *international professional associations*. The members of professional organizations would develop an awareness of both their national interests and their international interests. In this way a certain equilibrium would be achieved within both the professional group as a whole as within the individual minds of its members.

6. CHARLES E. MERRIAM (1874-1953): CIVILIZED POWER IN A PLURALISTIC WORLD

Merriam built a scientific "empire" in the United States, centred around the Chicago School. His ideal was to turn political science

238

into an interdisciplinary enterprise based on empirical research. But he remained a generalist himself, as well as an optimist, at times misled by his linear conception of history. In the midst of the second World War, for instance, he prophesied the abolition of war mainly because for him it was out of the question that humankind could lapse back to a lower level of civilization. It is for reasons as these that his work sank in oblivion. Moreover, his generation of scientists was followed by a wave of pessimism, personified by the immigrants that had fled from fascist Europe. These immigrant-refugees included Morgenthau whose theory of political Realism was to dominate the study of IR from the fifties to the seventies. The Realists disproved of the Idealism of the interbellum period, which implicitly included Merriam's Chicago School.

Merriam's political career modified much of his idealism. From 1905 onwards he was active in Chicago politics, where he was occupied taming the "invisible government" of big business and combatting corruption. During the first World War he ran a bureau in Italy that had as its objective the prevention of a communist revolution in that country. Under Roosevelt he worked in the National Resources Planning Board, a think-tank of the New Deal. Recurrent themes related to these political experiences are the problems of striking a balance between central control and the responsibilities of local authorities, and of balancing indoctrination and public education.

His political theory is mainly based on his American background, while the bulk of IR-theories (Realism in particular) is based on the European history. One of the most interesting differences between these two traditions is that the absence of a feudal and an aristocratic tradition in America led to a political agenda that was dominated by issues unknown in Europe.

In his political theory Merriam applied a multiple actor perspective; *the family of authority*. He stressed that political analysis had to be differentiated with respect to the multitude of individuals, groups and organizations that are seeking one another's loyalty in order to achieve their specific objectives.

He extended this logic to the analysis of international relations. On such grounds Merriam argued that a world order had to be based on democratic principles for it to be successful: it would be unthinkable that the struggle among the many actors for one another's loyalty could result in a clear-cut, universally approved victory for some of them.

Essential for the understanding of this struggle is the evolution of the societal role of violence. This evolution involves (a) the relation between social objectives (the ends of government) and the means to realize them (the tools of government), and (b) the legitimacy of violence as one of these means. When social objectives cannot be properly served by the use of violence or when less demanding options promise a similar result, the legitimacy of violence will decrease. Conversely, a decline in the legitimacy of violence makes violence more costly. Merriam argued that in democracies violence as a legitimate means to realize social objectives declined in value.

Power rests on four pillars: force, obedience, persuasion and participation. The power-pillars "force" and "participation" are not complementary: the more power depends on joint action, the less force is a reliable element of power.

7. DAVID MITRANY (1888-1977): FUNCTIONALISM AS STATECRAFT AND REVOLT

David Mitrany's life and work spans and connects the pre-war phase of Pluralism and the Pluralism of the 1950s and 1960s. He is generally known for his theory of functionalism, but less known is that he formulated functionalism in reaction to the emergence of global interdependence. Its emphasis on the technical management of issues is an attempt to go beyond political and ideological boundaries without disputing them. This was prompted by the transnational reality of international relations. Functionalism is a strategy of international organization and, ultimately, this strategy serves a normative end: to create a "working peace system".

240

Functionalism is based on the principles that (a) organizational form follows from social function and that (b) successful forms of cooperation in some issue-areas have a positive spill-over effect on the relations of the same actors in other issue-areas. Mitrany's functionalism has been criticized for making an artificial distinction between the technical and the political aspects of social problems and for being too deterministic in respect to the expectation of spill-over effects. Moreover, Mitrany neglected the social function of swindle and extortion; functionalists should specify for whom something is functional (actor specific) and to what purpose (issue specific).

The idea of functionalism has been inspired by the observation that, during the first World War, all belligerents made similar arrangements to deal with the unexpected economic character of the war, despite their ideological and political differences. A second incentive was formed by the American New Deal in which the issue-specific treatment of political problems proved to be effective. In *The Progress of International Government* (1933) he placed this in a historical context and he stressed the emergence of global interdependence as the main factor in the process.

An intriguing aspect of Mitrany's work is his ambiguity about the future role of the nation-state related to the question whether war can be abolished. On the one hand he argued that war would vanish because *the end of the state drew near*. After 1945 this argument was picked up by the integrationists. On the other hand he argued that war would vanish because *the metamorphosis of the state drew near*.

Though the prediction about the end of the nation-state turned out to be wrong, it was this aspect of his work which brought functionalism close to political Realists, especially Morgenthau. Morgenthau struggled with the future of the nation-state system, too, because nuclear weaponry had made him aware of the friction between the "ultima ratio" of military force in foreign policy and the "self-destructiveness" of military force; a friction that actually had been present throughout the twentieth century. Morgenthau saw a solution in supranational developments and these might be stimulated by functionalism.

241

Yet, overall Mitrany's work is inconsistent with the Realist paradigm. In 1933 he attacked the state-as-actor paradigm and the entire conception of foreign politics, defined as an articulated set of principles which are consistently executed by the Foreign Office during a period of government. In this respect he pointed at the increasing material interdependence between countries, which had grown to the point where it turned their formal separation into a myth.

This myth originated in the concept of sovereignty. But Mitrany recognized that its instalment in 1648 meant a pragmatic solution for one and a half century of wars. The pacification of Westphalia was achieved by denying the artificial cosmopolitan unity of the Middle Ages and by recognizing European pluralism. Here, Mitrany identified the paradox that growing systemic interdependence on the one hand stimulates fragmentation, self-development, individualism, in short, pluralism, while on the other hand it stimulates the integration of local communities into larger societies.

8. SAVED FROM OBLIVION: "NEW" INSIGHTS IN INTERDEPENDENCE

There are several reasons for the neglect of the tradition of the study of interdependence. The most important one is that when interdependence theory reappeared in the seventies, this had little to do with the kind of idealism that had been characteristic for political science during the interbellum. The concept re-entered political science in order to express the need to change the dominant concepts of the basic forces, relations and actors in world politics. This need was provoked by the experience that the state-centric theories of power politics had become too simplistic to be of assistance in understanding the complexity of the contemporary world. Interdependence was used essentially as a descriptive concept. But, because a change in the diagnosis greatly influences the therapy, normative ends and expectations about the influence of increasing interdependence on the chances of war reentered the discussion. Therefore, provided that one is aware of the liberal-christian and eurocentric way of thinking that was typical for the interbellum period, much can be learned from the early authors about interdependence.

The central political problem observed by the five authors is that the world has changed fundamentally while governmental mechanisms have remained unaltered. Social life in the twentieth century is much more dynamic than it was in the heyday of agricultural civilization: material conditions change faster than generations. Rapid change in the realm of technology affects the structure of society, and is characteristic for the present age. Mitrany's theory of functionalism has been a valuable attempt to incorporate this dynamics in political theory. It stresses that the technical imperative should be the decisive factor in social organization.

According to the authors, the neglect of global interdependence formed the root of many political problems. The first World War was a result of this neglect. It can be hypothesized that unwanted and unforeseen wars can be the result of increased systemic interdependence while they are caused by the failure to perceive this systemic interdependence.

The relationship between levels of interdependence and the chances of war is complicated by a process of social learning and experience. In its turn this process is more complex than the early authors of interdependence theory thought. In their view the main problem lay in the misunderstanding of reality: a proper analysis, leading to the awareness of mutual dependence in economic, political and military affairs, automatically implied the acceptance of these conditions. However, when interdependence is recognized, this merely means that the price of a policy is better understood in advance. Whether this price will be a decisive constraint on decisions to wage war does not only depend on the existing structure, but also on the presence of alternative policies, and the price of these.

The early authors formulated policies of interdependence that were directed against the conventional knowledge of statecraft. Angell and Merriam put their trust in "reason" when it came to the question how to achieve world order. They argued in favour of creating democratic internationalism, but how to get there remained unclear. Muir argued that sovereignty rights could be pooled or divided among governments, but he did not have a clear strategy as to how to limit state-sovereignty or the claims to it. Delaisi formulated a true policy of functionalist interdependence when he argued in favour of the deliberate propagation of a network of "international professional organizations". Mitrany's functionalism is the best developed strategy of the period, provided that it is not presented as an instrument of integration.

Two theses of the early writings should specifically be mentioned as "new" contributions to contemporary interdependence theory. The first concerns the observation that the increase of interdependence has led not only to an increased collectivization but also to an increased individualization. The process from medieval cosmopolitism to individualism and the process from parochial autarchy to world economy are both related to growing interdependence. The second concerns the observation that in complex, individualized societies political power rests more on participation than on force. This implies that an increase of constructional interdependence changes the nature of political power from power based on force towards power based on participation.

The general world view that emerges from the early writings on interdependence reinforces the thesis that the study of IR should focus on transnational relations rather than on interstate relations only.

Notes

1 THE CONCEPT OF INTERDEPENDENCE IN POLITICAL SCIENCE

1. The term "stable peace" refers to Kenneth Boulding's book with that title (Boulding, 1979). Stable peace is used here to refer to the absence of not only war, but also of the preparation of war and the threat and expectation of war. The opposite is unstable peace, in which there is no war either, though there is preparation for war, an expectation of war and, at times, actual threats of war. Compare Jaap de Wilde, "Interdependentie in het vredesonderzoek naar détente", *Transaktie*, vol. 18, 1989, nr. 3, pp. 209-224.

2. A rather important qualification concerning the OECD as an example of stable peace involves the dimension of time: for how long a period do the characteristics of stable peace have to exist and how pure should they be before peace can be labelled stable? Which are the factors on which the expectancies about the continuation or disruption of stable peace in the future are based? If 10% of the Japanese population expects war with the United States within 10 years, is it still stable peace that we are talking about? And how should we see this in case of 45% or 65% and 5, 20 or 50 years? Does it make a difference whether the war-expectancy is based solely on cultural pessimism ("war is inevitable, anyway, anyhow") or on a sober analysis of for instance the economic developments between Japan, the EC and North-America? Does it therefore make a difference *who* is expecting the war? War between France and the FRG certainly is unthinkable, but not

impossible; war between Japan and the United States is thinkable but not probable; where are the limits of stable peace situated? Additional research is required here. Despite these limitations as to analytical completeness, however, it is still justified to approach the OECD-countries from the point of view that the characteristics of stable peace can be applied to them. It would certainly be headlines-news if for instance the WEU unfolded a war scenario against the United States, Canada or Japan.

3. The concept of complex interdependence has been developed by Keohane and Nye (1977), pp. 24-37.
4. Aspen Institute International Group (1984), p. ii. John Jay McCloy (1896-1989) worked after World War II as a high commissioner of the USA in the occupied German territories and guided the transition from military to civilian government. As an advisor, he was also actively involved in solving the Cuban missile crisis (1962) and in reaching the Partial Test Ban Treaty (1963).
5. Senghaas (1990), pp. 11-14.
6. The Group of 77 was formed in 1964 at the first United Nations Conference on Trade and Development (UNCTAD I) and has since tried to stimulate South-South trade and to improve the general position of the developing countries in the world economy. In 1988, the Group of 77 consisted of 126 countries.
7. See: Shaw (1978); Jones and Willetts (1984), pp. 2-3.
8. See especially the work of Klaus Knorr (1977) and (1979). In The Netherlands F. Alting von Geusau and Jacques Pelkmans published a volume on this subject in 1982. See also Röling (1983).
9. See especially Jacobson (1984^2), Krasner (1983). An interesting review of the regime literature is given by Richard O'Meara (1984). See also Schrijver (1989) and Rood (1989).
10. Haas (1975), p. 830.
11. See e.g. Rosenau (1980), chapter 5: "The Tourist and the Terrorist: Two Extremes on the Same Transnational Continuum." (pp. 73-105.)
12. Compare Dürr (1987).
13. See on the political implications of drugtrade e.g. Kruijt (1988).
14. See about the rhetoric of interdependence also Nye (1976), pp. 130-132, Keohane and Nye (1977), pp. 6-8 and Sassoon (1981), p. 32.
15. In this respect the concept of interdependence shares a reputation with virtually all central concepts in political theory: concepts such as power, the national interest, actor, issue-area, exploitation, elite, regime, nation-state, politics, etcetera, are used with great ease but do not by definition mean the same to everyone.
16. See especially the critical account by Reynolds and McKinlay (1979). In the Dutch literature Jacques Pelkmans provided an account on the inaccurate use of the word interdependence as early as in 1972.

17. Methodologically, I started from the premise that every implicit and explicit definition of interdependence is relevant to its meaning. Next, I have looked at the common characteristics of these diverse interpretations, with the objective to develop a typology which is not far from the popular understanding of interdependence, but which also prevents confusion.
18. The German translation is given here to point at a subtlety which is hard to express in English. About the "ingredients" of this general definition the following: A social actor may consist of any individual or group that is able to contend for the disposition of a political stake. (Compare Mansbach and Vasquez (1981), p. 68.) A group may be called an actor when its behaviour can be explained as that of a single individual, instead of as the outcome of a social process going on within it. (This in turn can vary with the level of analysis in question.) Negatively defined, behaviour refers to any change in the state of an actor which cannot be explained exclusively by outside forces or physiological processes. (Compare De Vree (1982), p. 436.) Structural affect refers to these outside forces.
19. Oppenheimer (1955), p. 68; emphasis added. Originally from "Atomic Weapons and American Policy", a lecture given in February, 1953.
20. Senghaas (1989).
21. Clausewitz (1982), pp. 36-38. See also Jaap de Wilde, *Complexe interdependentie: een vreedzaam perspectief?*, Utrecht, research paper, RUU/RUG, 1985, pp. 36-50.
22. Haas and Whiting (1956, p. 7) and Y. Sakamoto's paper "The State of the Globe" (1976), quoted by Simai (1986), are among the few texts explicitly referring to positive interdependence.
23. Compare Haas (1975), p. 860 and Keohane and Nye (1977), p. 8. In the Dutch literature, see Hoefnagels (1978).
24. This is especially the case in Keohane and Nye (1977).
25. Quoted in *Department of State, Special Report* (1975), p. 9. Compare also Jones and Willetts (1984): "Faced with a practical and intellectual challenge from the South, Northern 'interdependencists' were, it would be argued, really doing no more than attempting to counter an adversarial conception of North-South relations with an approach that stressed the basic mutuality of interests amongst all groups of societies within the contemporary system." (p. 2.) Jones and Willetts call this a political stratagem.
26. Capitals are used to indicate when the terms Realism, Pluralism and Structuralism are used as the catch-all rubrics of the respective schools of thought. In low cast they refer to their actual manifestation.
27. See: Groom and Mitchell (1978); Kent and Nielsson (1980); Buzan and Jones (1981); Smith, Little and Shackleton (1981); Jones and Willetts (1984); Light and Groom (1985). In the Netherlands the same tripartition is applied in Soetendorp and Van Staden (1987); see especially the contributions of Van Staden, Leurdijk and Junne.

28. Banks (1985), p. 14.
29. Compare Muir (1933), pp. 39-41.
30. Banks (1985), p. 17.
31. According to his critics, Wallerstein's world system theory fits in the macro-sociological tradition of Max Weber and Karl Marx, and the historiographic tradition of Fernand Braudel.
32. See e.g. Leurdijk (1987), p. 39; Smith, Little and Shackleton (1981), pp. 117-119; and the examples given in chapter 2. pp. 43-45.
33. Banks (1985), p. 16.
34. Adapted from the *Yearbook of International Organizations 1988/89*, edited by the Union of International Associations, München, etc.: Saur Verlag, 1988. The figures relate to the so-called "conventional international bodies", that is to federations of international organizations, universal membership organizations, intercontinental membership organizations and regionally oriented membership organizations. If other sections are included, like for instance religious orders, autonomous conference series, internationally-oriented national organizations and intergovernmental agreements and treaties, the Yearbook of 1988/89 mentions a total of 4,038 IGOs and 24,904 INGOs.
35. There are some exceptions, like e.g. William T.R. Fox (1975) and David Baldwin (1980). Fox (1975), p. 598: "'Transnational relations', 'nation building' and 'political socialization' were as familiar to students of world politics of the Chicago school in the 1930s as they are to political scientists generally in the 1970s, though not always by the same names." Baldwin (1980), pp. 481-482: "In the twentieth century excellent scholarly discussions of international interdependence have been provided by Sir Norman Angell (1914), Francis Delaisi (1925), and Ramsay Muir (1933). All three works contain conceptual explication and empirical generalizations that are well worth the attention of contemporary scholars."
36. Rosenau (1980), p. 314.
37. Holsti (1988[5]), p. 5.
38. Carr, however, did not disapprove of Idealism, in the way Morgenthau did. In *The Twenty Year's Crisis* (1939) Carr portrays Idealism and Realism as equally important and indispensable parts of political science. Both are dialectically bound to each other, and the main thrust of his argument is that both elements should never be confused.
39. Rosenau (1980), p. 305.
40. Rosenau (1980), pp. 253, 256.
41. Smith, *et al* (1981), p. 13; emphasis added.

2 THE ERA OF GLOBAL INTERDEPENDENCE: WHEN DID IT START?

1. Van Ettinger, *et al* (1989), p. 11. Other vulnerable countries to a rising sea level are Indonesia, the Maladives, Mozambique, Gambia, Pakistan, Senegal, Surinam, Thailand and the Yangtse delta in China. Some metropoles are also very vulnerable, like Bangkok, Calcutta, Dacca, Hanoi, Karachi and Sjanghai. See Worldwatch Institute (1990).
2. The term "cognitive interdependence" is based on Russett and Starr's distinction between the *"conditions* of interdependence (the existence of linkages that hold the system together) and the *cognitions* of interdependence (people seeing or perceiving that interdependence exists)". Russett and Starr (1985), p. 499. See also Peter Willetts (1984) who relates interdependence to Festinger's cognitive consistency theory, Rosenau's theory of linkage politics and Mansbach and Vasquez' issue-based approach of world politics.
3. Sassoon (1981), p. 51.
4. "A New National Partnership", speech by Secretary of State Henry A. Kissinger at Los Angeles, January 24, 1975 (News release, Department of State, Bureau of Public Affairs, Office of Media Services, p. 1.); quoted in Keohane and Nye (1977), p. 3.
5. Interview by James Reston, *New York Times*, 13 October 1974; quoted in *Department of State, Special Report* (1975), p. 7, n30.
6. Presidents Nixon and Ford are both quoted in the *Department of State Special Report* (1975), pp. 7 and 4 respectively. For Haig, see: *Department of State Bulletin*, August 1981, p. 1 and June 1982, pp. 40-44. For Shultz, see: *Department of State Bulletin*, August 1982, pp. 49-51; December 1982, pp. 64-67; March 1983, pp. 68-75; June 1984, pp. 33-37 and March 1985, pp. 13-20; nr. 2128, 1987, pp. 16-18. For Reagan, see: *Department of State Bulletin*, November 1984, p. 60.
7. Mesarovic and Pestel (1974; second report to the Club of Rome), p. 29.
8. "Proposal for Atlantic Partnership: Address by the President at Independence Hall, Philadelphia, July 4, 1962" in Stebbins (1963), pp. 225-6.
9. Röling (1983), p. 16. Reference is made to: *World Affairs Council of Philadelphia*, "Declaration of Interdependence", October 24, 1975.
10. Muir (1933), p. vii.
11. Mitrany (1933), pp. 68, 175.
12. Angell (1909), pp. 41, 44-45.
13. In 1897 de Bloch published *The War of the Future in its Technical, Economic and Political Relations*. This quote has been taken from Tromp (1990), p. 5. Jean de Bloch (or Johann von Bloch, as he is called in German literature) lived from 1836 to 1902. He was a Polish banker and industrialist, and Privy Councillor in tsarist Russia. See Eisenbeiß (1990), pp. 372-373.

14. Mikhail Gorbachev's Address to Participants in the "International Forum for Nuclear-Free World, for Survival of Humanity", February 16, 1987, p. 6.
15. Translated from: Vadim Sagladin, paper presented at an international symposium on "Friedensbewahrung: Interdependenz als Strategie für den Frieden?", organized by the International Institute for Peace, Vienna, May 21, 1990.
16. See e.g. André Roelofs, "Beleid Sjevardnadze krijgt langzaam vorm", *Volkskrant*, October 27, 1989, p. 5.
17. Quoted by Flora Lewis in the *International Herald Tribune*, July 7, 1988, p. 4.
18. International Affairs Guest Club (1988), p. 131.
19. International Affairs Guest Club (1988), p. 135.
20. Artemiev, *et al* (1987).
21. *Department of State, Special Report*, nr. 17, Washington, July 1975; pp. 7-8. The report is based on Alker, Bloomfield and Choucri (1975).
22. Though it is misleading to speak of "natural" interdependence (it falsely suggests that the present levels of global interdependence exist separately from specific levels of civilization), the awareness of the tension between existing and optional levels is of crucial importance: it points at the tension between the existence of systemic interdependence and the possibility to cope with its perils by increasing interdependence of the functionalist or integrative types. See also chapter 8, p. 219.
23. Shulman (1973), p. 48.
24. "Pope Says a 'Better Era' Is Coming", *International Herald Tribune*, June 8, 1989.
25. Muir (1933), p. 2.
26. Sprout and Sprout (1971), p. 420.
27. Muir (1933), p. 3.
28. Staley (1939), p. 11.
29. (ICBM = intercontinental ballistic missile.) Mind the reverse of the process which lurks in the balance between travelling time, the amount of fresh impressions and the psychological processing of these impressions. The Bostoner who travels round the world in five days, hardly enlarges his horizon: either he sees more than he can digest, or he sees only airports and American-styled hotels.
30. Muir (1933), pp. 7-8.
31. The term "perils of interdependence" has been introduced by Ramsay Muir in 1933. What he understood these perils to be is discussed in chapter 4, pp. 109-112.
32. Haas and Whiting (1956), pp. 3, 12-14. The tendency of increased sub-groupism, as observed by Rosenau (1980), fits in this picture.
33. Muir (1933), p. 54.
34. Rosenau (1980), p. 112.

35. Simai (1986), p. 454.
36. Compare Oliver (1982), pp. 386-387, who is quoting Rousseau: "They [the European states] touch each other at so many points, that not one of them can move without giving a jar to all the rest." A quite appropriate description of confrontational interdependence.
37. Mitrany (1933), p. 45.
38. Mitrany (1933), p. 46.
39. Joll (1982), pp. 218-219.
40. Waltz (1979), p. 140. Waltz does not tell us, however, that Briggs used the word "interdependence" in a strict economic context, as the opposite of "planning" and "interventionism". By the "belle époque" of interdependence she meant the specific economic system of laissez-faire which was based on "the separation of economics and politics" (p. 43) and which was "unique as well as mortal" (p. 39). See Briggs (1968).
41. Waltz (1979), pp. 158-159.
42. Keohane and Nye (1972); East and Salomonsen (1981).
43. Compare Hartley (1987).
44. The phrase has been taken from Banks (1985).

3 NORMAN ANGELL (1872-1967): ANCESTOR OF INTERDEPENDENCE THEORY

1. Earlier drafts of this chapter appeared in *Transaktie*, vol. 16, nr. 4, 1987, pp. 246-261 ("Norman Angell: stamvader van de interdependentie gedachte"), and in Rosenau and Tromp (1989), pp. 13-30.
2. According to Philip Supina (1972), p. 164, Sir Richard Garton had made a fortune in the manufacture of brewer's yeast. He was active in philanthropy and conservative politics.
3. Angell (1951), p. 164.
4. Miller (1986), p. 7-8. *Who was Who 1961-1970*, vol. 6. The successful distribution of *The Great Illusion* was made possible by a secret subsidy from the Carnegie Peace Endowment of $ 36,000 in December, 1911. See Supina (1972), pp. 161, 164.
5. Norman Angell, "Yesterday and Tomorrow", *War and Peace*, no. 1, 1914, quote taken from Miller (1986), p. 11.
6. There is some confusion concerning in exactly which year *The Great Illusion* first appeared. The indications vary from 1908 to 1912. Miller claims that the first edition dates from 1910 and, indeed, this edition opens with the observation that it is an expanded version of the pamphlet that appeared in 1909 (the pamphlet itself not being dated). In *The Great Illusion - Now* (a reprint in 1938), however, Angell gives 1908 as the publication date, and in his memoir, *After All* (1951), he mentions 1908 for the pamphlet and 1909

for the book. As Angell had a lot of trouble in finding a publisher, it is most plausible that the pamphlet was written in 1908, but not published before 1909, which is in conformance with Miller's reading.

7. Reynolds (1986), p. 261. Christian Lange was the Committee Chairman.
8. Miller (1986), p. 79.
9. This study is primarily based on *The Great Illusion - Now* (1938). In this book, Angell expanded upon his earlier ideas. To demonstrate that they were still relevant, he included a thorough summary of the various versions of *The Great Illusion* that appeared between 1910 and 1914. I have also consulted the unabridged (second) edition of 1910 as well as a copy of the original pamphlet *Europe's Optical Illusion* (not dated, probably 1909), *The Political Conditions of Allied Success* (1918), *Peace With the Dictators?* (1938), and his autobiography *After All* (1951). Further biographical information was taken from Miller (1986).
10. Angell (1951), p. 147 and Miller (1986), p. 4. See about this early phase in Angell's life also chapter 4, pp. 95-96.
11. Norman Angell, *The Great Illusion - 1933*, William Heineman, London, 1933, p. 370; quote taken from Miller (1986), p. 20.
12. Miller (1986), pp. 22-23.
13. Angell (1938), pp. 70, 281-282.
14. Taylor (1980), p. 65.
15. See Morgenthau (1978^5), pp. 3-4; see also chapter 6, p. 159.
16. Angell (1938), p. 270.
17. Angell (1938), pp. 17-18.
18. Wilfried Eisenbeiß mentions three main axioms that were debated, instead of two: 1. the illusion that welfare depends on military power; 2. the illusion that territorial acquisitons by definition increase the national welfare; 3. the illusion that the military and economic repression of a foreign country is profitable for the people in the home country. The first point fits in the national superiority axiom; the other two fit in the conquest pays axiom. Compare Eisenbeiß (1990), pp. 378-379.
19. Angell (1938), pp. 75, 17.
20. Morgenthau (1978^5), p. 52.
21. Modelski (1972), p. 234.
22. Goldstein (1988), p. 363.
23. Grieves (1977), p. 93.
24. Steinweg (1990), p. 13. "Die umfangreiche Werke der Kriegskritiker Johann v. Bloch und Norman Angell ... stellen den zukünftigen, auf industrieller Basis geführten Krieg mit seinen gegenüber dem 19. Jahrhundert extrem gesteigerten Zerstörungen als dermaßen verheerend dar, und zwar gleichermaßen für Sieger und Besiegte, *daß ein aus Machtkalkülen heraus geführter Krieg völlig undenkbar erschien.*" (emphasis added). Note that the article on Angell in this volume by Eisenbeiß gives a more balanced impres-

sion of his work.

25. Rosecrance (1989), pp. 49-50.
26. Miller (1986), pp. 9, 79. Miller refers to Barbara Tuchman, *The Guns of August* (1964), p. 24; Albert Wohlstetter, "Threats and Promises of Peace: Europe and America in the New Era", *Orbis*, vol. 17, nr. 4, 1974, p. 114. Angell (1951), pp. 150 ff. Carr (1939), pp. 35-36, 51, 56, 147.
27. Angell (1938), p. 77.
28. Angell (1938), p. 149.
29. Navari (1989), p. 348.
30. Angell (1938), p. 141.
31. Angell (1938), p. 144.
32. Angell (1938), pp. 154, 156.
33. Angell (1938), pp. 116, 157.
34. Dougherty and Pfaltzgraff (1971), p. 159; based on J.H. Jones, *The Economics of War and Conquest*, London: King & Son, 1915, p. 25.
35. See chapter 5.
36. Angell (1938), p. 64.
37. Angell (1938), p. 121.
38. Norman Angell, *America and the New World-State: A Plea for American Leadership in International Organisation*, Putnam & Sons, New York, 1915, pp. 32-34; quotations in this section are taken from Miller (1986), p. 108.
39. Angell (1938), pp. 225-226.
40. Navari (1989), p. 342. She goes on to say that, because of this shift, Angell is an important forbear of Keohane, Nye, Deutsch and Morse, who, in her view, all are structural functionalists.
41. Angell (1918), p. 4.
42. Angell (1938), pp. 279-280.
43. Angell (1938), pp. 16, 19, 236-237.
44. Angell (1938), p. 278.
45. Angell (1938), pp. 279-280. See also Angell, *Peace with The Dictators?* (1938).
46. Angell (1938), p. 280. The nucleus of this Defensive Confederation was to be formed by Britain, France, Russia, China, drawing in later, Poland, Yugoslavia and Rumania.
47. Angell (1938), pp. 89-90.
48. Angell (1938), pp. 45, 70. See also Hitler (1932), pp. 154, 742, 767.
49. Angell (1938), pp. 30-31.
50. Angell (1938), p. 53.
51. Angell (1938), pp. 53-54.
52. Angell (1938), both quotations p. 55.
53. Angell (1938), pp. 57-58.
54. Angell (1938), p. 61.
55. Angell (1938), p. 16.
56. Angell (1912 edition of the *The Great Illusion*), p. 132. See Navari (1989), p.

351.

57. Angell (1938), p. 256.
58. Angell (1938), p. 281.
59. Angell (1938), p. 163.
60. Angell (1938), p. 232.
61. Angell (1938), p. 62.
62. Taylor (1977), pp. 158-159 and 161. Several strategists feared that Great Britain wished to destroy American industry, and the idea was taken seriously by politicians, according to Taylor.
63. Angell (1938), p. 229.
64. Angell (1938), p. 264; emphasis added.
65. SIPRI Yearbook (1990), pp. 393: "A major armed conflict is defined as 'a prolonged combat between the military forces of two or more governments or of one government and the organized armed opposition forces, involving the use of manufactured weapons and incurring battle-related deaths of at least 1000 persons'."
66. Angell (1938), p. 108.
67. Angell (1938), p. 228.
68. Angell (1938), p. 228.
69. Angell (1938), p. 215.
70. Angell (1938), p. 248.
71. It is noteworthy in this respect that Charles Merriam observed that "the largely increased leisure of the mass of the community" gave people more time for politics. In his view, this change was one of the factors that created a new political world. Merriam (1931), p. 3.
72. Angell (1938), p. 105.
73. Angell (1938), p. 271. This debate about democracy was typical for the spirit of the time. Delaisi and Merriam, for instance, were likewise struggling with the discrepancy between the ideal and the reality of democracy. Compare chapter 5 and 6.
74. The criticism that Angell counted too much on rational decision making was formulated, among others, by Bert Röling. He was wrong in arguing that Angell neglected war as an unwanted, unintended catastrophy but right in arguing that it was Angell's illusion that rational calculations would exert a decisive influence on the behaviour of governments. See Röling (1967), p. 105.
75. Angell (1938), p. 164.
76. Navari (1989), p. 342.

4 RAMSAY MUIR (1872-1941) AND THE LESSONS OF THE FIRST WORLD WAR

1. Muir (1933), p. vii, quoted by Diebold (1983), p. 121. Diebold's valedictory address "The United States in the World Economy: A Fifty Year View" has been published in both *Development and Peace*, vol. 4, Autumn 1983, pp. 115-127 and *Foreign Affairs*, vol. 62, Fall 1983, nr. 1, pp. 81-104. The texts are slightly different. In this chapter reference is made to the version in *Development and Peace*.
2. The only other quotation I have come across is by David Baldwin (1980) pp. 481-482 (see note 35, chapter 1).
3. Muir in Hodgson (1943), p. 2. Stuart Hodgson edited the existing parts of Muir's autobiography, together with biographical essays by his colleagues and friends: Sir Walter Layton, Dr. Ernest Barker, Dr. George Stead Veitch, Major H.E. Crawfurd, Sir Ernest Simon, G. Garvill, Lord Meston, Maurice Gorham, Mrs. George Black, Sydney Brown, and Capt. Godfrey.
4. Muir (1933), p. xii. Compare Merriam, who in a similar context wrote that "Plato with his ideal state of 5,040 persons and Aristotle with his city of 10,000 will not help much at this point". Merriam (1939), p. 93.
5. Muir (1933), p. xii.
6. Muir in Hodgson (1943), p.103.
7. Hodgson (1943), pp. 100-106.
8. Muir in Hodgson (1943), p. 53.
9. In 1926, Muir travelled through the United States again. This time he was sent by the Liberal Industrial Inquiry to report about the American industrial situation. Now, he was awake: "As caste revolted him in India, so the colour ban shocked him in the States." Hodgson (1943), pp. 133-134. Struck by the lawlessness in the USA, he wrote *America the Golden* (1927), in which he analysed the production model, nowadays known as Fordism, under the denominator of "Detroitism".
10. Muir in Hodgson (1943), p. 42.
11. Miller (1986), pp. 3-4. Angell (1951), pp. 1-31, 86-87.
12. Muir in Hogdson (1943), p. 108. He worked this out in three books, *The Expansion of Europe* (1916), *National Self-Government* (1917) and *Nationalism and Internationalism* (1917) and thereby developed more and more into a publicist rather than a historian.
13. Hodgson (1943), p. 110.
14. Hodgson (1943), p. 148.
15. Hodgson (1943), p. 181.
16. Hodgson (1943), pp. 183-184.
17. With 158 seats in 1924, the Liberals did actually obtain some influence by supporting the Labour cabinet of James Ramsay MacDonald. (The Conservatives had 250 seats; Labour had 191.) But, as a result of the Campbell affair

(the release of the communist editor of *The Workers Weekly*), and the publication of the notorious Sinoviev letter (which revealed the connection of the Comintern with the British revolutionary movement), shortly after the official recognition of the Soviet-Union in February 1924, the government fell in the same year it was formed. In October the Conservatives won a landslide victory, resulting in the second cabinet of the Conservative Baldwin (1924-1929). The second cabinet MacDonald (1929-1931) again depended on support from the Liberals, but with a less fortunate division of seats: 287 seats for Labour and 59 for the Liberal Party (the Conservatives had 216 seats).

18. Hodgson (1943), p. 149.
19. From "The New Liberalism" (undated), quoted in Hodgson (1943), p. 213.
20. Compare Johann Galtung's analysis of the Western cultural tradition in respect to conceptions of peace. Galtung (1980), pp. 415-431.
21. Muir (1917), p. 224.
22. Muir (1933), pp. 2-7. See also chapter 2, pp. 50-52.
23. All quotes in this section are taken from Muir (1933), pp. 8-12.
24. Muir (1933), p. 20.
25. B. van Praag and Mrs. A. Hagenaars have developed a method, known as the Leiden Poverty Line, the LPL-norm. Here, poverty is being calculated not merely in terms of income distribution but in terms of social factors: the social environment is the main point of reference. Van Praag: "A Dutch citizen is comparing his income and prospects with those of other Dutch citizens, and not with those of a farmer in Portugal. ... The man in Portugal compares himself with his environment, too. If he has no running water while his neighbours have, he feels himself to be poor." (*De Volkskrant*, October 26, 1989; translation jdw).
26. When Keohane and Nye, in 1977, improved interdependence theory by their discussion of the sensitivity and vulnerability costs, which are latently inherent to interdependent relations, they omitted this important aspect of social resilience. This aspect might be labelled "habituation costs", which are essentially of a psychological nature.
27. Muir (1933), p. 102.
28. Rosecrance (1981), p. 700.
29. Muir (1933), pp. 12-13.
30. A. de Swaan, "Nederland Wereldland", *NRC/Handelsblad*, April 2, 1988; translation jdw; emphasis added. See also De Swaan (1989), pp. 251-257.
31. In chapter 7 about the work of David Mitrany this discussion is continued in the description of the paradox of growing interdependence. This paradox is that growing interdependence leads both to integrative and to disintegrative processes. See especially pp. 191-194.
32. Muir (1933), p. 14.
33. Muir's observations about the doctrine of the reign of law equal Norman

Angell's plea for democratic internationalism (see chapter 3, pp. 80-83) and Merriam's observation about the changing nature of political power, from force to participation (chapter 6, pp. 167-169).

34. In *When the State Kills* (1989), Amnesty International mentions a total of 3.399 executions from 1985 to the first half of 1988. Eighty-three percent of these registered executions took place in: Iran (> 743); South Africa (> 537); the People's Republic of China (> 500); Nigeria (> 439); Somalia (> 150); Saudi Arabia (> 140); Pakistan (> 115); United States of America (> 66); Soviet-Union (> 63); Malaysia (> 52). In addition, Amnesty adds that it receives yearly reports of hundreds of executions in Iraq, but that the exact figures are unknown.

35. For the Dutch police actions, see e.g. Tessel Polman, "The Dutch Colonial War 1945-1950 and the Soldier as the Adventurous Social Worker", paper presented at the Conference on "Social History of War Enthusiasm", Polemological Institute, University of Groningen, October 12-14, 1988. See also Robert Lawrence's account of his experiences in the Falkland/Malvinas War of 1982. (Lawrence, 1988).

36. It is typical that the Islamic regimes that are less sensitive to world public opinion in this respect are focusing more on the conditions of the sixth century, when Mohammed lived, than on the twenty-first century that lies ahead of us.

37. Muir (1933), p. 56.

38. Muir (1933), p. 80.

39. Muir (1933), p. 124.

40. Muir (1933), p. 100.

41. Muir (1933), p. 106.

42. Muir (1933), p. 103. "[T]he doctrine of sovereignty is that in every State there must somewhere reside a definite, recognisable, unlimited and indivisible power, from which all lesser powers within the State derive their authority, and which all citizens of the State habitually obey. If no such supreme power exists, then the State will not be truly a State, and will dissolve into anarchy." (pp. 103-104).

43. Muir (1933), p. 126.

5 FRANCIS DELAISI (1873-1947): A FRENCHMAN'S VIEW OF GLOBAL INTERDEPENDENCE

1. Delaisi (1925), p. 110.

2. Delaisi (1925), p. 269.

3. Delaisi (1925), pp. 138-140 as quoted by Muir (1933), pp. 21-22. The satirical manner in which the unawareness of the internationalization of daily life is illustrated resembles the education programmes that were made in the

seventies, especially by the UNESCO. See e.g. Graves, Dunlop and Torney-Purta (1984); in particular Ch.6 'Interdependence and Development' by James Dunlop.

4. *Dictionnaire de biographie Française,* Paris: Libraire Letouzey et Ané, vol. 10, 1965, pp. 653-655. The other bibliographical data are taken from the *National Union Catalog, Pre-1956 Imprints* (NUC), vol. 137, 1971 (The NUC incorrectly gives 1874 as Delaisi's date of birth and does not give the date of his death, but it does give a extensive list of publications by Delaisi.)

5. The quote is taken from Domela Nieuwenhuis (1911/12), pp. 58-59 (translation jdw) who edited a shortened Dutch version of Delaisi's *La démocratie et les financiers.* F. Domela Nieuwenhuis (1846-1919) was one the most important Dutch socialists at the turn of the century. In 1881 he founded the social democratic union, the "Socialistisch Democratische Bond". This union split off from the more moderate union of workers, the "Algemeen Nederlands Werkliedenverbond" (1871), and was a forerunner of the "Nederlands Verbond van Vakverenigingen (NVV)" (1906).

6. Domela Nieuwenhuis (1911/12), pp. 8-9; translation jdw.

7. The Dawes-plan ("business, not politics") was meant to regulate the German reparations after the failure of Poincaré's Ruhr policy. In the Pact of Locarno, Germany recognized the inviolability of its western borders and accepted the principle of arbitration in case of disputes with Belgium, France, Poland and Czechoslavakia. Though the Eastern border of Germany was not definitely decided on, Germany recognized the defensive pacts between France and Poland and Czechoslovakia and proclaimed not to change the borderlines by force.

8. The report was presented at the "V-ème Assemblé générale" of the "Comité fédéral de coopération européenne", Paris, July 4-6, 1932.

9. Delaisi, *Expéditions coloniales; leurs dessous, leurs atrocités,* Paris: Malraux, Galtier-Boissière, 1936, 68 pp.

10. *Die Revolution der europäische Wirtschaft,* Stuttgart: Deutsche Verlags-anstalt, 1943; a translation of *La révolution européenne,* Bruxelles/Paris: Les Editions de la Toison d'or, 1942, 298 pp.. The contents of the book were not specifically pro-German.

11. See Delaisi (1911). The pamphlet was translated in German, English, Spanish, Dutch and esperanto. In this chapter reference is made to the German translation. Striking is that these translations, except the Spanish one which was also published in 1911, appeared during the war and not before it. "Der kommende Krieg", "The Coming War" and "De huidigen oorlog in 1911 voorspeld door den Franschen socialist François Delaisie" all appeared in 1915. The American edition and "La venonto milito" were published in 1916.

12. Delaisi (1915), pp. 12-14, 17.

13. Delaisi (1915), pp. 38-39.

14. Delaisi (1915), pp. 1-2.
15. Delaisi (1915), pp. 46-48.
16. Delaisi (1915), pp. 3-5.
17. Delaisi (1915), p. 32.
18. Delaisi (1915), p. 18.
19. Delaisi (1915), pp. 19-21.
20. Delaisi (1915), pp. 11-12; translation jdw. See also pp. 5-8.
21. Delaisi (1915), p. 21; translation jdw.
22. Delaisi (1925) p. 272.
23. Delaisi (1915), pp. 7-8, 14.
24. Delaisi (1925), p. 422. In her article on Angell, Cornelia Navari pointed in this respect at the work of Organski and Kugler, who demonstrated that countries accrue no long term growth through victory in war. In case of the two world wars they even observed that, twelve to fourteen years after the war, the defeated countries tended to do better than the victors. This they called the "phoenix factor". Navari (1989), p. 352; based on A.F.K. Organski and J. Kugler, "The Cost of Major War: the Phoenix Factor", *American Political Science Review*, vol. 71, 1977, pp. 1347-1366.
25. Delaisi (1925), p. 399.
26. Delaisi (1925), pp. 391-392.
27. Delaisi (1925), pp. 428-429.
28. Delaisi (1925), p. 438.
29. Domela Nieuwenhuis (1911/12), p. 71.
30. Delaisi (1925), p. 373.
31. Delaisi (1925), p. 87.
32. Delaisi (1925), p. 11.
33. Delaisi (1925), pp. 19-20, 23-24.
34. Delaisi (1925), p. 30.
35. Delaisi (1925), p. 83.
36. Delaisi (1925), p. 87.
37. Delaisi (1925), p. 257; see also pp. 85-86.
38. Delaisi (1925), p. 84.
39. Delaisi (1925), p. 259.
40. Delaisi (1925), pp. 255-256.
41. Compare chapter 7 on Mitrany (pp. 191-194) in which it is explained that these contradictory forces were both the result of an increasing interdependence. See also chapter 8, pp. 223-224.
42. Delaisi (1925), p. 256.
43. Delaisi (1925), pp. 265-267.
44. Delaisi (1925), pp. 263-264.
45. Delaisi (1925), p. 391.
46. Delaisi (1925), p. 270.
47. Delaisi (1925), pp. 391, 422.

48. Delaisi (1925), p. 261.
49. Delaisi (1925), pp. 261-262. In a note he added that Saint-Simon had foreseen this "logical consequence" of industrialism: in 1816 Saint-Simon had written that "wars are harmful even to the victor" and that, in order to prevent them, a "European parliament" was needed consisting of industrialists and scientists. Compare James Joll (1982), p. 216: "Saint-Simon's view of the new technocratic international order seemed far from realisation at the time of his death in 1825, but a century-and-a-half later in an age when there is, for better or for worse, a European Parliament and when a technocratic European community is perhaps developing ... when much of our educational and cultural life depends on the charity of great international foundations and the economic development of the world is in the hands of large multinational corporations, we are perhaps justified in wondering whether in fact Saint-Simon has not turned out to be a better prophet than Karl Marx."
50. Compare David Easton's definition of politics: politics is about the authoritative allocation of values.
51. Delaisi (1925), pp. 442-446.
52. Marxists and socialists had correctly understood the principle of international solidarity, Delaisi argued, but they had underestimated the power of local interests. Bourgeois pacifists concentrated too much on juridical aspects; they treated sovereign nations too much as if they were autonomous individuals. Delaisi (1925), p. 408.
53. Delaisi (1925), p. 392.
54. Delaisi (1925), p. 406.
55. Delaisi (1925), pp. 394-399.
56. Delaisi (1925), p. 399.
57. Delaisi (1925), pp. 400-403.
58. Delaisi (1925), pp. 403-405.
59. Delaisi (1925), pp. 409-410.
60. Delaisi (1925), pp. 410-411; emphasis added.
61. Delaisi (1925), p. 414.
62. See note 52 of this chapter.
63. Delaisi (1925), p. xiv.
64. Delaisi (1925), pp. 417-418.
65. Coincidentally, Angell also used a sailor's metaphor in respect to interdependence. In *The Foundations of International Polity* (1914), p. 17, he wrote: "The boat was leaky, the sea heavy, and the shore a long way off. It took all the efforts of one man to row, and of the other to bale. If either had ceased both would have drawned. At one point the rower threatened the baler that if he did not bale with more energy he would throw him overboard; to which the baler made the obvious reply, that if he did, he (the rower) would certainly drawn also. And as the rower was really dependent upon the baler,

and the baler upon the rower, neither could use force against the other."
(the quote is taken from Navari (1989), p. 344.)

6 CHARLES E. MERRIAM (1874-1953): CIVILIZED POWER IN A PLURALISTIC WORLD

1. Little (1980a), p. 18.
2. Karl (1974), p. viii.
3. Little (1980a), p. 10, n.19 and Little (1980b), p. 167.
4. According to Crick (1959), Merriam's first publications, *A History of Sovereignty Since Rousseau* (1900), *A History of American Political Theories* (1903) and *American Political Ideas* (1920), still fit in this nineteenth century tradition.
5. Karl (1974), p. 297.
6. Crick (1959), pp. v, 148, 152.
7. Merriam (1942), p. 10.
8. Karl (1974), pp. 144, 171-173; Merriam (1942), pp. vi-vii, 10-11. This ambitious plan, "Studies in the Making of Citizens; A Series of Monographs on Civic Education", involved the education systems in Great Britain, the Soviet-Union, Austria-Hungary, Germany, France, the "Duk-Duks of Melanesia", Switzerland, the United States and Italy. But the cooperation with the Europeans turned out a failure.
9. Merriam (1942), p. vi; Karl (1974), pp. 106-107.
10. Karl (1974), p. 147.
11. Karl (1974), p. 288.
12. Thompson (1980), pp. 63-64.
13. Karl (1974), p. 288.
14. Fox (1975), p. 597.
15. Crick (1959), p. vi.
16. Karl (1974), p. 294.
17. Karl (1974), p. 294.
18. Karl (1974), pp. 295-296.
19. Fox (1975), p. 600.
20. Nobel (1985), p. 16, translation jdw.
21. Nobel (1985), p. 15. Nobel founds this opinion on K.W. Thompson, *Interpreters and Critics of the Cold War*, Washington, 1978, pp. 73-77.
22. In contrast to this observation, Richard H. Leach mentions a poll (held in 1963) among members of the American Political Science Association (of which Merriam had been president) in which Merriam was rated the most important political scientist of the pre-war period. But this does not imply that he also ranked high in the post-war period. See the biographical note of Leach in Merriam (1939), p. vi.

23. Holsti (1988[5]), p. 5.
24. Nobel (1985), p. 14; based on G.L. Kirk, *The Study of International Relations in American Colleges and Universities*, New York, 1947.
25. Morgenthau (1978[5]), pp. 3-4.
26. For the debate on idealism versus realism see also chapter 3 on Norman Angell, pp. 83-87, and chapter 7 on Mitrany, pp. 187-191.
27. Merriam (1945), pp. vii-viii.
28. Merriam (1945), pp. 262-263.
29. Karl (1974), pp. 40, 211.
30. Quoted by Karl (1974), p. 103.
31. Karl (1974), p. 88.
32. Karl (1974), p. 90.
33. Karl (1974), p. 104.
34. On the New Deal, see also chapter 7, pp. 174-175.
35. Quoted by Karl (1974), p. 239.
36. Karl (1974), p. 241.
37. Crick (1959), p. 134.
38. Karl (1974), p. 200.
39. Karl (1974), p. 169.
40. Karl (1974), p. 191.
41. Crick (1959), p. 154.
42. Willetts (1989), p. 196.
43. Willetts (1989), p. 196.
44. Compare De Vree (1982), pp. 42, 436-437, whose system's theory of IR is making use of this difference between atomic systems and compound systems. De Vree defined an atomic system as "A social system, whose behaviour is explained as that of a single individual, instead of as the outcome of a social process going on within it", and a compound system as: "Any system made up of atomic systems or other compound systems, whose behavioural state is to be explained as the outcome of social processes between its member-systems, rather than from information, values and expectations of the system as such."
45. See about the paradigm debate, chapter 1, pp. 30-37.
46. Merriam (1945), chapter 1, especially pp. 11, 17.
47. Fox (1975), pp. 597-598.
48. Lijphart (1976[2]), chapter 10 "De theorie van het Pluralisme", pp. 189-203.
49. Merriam (1945), p. 17; see also pp. 39-40, 72-73.
50. Rosenau (1989), p. 31.
51. Merriam (1945), p. 8.
52. Merriam (1945), p. 18.
53. Merriam (1945), p. 33. He referred to Q. Wright, *A Study of War* (2 vols., 1942); A. Vagts, *A History of Militarism* (1937); E. Mead Earle, *Makers of Modern Strategy* (1943) and to his own "The Organization of Violence" in

Merriam (1939), pp. 1-22.
54. Merriam (1945), p. 271; see also pp. 23-24, 280. Though this clearly implies an awareness of increasing global interdependence, this concept was seldom used by Merriam; let alone that Merriam defined interdependence, as is maintained by Nobel (1989), p. 214.
55. Merriam (1945), p. 24.
56. Merriam (1945), pp. 271-272.
57. In *Prologue to Politics* (1939), however, Merriam spent a whole chapter defining his ideal state without evading these pitfalls. See Merriam (1939), pp. 44-75.
58. Merriam, *Public and Private Government* (1944), p. 73; quoted by Fox (1975), p. 605.
59. Merriam (1941), chapter III, "Democracy and World Order", pp. 52-72; quotations pp. 54-55.
60. See chapter 3, pp. 87-88.
61. Merriam (1945), p. 33.
62. Merriam (1945), p. 6. This definition fits very well into the theory of functionalism.
63. See chapter 7, pp. 180-182.
64. Merriam (1942), p. 19. See also Merriam (1939), p. 75.
65. Merriam (1945), p. 18. Note that this description comes remarkably close to Krasner's definition of international regimes: Regimes "are sets of implicit or explicit principles, norms, rules, and decision-making procedures around which actors' expectations converge in a given area of international relations." Krasner (1983), p. 2. In this terminology, Merriam thus stated that the conditioning factor of government is the regime in which it functions.
66. Merriam (1945), pp. 285-287.
67. Merriam (1945), p. 37. Note that even in this neat, mechanically organized structure the fourth pillar can be of decisive importance: mercenaries and unmotivated conscripts are surely less willing to sacrifice their lives than fanatics fighting a holy war.
68. Karl (1974), p. 251; based on Merriam's chapter "The Poverty of Power" in *Political Power* (1934).
69. Merriam (1945), p. 67.
70. Merriam (1945), p. 267.

7 DAVID MITRANY (1888-1977): FUNCTIONALISM AS STATECRAFT AND REVOLT

1. Quoted by Thompson (1980), p. 203.
2. Mitrany (1975a), p. 241.

3. Mitrany (1975a), p. 240.
4. In 1990, at the special meeting of the EC in Dublin, the Dutch prime-minister Ruud Lubbers made use of exactly the same rhetoric when he launched a proposal to form a pan-European energy community. "After the second World War, the foundation of the ECSC was the symbol of the ideal to ban war (especially between France and Germany); in the same way the foundation of a European energy community may contribute to prevent the construction of new walls in Europe", *De Volkskrant*, June 26, 1990, translation jdw.
5. Keohane and Nye (1987), p. 729.
6. Taylor in Mitrany (1975), p. xviii. Reference is made to Keohane and Nye (1972).
7. Mitrany's autobiography is included in Mitrany (1975a), pp. 3-82. The quote is taken from p. 4.
8. Mitrany (1975a), p. 8.
9. Mitrany (1975a), p. 136; see also p. 17.
10. Mitrany (1975a), p. 26.
11. Several measures taken in the New Deal provoked conflicts between the Roosevelt Administration and the Supreme Court because of their constitutional implications. Mitrany's papers on federalism and constitutionalism versus functionalism are based on these controversies. See also chapter 6, pp. 154-156.
12. Burton (1975), p. 240.
13. De Vree (1972), p. 38.
14. Mitrany (1975a), p. 19.
15. Mitrany (1975a), p. 19.
16. Mitrany (1975a), pp. 20-25.
17. Mitrany (1966), p. 62.
18. Mitrany (1975a), p. 31.
19. See on this subject Hodges (1975), especially p. 225.
20. Compare Groom and Taylor (1975), p. 6.
21. Mitrany (1966), pp. 70-73. In this respect a direct link can be established with the so-called issue-structure approach developed by Richard Mansbach and John Vasquez. See Mansbach and Vasquez (1981).
22. See e.g. De Vree (1972), pp. 41, 44-45 and Groom (1975), p. 99.
23. A. Zimmern, *The League of Nations and the Rule of Law, 1818-1935*, London: Macmillan, 1936, pp. 322-323; quoted by De Vree (1972), p. 39. According to Thompson (1980), p. 203 the roots of Mitrany's work are indeed as diverse as is suggested here by Zimmern.
24. Groom and Taylor (1975), p. 4. See also Taylor (1975), p. xi: "Functionalism holds that violence has its roots in the social and economic circumstances of people."
25. Mitrany (1975a), pp. 35-36.

26. Compare Groom and Taylor (1975), pp. 1-4; Eastby (1985), pp. 7-9, 37; Thompson (1980), p. 215.
27. Carr (1942), p. 63.
28. Carr (1942), pp. 168-169.
29. Thompson (1980), p. 208.
30. Mitrany (1933), p. 17. See also Eastby (1985), p. 3.
31. Mitrany (1975a), p. 34.
32. Taylor in Mitrany (1975a), p. x. In the volume on functionalism, which he edited with John Groom, he argued similarly: "The functionalist strategy depends upon a belief that there are indeed a number of carrots which are juicier than the nation state, and that they will flourish in a working peace system." Taylor (1975), p. 89.
33. Mitrany (1975b), pp. 27-28.
34. Pentland (1975), p. 15.
35. Morgenthau in Mitrany (1966), pp. 9, 11.
36. Morgenthau (1978[5]), p. 10.
37. Morgenthau in Mitrany (1966), p. 9.
38. See Angell (1918).
39. Morgenthau (1978[5]), pp. xiv, xv.
40. Morgenthau in Mitrany (1966), p. 9; emphasis added.
41. Von Clausewitz reached these conclusions by applying the logic of confrontational interdependence. See chapter 1, p. 24.
42. Morgenthau in Mitrany (1966), p. 10.
43. Morgenthau (1978[5]), p. 553; emphasis added.
44. Morgenthau (1978[5]), p. 126.
45. Groom and Taylor (1975), p. 1.
46. Groom and Taylor (1975), p. 2.
47. Groom and Taylor (1975), p. 3; Groom (1975), p. 110: "'functionalist' ideas were quite common among anarchist writers of the nineteenth century. ... Moreover, modern anarchism with its emphasis on responsiveness, participation, consensus and the transactional basis for organisation has much in common with the functionalist mode."
48. Eastby (1985), p. 32.
49. Eastby (1985), p. ix. Another disappointing aspect of this volume is that, in contrast to its suggestive title *Functionalism and Interdependence*, the concept of interdependence does not play any role of interest. The few passages in which the word occurs (pp. xiii-note 15, 8, 89-90) do not add a thing to the debate.
50. Morgenthau mentioned the following common interests of humanity: "physical survival through avoidance of nuclear war and non-proliferation of nuclear weapons, protection of the natural environment and economic well-being through the control of trade, the monetary system, and the global corporations." Morgenthau (1978[5]), p. 515.

51. Morgenthau (1978[5]), pp. 515, 518.
52. Mitrany (1975a), pp. 216-217.
53. Mitrany (1966), p. 30.
54. Thompson (1980), p. 213.
55. Morgenthau in Mitrany (1966), p. 9.
56. Mitrany (1966), p. 68.
57. Mitrany (1966), pp. 25-26. See also Mitrany (1975a), pp. 185-186.
58. Mitrany (1933), p. 43.
59. Mitrany (1933), p. 23. Nys indeed mentions the figure of 2.000 sovereigns in the year 1500 but does not give a further source. See Nys (1912), p. 395.
60. Mitrany (1966), p. 131.
61. See chapter 1, p. 17.
62. Mitrany (1933), p. 20; see also p. 33. Fourty-four years later, the same thesis was formulated again by Keohane and Nye, with the difference that they maintained that in the past the distinction between domestic and international politics had really existed. The blurring of state borders in their view was a recent phenomenon. Keohane and Nye (1977), pp. 25, 33-34.
63. Mitrany (1933), pp. 97-102.
64. Mitrany (1933), pp. 56-57.
65. Mitrany (1933), p. 102. Compare Tromp (1981), pp. 69-70.
66. Mitrany (1933), p. 127. Mitrany took this quote from a statement made in 1930 by a certain Dr. Bailey of the University of London. (I have not traced the original source.)
67. Mitrany (1933), pp. 67-68.
68. Mitrany (1933), p. 118.
69. Mitrany (1933), p. 101.
70. Mitrany (1933), p. 56. Compare chapter 5, pp. 131-135.
71. Compare Rosecrance (1989).
72. Wallace and Singer (1970), p. 277.
73. Over against the German and Italian unification there is the disintegration of the Austrian-Hungarian empire and the Ottoman empire, and over against the present unification of the two German states there is the possible disintegration of Yugoslavia and the Soviet-Union.
74. Mitrany (1966), p. 27.
75. Mitrany (1933), p. 117.
76. Mitrany (1933), pp. 89-90; Mitrany (1966), pp. 131, 164.
77. See chapter 1, table 2, p. 36. A review of hypotheses about the role of INGOs which is still very useful for peace research can be found in Judge and Skjelsbaek (1975), especially pp. 209-217.
78. Mitrany (1933), pp. 92-93.
79. See about the relationship between domestic and international conflicts e.g. Rosenau (1964).
80. Burton (1975), pp. 238-240.

81. Mitrany (1966), p. 146.
82. Mitrany (1966), p. 62.
83. Taylor (1975), p. xiv.
84. This point is missed by critics of the interdependence thesis, and often by adherents, too. See e.g. Haas (1987), pp. 111-112.
85. Thompson (1980), p. 213.

8 SAVED FROM OBLIVION: "NEW" INSIGHTS IN INTERDEPEN-DENCE

1. Parts of this chapter have been published in Jaap de Wilde, "Promises of Interdependence: Risks and Opportunities", *Bulletin of Peace Proposals*, vol. 19 (1988) nr. 2, pp. 159-166.
2. See, for instance, Leurdijk (1987), p. 59 where it is said that interdependence was seen as "nieuwlichterij", sheer modernism.
3. See e.g. Waltz (1979) p. 140. In the Dutch literature this argument can be found in a recently published handbook on IR, edited by Soetendorp and Van Staden. See in particular: Leurdijk (1987), p. 51; Pijpers (1987), pp. 197-198, 202; Koch (1987), pp. 261-262.
4. There are a few exceptions to this general observation. Some authors have stressed the continuity in thought about interdependence, while other scholars, who studied the interbellum period for historical reasons, touched upon its tradition. These include: Fox (1975), Baldwin (1980), Thompson (1980), Miller (1986).
5. See De Lange (1983), p. 257 (who referred to Bernard Brodie, *War and Politics*, London, 1974, p. 322).
6. Carr's *The Twenty Year's Crisis* is the only pre-war volume on IR that ranked high on a list of "assigned or suggested sources" mentioned in 178 syllabi on IR in the USA in 1973-1974. Rosenau (1980), p. 256.
7. Haas (1975), p. 852; emphasis in the original.
8. The paradigm is most manifest in the work of Muir, while its traces are weakest in the work of Angell and Mitrany. In Merriam's work liberal-christian elements are very evident but, obviously, eurocentrism is less manifest. Though Delaisi was a syndicalist, liberalism, of all aspects, was most manifestly present in his work.
9. Here, Delaisi is partly an exception because, in 1936, he wrote a book about the atrocities in the colonies.
10. The word "could" should be stressed, because it is not so that every decision or every event has such a worldwide impact. But important for politics is that there are events and decision which *can* have worldwide consequences. One of the unsolved problems of political science is the development of a typology of variables that determine whether a specific event will have an

impact on world politics or whether it is only of local importance. Put differently: the demarcations of micro- and macro-politics have not yet been defined.

11. See about this development of warfare e.g. Earle (1973^2), Spits (1971), Howard (1976) and Tromp (1986).

12. The main antagonists of an interdependence policy in this respect are policies of imperialism and policies of isolationism. Policies of imperialism are attempts to end interdependence: the actor pursuing them tries to increase his or her own independence ("unabhängigkeit") by reducing the independence ("selbständigkeit") of other actors. Policies of isolationism are also attempts to end interdependence: the actor who pursues them tries to increase his or her own independence by reducing the relations with other actors to a minimum. Both types of policy are attempts to reduce the complexity of politics by reducing pluralism.

13. This concern has in the meantime been institutionalized in several institutions, especially UNESCO.

14. See Elias, *Über den Prozess der Zivilisation* (1939) and *What is Sociology?* (1978).

15. Staley (1939).

16. See e.g. the work of Hans Kelsen, Alfred von Verdross, J. Novicow and E. Nys.

17. The term interdependence calculus is taken from Mansbach and Vasquez (1981), pp. 75-76.

Bibliography

Alker, Hayward R., L.P. Bloomfield and N. Choucri, *Analyzing Global Inter-dependence*, Cambridge, Mass., 1975.

Alting von Geusau, F.A.M. and Jacques Pelkmans (eds), *National Economic Security: Perceptions, Threats and Policies*, Tilburg: John F. Kennedy Institute, 1982.

Angell, Norman, *Europe's Optical Illusion*, London: Simpkin, Marshall, Kent & Co., not dated, ?1909.

Angell, Norman, *The Great Illusion. A Study of the Relation of Military Power to National Advantage*, London: Heinemann, (1910) 1910^2.

Angell, Norman, *The Political Conditions of Allied Success. A Plea for the Protective Union of the Democracies*, New York, London: Putnam & Sons, 1918.

Angell, Norman, *Peace With the Dictators?*, London: Hamish Hamilton, 1938.

Angell, Norman, *The Great Illusion - Now*, Harmondsworth: Penguin Books, 1938.

Angell, Norman, *After All. The Autobiography of Norman Angell*, London: Hamish Hamilton, 1951.

Artemiev, I., et al., "International Economic Security" paper prepared for the Anglo-Soviet experts' meeting on problems of international economic security between IMEMO and RIIA, Moscow, September 21, 1987.

Aspen Institute International Group, Statement of the, *Managing East-West Conflict: A Framework for Sustained Engagement*, New York: Aspen Institute for Humanistic Studies, 1984.

Baldwin, David A., "Interdependence and Power: A Conceptual Analysis", *International Organization*, vol. 34, 1980, no. 4, pp. 471-506.

Banks, Michael, "The Inter-Paradigm Debate" in Light and Groom (1985), pp. 7-26.

Boulding, Kenneth E., *Stable Peace*, Austin: University of Texas Press, 1979.

Briggs, Asa, "The World Economy: Interdependence and Planning" in C.L. Mowat (ed), *The New Cambridge Modern History. Volume XII. The Shifting Balance of World Forces, 1898-1945*, London/New York: Cambridge University Press, 1968, pp. 37-86.

Burton, John W., "Functionalism and the Resolution of Conflict" in Groom and Taylor (1975), pp. 238-249.

Buzan, Barry and R.J. Barry Jones (eds), *Change and the Study of International Relations. The Evaded Dimension*, New York: St. Martin's Press, 1981.

Carr, Edward H., *The Twenty Years' Crisis, 1919-1939. An Introduction to the Study of International Relations*, London: Macmillan, (1939) 1940^2.

Carr, Edward H., *Conditions of Peace*, New York: The Macmillan Company, 1942.

Carr, Edward H., *The New Society*, London: Macmillan, St. Martin's Press, (1951), 1969.

Clausewitz, Carl von, *Over de oorlog*, Bussum/Antwerpen: Het Wereldvenster/Standaard Wetenschappelijke Uitgeverij, 1982 (translation of *Vom Kriege*, part I, II and III, originally published in 1832, 1833 and 1834).

Crick, Bernard, *The American Science of Politics. Its Origins and Traditions*, London: Routledge & Kegan Paul, 1959.

Delaisi, Francis, *Der kommende Krieg*, Berlin: Verlag E.S. Mittler, 1915 (translation of *La guerre qui vient*, Paris: Edition de la "Guerre Sociale", 1911).

Delaisi, Francis, *Political Myths and Economic Realities*, Washington/London: Kennikat Press, 1971 (first published in England in 1925 by N. Douglas and by Williams & Norgate, and in the USA by The Viking Press in 1927; originally published as *Les contradictions du monde moderne*, Paris: Payot, 1925).

Delaisi, Francis, *La Révolution Européenne*, Bruxelles/Paris: Les Editions de la Toison d'Or, 1942.

Department of State, "Toward a Strategy of Interdependence", *Department of State, Special Report*, Washington, July 1975, no. 17.

Diebold, William, Jr., "The United States in the World Economy: A Fifty-Year View", *Development and Peace*, vol. 4, 1983, pp. 115-127 (also in *Foreign Affairs*, vol. 62, 1983, no. 1, pp. 81-104).

Domela Nieuwenhuis, F., *De demokratie en de financiers; de werkelijke meesters der wereld*, Amsterdam: W. ten Hoorn, not dated, ?1911/1912 (shortened version and translation of Francis Delaisi, *La Democratie et les Financiers*, 1911).

Dougherty, James E. and Robert L. Pfaltzgraff, Jr., *Contending Theories of International Relations*, Philadelphia, etc.: J.B. Lippincott, 1971.

Dunlop, O.J., "Interdependence and Development" in Graves, Dunlop and Torney-Purta (1984), pp. 105-132.

Dürr, Hans-Peter, "Kooperation statt Konfrontation. Plädoyer für ein 'Global Challenges Network'", *Blätter für deutsche und internationale Politik*, 1987, no. 8, pp. 1029-1042.

Earle, Edward Mead (ed), *Makers of Modern Strategy. Military Thought from Machiavelli to Hitler*, Princeton: Princeton University Press, (1943), (1971) 1973[2].

East, M. and L.H. Salomonsen, "Adapting Foreign Policy Making to Interdependence: A Proposal and some Evidence from Norway", *Cooperation and Conflict*, vol. 16, 1981, no. 3, pp. 165-182.

Eastby, John, *Functionalism and Interdependence. The Credibility of Institutions, Policies and Leadership. Volume 3*, With a preface by Kenneth W. Thompson, Lanham, New York, etc.: University Press of America, 1985.

Eisenbeiß, Wilfried, "Einsicht vor der Zeit: Der seit 1900 sinnlose Krieg. Uber die Schriften der Kriegskritiker Johann von Bloch und Norman Angell" in Steinweg (1990), pp. 369-401.

Ettinger, Jan van, T. Hans Jansen and Catrinus J. Jepma, "Climate, Environment and Development", *Development & Security*, 1989, no. 27.

Fox, William T.R., "Pluralism, the Science of Politics, and the World System", *World Politics*, vol. 27, 1975, no. 4, pp. 597-611.

Galtung, Johann, *Peace Problems: Some Case Studies. Essays in Peace Research, vol. V*, Copenhagen: Christian Ejlers, 1980.

Goldmann, Kjell and Gunnar Sjöstedt (eds), *Power, Capabilities, Interdependence: Problems in the Study of International Influence*, Beverly Hills/London: Sage Publications, 1979.

Goldstein, Joshua, *Long Cycles: Prosperity and War in the Modern Age*, London: Yale University Press, 1988.

Graves, N.J., O.J. Dunlop and J.V. Torney-Purta (eds), *Teaching for International Understanding, Peace and Human Rights*, Paris: Unesco, 1984.

Grieves, Forest L., *Conflict and Order. An Introduction to International Relations*, Boston, etc.: Houghton Mifflin, 1977.

Groom, A.J.R. and Paul Taylor (eds), *Functionalism. Theory and Practice in International Relations*, London: University of London Press, 1975.

Groom, A.J.R., "Functionalism and World Society" in Groom and Taylor (1975), pp. 93-111.

Groom, A.J.R. and C.R. Mitchell (eds), *International Relations Theory: A Bibliography*, New York/London: Nichols/Francis Pinter, 1978.

Haas, Ernst B. and Alan Whiting, *Dynamics of International Relations*, New York, etc.: McGraw Hill Book Comp., 1956.

Haas, Ernst B., "Is There a Hole in the Whole? Knowledge, Technology, Interdependence, and the Construction of International Regimes", *International Organization*, vol. 19, 1975, no. 3, pp. 827-875.

Haas, Ernst B., "War, Interdependence and Functionalism" in Väyrynen (1987), pp. 108-126.

Hartley, Anthony, "Does the Ambassador Have a Future?", *Encounter*, March

1987, pp. 23-30.

Heathcote, N., "Neofunctional Theories of Regional Integration" in Groom and Taylor (1975), pp. 38-52.

Hitler, Adolf, *Mein Kampf*, München: Verlag Franz Eher Nachfolger, 1932 (first ed. Band I 1925, Band II 1927).

Hodges, M., "Functionalism and Multinational Companies" in Groom and Taylor (1975), pp. 225-237.

Hodgson, Stuart (ed), *Ramsay Muir. An Autobiography and Some Essays*, London: Lund Humphries & Co., 1943.

Hoefnagels, Marjo, "Interdependentiepatronen in het internationale systeem", report to the Dutch Commission on Research of Non-violent Con-flictmanagement (Begeleidingsgroep inzake het onderzoek op het gebied van de geweldloze conflictoplossing), Brussel: Centrum voor Polemologie, 1978.

Holsti, Kal J., *International Politics. A Framework for Analysis*, Englewood Cliffs: Prentice Hall, (1967) 1988[5].

Howard, Michael, *War in European History*, Oxford, etc.: Oxford University Press, 1976.

Hsiao, Kung Chuan, *Political Pluralism: A Study in Contemporary Political Theory*, New York: Harcourt, Brace, 1927.

International Affairs Guest Club, "The Soviet Union in an Interdependent World", *International Affairs (Moscow)*, May 1988, pp. 130-143.

Jacobson, H.K., *Networks of Interdependence: International Organizations and the Global Political System*, New York: A.A. Knopf, (1979) 1984[2].

Joll, James, "The Ideal and the Real: Changing Concepts of the International System, 1815-1982", *International Affairs*, vol. 58, 1982, no. 2, pp. 210-224.

Jones, R.J. Barry and Peter Willetts (eds), *Interdependence on Trial. Studies in the Theory and Reality of Contemporary Interdependence*, New York: St. Martin's Press, 1984.

Judge, A.J.N. and K. Skjelsbaek, "Transnational Associations and Their Func-tions" in Groom and Taylor (1975), pp. 190-224.

Junne, G., "Benaderingen die uitgaan van klassentegenstellingen" in Soeten-dorp and Van Staden (1987), pp. 65-99.

Karl, Barry D., *Charles E. Merriam and the Study of Politics*, Chicago/London: University of Chicago Press, 1974.

Kent, R.C. and G.P. Nielsson (eds), *The Study and Teaching of International Relations*, London/New York: Pinter/Nichols, 1980.

Keohane, Robert O. and Joseph S. Nye, Jr. (eds), *Transnational Relations and World Politics*, Cambridge, Mass.: Harvard University Press, 1972.

Keohane, Robert O. and Joseph S. Nye, Jr., *Power and Interdependence: World Politics in Transition*, Boston: Little, Brown, 1977.

Keohane, Robert O. and Joseph S. Nye, Jr., "Power and Interdependence Revisited", *International Organization*, vol. 41, 1987, no. 4, pp. 725-753.

Knorr, Klaus and F.N. Trager (eds), *Economic Issues and National Security*,

Lawrence, Kansas: Allen Press, 1977.

Knorr, Klaus, "Economic Interdependence and National Security" in Knorr and Trager (1977), pp. 1-18.

Knorr, Klaus, "National Power in an Economically Interdependent World" in Goldman and Sjöstedt (1979), pp. 167-191.

Koch, Koen, "Structuralisme en internationale systemen: het neorealisme van Kenneth N. Waltz" in Soetendorp and Van Staden (1987), pp. 243-269.

Krasner, Stephan D. (ed), *International Regimes*, Ithaca/London: Cornell University Press, 1983.

Krasner, Stephan D., "Structural Causes and Regime Consequences. Regimes as Intervening Variables" in Krasner (1983), pp. 1-21.

Kruijt, Peter E., "Internationale drugshandel, georganiseerde misdaad en politiek extremisme: een huwelijk van geld en geweld", *Transaktie*, vol. 17, 1988, no. 1, pp. 38-52.

Lange, Herman de, *De bewapeningswedloop tussen de Verenigde Staten en de Sovjetunie, 1945-1983*, Leeuwarden: Eisma, 1983.

Laski, H.J., "The Pluralistic State" in H.J. Laski, *The Foundation of Sovereignty and Other Essays*, New York: Harcourt, Brace, 1921.

Lawrence, Robert, *When the Fighting is Over*, London: Bloomsbury, 1988.

Leurdijk, J. Henk, "De analyse van de wereldgemeenschap" in Soetendorp and Van Staden (1987), pp. 37-64.

Light, Margot and A.J.R. Groom (eds), *International Relations. A Handbook of Current Theory*, London: Francis Pinter, 1985.

Lijphart, Arend, *Verzuiling, pacificatie en kentering in de Nederlandse politiek*, Amsterdam: J.H. De Bussy, (1968) 1976; (revised version of *The Politics of Accomodation. Pluralism and Democracy in the Netherlands*, Berkeley: University of California Press, 1968).

Little, Richard, "The Evolution of International Relations as a Social Science" in Kent and Nielsson (1980), pp. 1-27.

Little, Richard, "A Paradigmatic Approach to Teaching International Relations to Mid-Career Students" in Kent and Nielsson (1980), pp. 156-171.

Mansbach, Richard W. and John A. Vasquez, *In Search of Theory. A New Paradigm for Global Politics*, New York: Columbia University Press, 1981.

Mayall, J., "Functionalism and International Economic Relations" in Groom and Taylor (1975), pp. 250-277.

McKnight, A., "Functionalism and the Specialised Agencies" in Groom and Taylor (1975), pp. 162-172.

Merriam, Charles E., *A History of American Political Theories*, With a new introduction by Robert E. Merriam, New York/London: Johnson Reprint Corp., (1903) 1968.

Merriam, Charles E., *The American Party System. An Introduction to the Study of Political Parties in the United States*, New York: Macmillan Company, 1922.

Merriam, Charles E., *New Aspects of Politics*, Chicago: University of Chicago Press, (1925) 1931.

Merriam, Charles E., *Civic Education in the United States*, Report of the Commission on the Social Studies, part VI, New York: Charles Scribner's Sons, 1934.

Merriam, Charles E., *Prologue to Politics*, With a Preface by Glenn Negley, New York/London: Johnson Reprint Corp., (1939) 1970.

Merriam, Charles E., *On the Agenda of Democracy*, Cambridge, Mass.: Harvard University Press, 1941.

Merriam, Charles E., "The Education of Charles E. Merriam" in White (1942), pp. 1-24.

Merriam, Charles E., *Systematic Politics*, Chicago: University of Chicago Press, 1945.

Mesarovic, Mihailo and Eduard Pestel, *Mankind at the Turning Point*, London: Hutchinson, 1974.

Miller, J.D.B., *Norman Angell and the Futility of War. Peace and the Public Mind*, London: Macmillan, 1986.

Mitrany, David, *The Problem of International Sanctions*, London, etc.: Oxford University Press, 1925.

Mitrany, David, *The Progress of International Government*, New Haven: Yale University Press, 1933.

Mitrany, David, *A Working Peace System*, Chicago: Quadranglite Books, 1966.

Mitrany, David, *The Functional Theory of Politics*, London: Martin Robertson, 1975.

Mitrany, David, "A Political Theory for the New Society" in Groom and Taylor (1975), pp. 25-37.

Mitrany, David, "The Prospect of Integration: Federal of Functional?" in Groom and Taylor (1975), pp. 53-78.

Modelski, George A., *Principles of World Politics*, New York/London: The Free Press/Collier-Macmillan, 1972.

Morgenthau, Hans J., *Politics Among Nations. The Struggle for Power and Peace*, New York: A.A. Knopf, (1948) 1978[5].

Muir, Ramsay, *Nationalism and Internationalism. The Culmination of Modern History*, London: Constable & Co., 1917.

Muir, Ramsay, *The Interdependent World and Its Problems*, Washington, London: Kennikat Press, (1933) 1971.

Navari, Cornelia, "The Great Illusion Revisited: The International Theory of Norman Angell", *Review of International Studies*, 1989, no. 15, pp. 341-358.

Nobel, Jaap W., *De utopie van het realisme. De machtstheorie van Hans J. Morgenthau en de kritiek op het Amerikaanse beleid in de koude oorlog*, Amsterdam: Jan Mets, 1985.

Nobel, Jaap W., "The Paradigm Debate in International Relations" in Rosenau and Tromp (1989), pp. 211-219.

Nye, Joseph S., "Independence and Interdependence", *Foreign Policy*, Spring 1976, no. 22, pp. 129-161.

Nys, Ernest, *Le droit international. Les principes, les théories, les faits*, (3 vols.) Bruxelles: M. Weissenbruch, 1912.

274

OECD, *From Marshallplan to Global Interdependence*, Paris: OECD, 1978.

OECD, *Economic and Ecological Interdependence: A Report on Selected Environmental and Resource Issues*, Paris: OECD, 1982.

OECD, *Interdependence and Co-operation in Tomorrow's World. A Symposium Marking the Twenty-fifth Anniversary of the OECD*, Paris: OECD, 1987.

Oliver, J.K., "The Balance of Power Heritage of 'Interdependence' and 'Traditionalism'", *International Studies Quarterly*, vol. 26, 1982, no. 3, pp. 373-396.

O'Meara, Richard L., "Regimes and their Implications for International Theory", *Millennium*, vol. 13, 1984, no. 3, pp. 245-264.

Oppenheimer, J.R., *The Open Mind*, New York: Simon and Schuster, 1955.

Pelkmans, Jacques, "Een analyse van interdependentie", *Internationale Spectator*, vol. 26, 1972, no. 9, pp. 847-872.

Pentland, Ch., "Functionalism and Theories of International Political Integration" in Groom and Taylor (1975), pp. 9-24.

Pijpers, Alfred E., "Internationale integratie en de functionalistische verleiding" in Soetendorp and Van Staden (1987), pp. 189-212.

Reynolds, Ph.A. and R.D. McKinlay, "The Concept of Interdependence: Its Uses and Misuses" in Goldmann and Sjöstedt (1979), pp. 141-167.

Reynolds, R.C., "Nobel Prize Laureates - Norman Angell (1933)", *World Encyclopedia of Peace*, vol. 4, 1986, pp. 261-264.

Röling, B.V.A., "Ontwikkeling van het denken over oorlog en vrede", *Maandblad Oost-West*, vol. 6, 1967, no. 4, pp. 103-109.

Röling, B.V.A., "Veiligheid", *Ontwikkeling & Veiligheid*, 1983, no. 6.

Rood, Jan Q.Th., "The Functioning of Regimes in an Interdependent World" in Rosenau and Tromp (1989), pp. 61-82.

Rosecrance, Richard, "International Theory Revisited", *International Organization*, vol. 35, 1981, no. 4, pp. 691-713.

Rosecrance, Richard, "War, Trade and Interdependence" in Rosenau and Tromp (1989), pp. 48-57.

Rosenau, James N. (ed), *International Aspects of Civil Strife*, Princeton, N.J.: Princeton University Press, 1964.

Rosenau, James N. (with Gary Gartin, Edwin P. McClain, Dona Stinziano, Richard Stoddard and Dean Swanson), "Of Syllabi, Texts, Students, and Scholarship in International Relations: Some Data and Interpretations on the State of a Burgeoning Field" in Rosenau (1980), pp. 242-314 (originally published in *World Politics*, vol. 29, 1977, pp. 263-341).

Rosenau, James N., *The Study of Global Interdependence. Essays on the Transnationalization of World Affairs*, New York/London: Nichols/Francis Pinter, 1980.

Rosenau, James N. and Hylke W. Tromp (eds), *Interdependence and Conflict in World Politics*, Aldershot, etc.: Avebury, 1989.

Rosenau, James N., "Subtle Sources of Global Interdependence. Changing Criteria of Evidence, Legitimacy, and Patriotism" in Rosenau and Tromp

(1989), pp. 31-47.

Russett, Bruce and Harvey Starr, *World Politics. The Menu for Choice*, San Francisco: W.H. Freeman and Co., (1981) 1985^2.

Sassoon, Joseph, "Interdependence in the International System. A Survey of the Literature", *Lo Spettatore Internazionale*, vol. 16, 1981, no. 1, pp. 29-55.

Schrijver, Nico, "International Organisation for the Management of Interdependence" in Rosenau and Tromp (1989), pp. 100-114.

Senghaas, Dieter, "Die Interdependenz-Problematik in der Analyse internationaler Politik und internationaler Beziehungen" paper, 1989.

Senghaas, Dieter, *Europa 2000: Ein Friedensplan*, Frankfurt a/M: Suhrkamp, 1990.

Shaw, T.M., "Dependence to (Inter)dependence: Review of the Debate on the (New) International Economic Order", *Alternatives*, 1978, no. 4, pp. 557-578.

Shulman, Marshall D., "Toward a Western Philosophy of Coexistence", *Foreign Affairs*, vol. 52, October 1973, pp. 35-58.

Simai, Mihaly, "Interdependence, International", *World Encyclopedia of Peace*, vol. 1, 1986, pp. 454-456.

SIPRI, *SIPRI Yearbook 1990. World Armaments and Disarmament*, Oxford, etc.: Oxford University Press, 1990.

Smith, Michael, Richard Little and Michael Shackleton (eds), *Perspectives on World Politics*, London: Croom Helm for the Open University Press, 1981.

Soetendorp, R.B. and A. van Staden (eds), *Internationale betrekkingen in perspectief*, Utrecht: Het Spectrum, 1987.

Spits, F.C., *De metamorfose van de oorlog in de achttiende en negentiende eeuw*, Assen: Van Gorcum, 1971.

Sprout, Harold and Margaret Sprout, *Toward a Politics of the Planet Earth*, New York: Van Nostrand, 1971.

Staden, A. van, "De heerschappij van staten: het perspectief van het realisme" in Soetendorp and Van Staden (1987), pp. 13-36.

Staley, Eugene, *World Economy in Transition: Technology vs. Politics, Laissez Faire vs. Planning, Power vs. Welfare*, New York: Council on Foreign Relations, 1939.

Stebbins, R.P. (ed), *Documents on American Foreign Relations, 1962*, New York: Harper & Row, 1963.

Steinweg, Reiner (ed), *Lehren aus der Geschichte? Historische Friedensforschung*, Frankfurt am Main: Suhrkamp, 1990.

Supina, Philip D., "The Norman Angell Peace Campaign in Germany", *Journal of Peace Research*, vol. 9, 1972, pp. 161-164.

Swaan, Abram de, *Zorg en de staat. Welzijn, onderwijs en gezondheidszorg in Europa en de Verenigde Staten in de nieuwe tijd*, Amsterdam: Bert Bakker, 1989 (translation of *In Care of the State. Health Care, Education and Welfare in Europe and the USA in the Modern Era*, 1988).

Taylor, A.J.P., *How Wars Begin*, London: Futura Publications, (1977), 1980.

Taylor, Paul, "Functionalism and Strategies for International Integration" in Groom and Taylor (1975), pp. 79-92.

Taylor, Paul, "The Development of the Theory of International Organisation: The Four Phases of Writing" in Kent and Nielsson (1980), pp. 59-77.

Thompson, Kenneth W., *Masters of International Thought. Major Twentieth-Century Theorists and the World Crisis*, Baton Rouge, London: Louisiana State University Press, 1980.

Tromp, Hylke W., "Statenanarchie of interdependentie?", *Transaktie*, vol. 10, 1981, no. 1, pp. 67-92.

Tromp, Hylke W., *In staat van oorlog*, Amsterdam: Contact, 1986.

Tromp, Hylke W., "Commentaar: Bij het einde van de koude oorlog", *Transaktie*, vol. 19, 1990, no. 1, pp. 1-6.

Väyrynen, Raimo (ed) in collaboration with Dieter Senghaas and Christian Schmidt (ISSC Issue Group on Peace), *The Quest for Peace. Transcending Collective Violence and War among Societies, Cultures and States*, London, etc.: Sage Publications, 1987.

Vree, Johan K. de, *Political Integration. The Formation of Theory and Its Problems*, The Hague/Paris: Mouton & Co., 1972.

Vree, Johan K. de, *Foundations of Social and Political Processes. The Dynamics of Human Behaviour, Politics, and Society. Volume 1: Theory*, Bilthoven: Prime Press, 1982.

Wallace, M. and J.D. Singer, "Intergovernmental Organization in the Global System, 1816-1964", *International Organization*, vol. 24, 1970, no. 2, pp. 239-282.

Waltz, Kenneth N., *Theory of International Politics*, Reading, Mass.: Addison-Wesley, 1979.

Weiss, Th. and J. Siotis, "Functionalism and International Secretariats: Ideology and Rhetoric in the UN Family" in Groom and Taylor (1975), pp. 173-189.

White, Leonard D. (ed), *The Future of Government in the United States. Essays in Honor of Charles E. Merriam*, Chicago: University of Chicago Press, 1942.

Wilde, Jaap H. de, "Interdependentie in het vredesonderzoek naar détente", *Transaktie*, vol. 18, 1989, no. 3, pp. 209-224.

Wilde, Jaap H. de, "A Short History of Global Interdependence", *Development & Security*, 1989, no. 28.

Willetts, Peter, "The Politics of Global Issues: Cognitive Actor Dependence and Issue Linkage" in Jones and Willetts (1984), pp. 83-110.

Willetts, Peter, "Interdependence: New Wine in Old Bottles" in Rosenau and Tromp (1989), pp. 195-210.

Worldwatch Institute, *State of the World 1990*, New York/London: W.W. Norton, 1990.

Index